T0285811

CROSS WINDS

ADVANCE PRAISE FOR THE BOOK

'Former foreign secretary Vijay Gokhale, who has authored a string of academically rigorous examinations of twentieth-century China and India, has written a remarkable study of the effects of rival US and British approaches to the Asian order after World War II on China policy, Taiwan, and on Indian, US and British diplomacy and policy. The book tells the story with verve and clarity, of differing British and American approaches to Asia east of India, and of newly independent India's reactions and approach at the time, through four pivotal policy decisions on China. Populated by larger-than-life characters, this admirable work of contemporary history, based on a close reading of the archives and other evidence, casts new light on a pivotal period. It has immediate resonance today, seventy years later, when Taiwan has acquired new geopolitical salience, and the Asian order is once again contested due to the China–US rivalry and China's rise to power. A book that deserves to be widely read for the lessons it offers about the defence of India's interests in troubled times'—Shivshankar Menon, former national security adviser

'Vijay Gokhale's rare exploration of the intersection between India's China policy in the first decade after Independence and the tension between a Britain in decline and an America on the rise offers rich rewards. *Crosswinds* presents deep insights into New Delhi's troubled approach to Beijing and a valuable template to reflect on the future of India's China ties amid the renewed turbulence in the relations between the great powers. Gokhale's accessible and fascinating diplomatic history is a must-read for all students of India's foreign policy'—C. Raja Mohan, visiting research professor, Institute of South Asian Studies, National University of Singapore

'Vijay Gokhale presents a must-read account of India's diplomatic engagements with the United States, Britain and China in the Far East in the 1950s. He lucidly argues that India showed strategic clarity in seeking a partnership with China and demonstrates how its personality-driven diplomacy made it vulnerable to manipulation'—Samir Saran, president, Observer Research Foundation

'Vijay Gokhale's *Crosswinds* is a masterly survey of the Anglo–American rivalry over managing an emergent Asia in the early post-war era. By skilfully marrying archival sources with secondary literature, he has unveiled the successes and shortcomings of Indian diplomacy at a critical moment in global politics to yield lessons that are pertinent to this day. A remarkable work that leaves both practitioners and students of international politics in his debt'—Ashley Tellis, Tata Chair for Strategic Affairs, Carnegie Endowment for International Peace

CROSS WINDS

NEHRU, ZHOU AND THE ANGLO–AMERICAN COMPETITION OVER CHINA

VIJAY GOKHALE

VINTAGE
An imprint of Penguin Random House

VINTAGE

USA | Canada | UK | Ireland | Australia
New Zealand | India | South Africa | China | Singapore

Vintage is part of the Penguin Random House group of companies
whose addresses can be found at global.penguinrandomhouse.com

Published by Penguin Random House India Pvt. Ltd
4th Floor, Capital Tower 1, MG Road,
Gurugram 122 002, Haryana, India

Penguin
Random House
India

First published in Vintage by Penguin Random House India 2024

Copyright © Vijay Gokhale 2024

All rights reserved

10 9 8 7 6 5 4 3 2 1

ISBN 9780670099917

Typeset in Adobe Garamond Pro by MAP Systems, Bengaluru, India
Printed at Thomson Press India Ltd, New Delhi

www.penguin.co.in

MIX
Paper from
responsible sources
FSC® C010615

Contents

For Sahaj

Principal Characters

The United States of America

FRANKLIN D. ROOSEVELT, 32nd President of the US, 1933–45

HARRY S. TRUMAN, 33rd President of the US, 1945–53

DWIGHT D. EISENHOWER, 34th President of the US, 1953–61

GEORGE C. MARSHALL, Special Representative to China (1945–46), US Secretary of State (January 1947–January 1949)

DEAN ACHESON, US Secretary of State, 1949–53

JOHN FOSTER DULLES, US Secretary of State, 1953–59

GENERAL WALTER BEDELL-SMITH, US Under Secretary of State, 1953–54

MAJOR GENERAL PATRICK J. HURLEY, Special Representative, US Ambassador to Nationalist China, October 1944–November 1945

JOHN LEIGHTON STUART, US Ambassador to Nationalist China, July 1946–August 1949

LOY HENDERSON, US Ambassador to India, 1948–51

CHESTER BOWLES, US Ambassador to India, 1951–53

GEORGE ALLEN, US Ambassador to India, 1953–54

JOHN SHERMAN COOPER, US Ambassador to India, 1955–56

ELLSWORTH BUNKER, US Ambassador to India, 1956–61

U. ALEXIS JOHNSON, US Ambassador to Czechoslovakia (1954–57) and US Negotiator for the Warsaw Talks

The United Kingdom

CLEMENT ATTLEE, Prime Minister, 1945–51

WINSTON CHURCHILL, Prime Minister, 1951–55

ANTHONY EDEN, Deputy Prime Minister and Foreign Secretary (1951–55), Prime Minister (1955–57)

HAROLD MACMILLAN, Foreign Secretary (1955), Prime Minister (1957–63)

JOHN SELWYN LLOYD, Foreign Secretary, 1955–60

ROGER MAKINS, Britain's Ambassador in Washington, 1953–56

HAROLD CACCIA, Britain's Ambassador in Washington, 1956–61

HUMPHREY TREVELYAN, Britain's Chargé d'Affaires in the People's Republic of China, 1954–55

ARCHIBALD NYE, British High Commissioner in India, 1950–52

ALEXANDER CLUTTERBUCK, British High Commissioner in India, 1952–55

MALCOLM MACDONALD, British High Commissioner in India, 1955–60

India

JAWAHARLAL NEHRU, Prime Minister and Foreign Minister of India, 1947–64

K.M. PANIKKAR, India's Ambassador to Nationalist China (1947–49) and to the People's Republic of China (1950–52)

V.K. KRISHNA MENON, India's High Commissioner to the United Kingdom (1947–52) and Permanent Representative of India to the United Nations (1952–62), Defence Minister (1957–62)

GAGANVIHARI LAL MEHTA, India's Ambassador to the United States of America, 1952–58

VIJAYALAKSHMI PANDIT, India's Ambassador to the United States of America (1949–51) and High Commissioner in London (1956–61)

GIRIJA SHANKAR BAJPAI, Secretary General of the Ministry of
External Affairs, 1947–52

N.R. PILLAI, Secretary General of the Ministry of External
Affairs, 1953–59

K.P.S. MENON, Foreign Secretary (1948–52), Ministry of
External Affairs

SUBIMAL DUTT, Foreign Secretary (1955–61), Ministry of
External Affairs

N. RAGHAVAN, India's Ambassador to China, 1952–55

G. PARTHASARATHI, India's Ambassador to China, 1958–61

People's Republic of China

MAO ZEDONG, Chairman of the Communist Party of
China, 1949–76

ZHOU ENLAI, Foreign Minister of China (1949–58) and Premier
of the State Council (1954–76)

WANG BINGNAN, China's Ambassador to Poland and Negotiator
at the Warsaw Talks

Preface

The Second World War ended in August 1945, and with it the pre-war global order vanished. Two major powers—the United States of America (US) and the Union of Soviet Socialist Republics (USSR)—eclipsed the European domination of the world order. In Europe, the two new powers began a fierce competition that would shape the foreign policies of all countries on that continent. In the Asia-Pacific, however, the defeat of the Japanese empire initially left a power vacuum. The US, as the dominant military power, was seeking to build a new Pacific order based on democratic values and open trading arrangements that served its new security and economic interests. But the European powers wished to reimpose the old colonial order that they had been forced to abandon at the hands of Japan, and to reclaim their territorial possessions and trading privileges. Chief among these powers was the British empire that had dominated the Indo-Pacific until the 1930s. It had been a junior partner of the US in the Second World War but was unwilling to cede economic and commercial space to it in post-war Asia.

China was the lynchpin of their respective strategies. The US had supported the Republic of China militarily and politically throughout the Second World War. It had insisted, over the heads of the British imperialists, to accord China the status of a 'Great Power' at the Moscow Summit in 1943. Having no large commercial or economic stakes in China before 1939, it framed its China policy in moral and political terms. President Franklin D. Roosevelt, who was the architect of America's new China policy, believed that a democratic, united and peaceful China, albeit under President Chiang Kai-shek who was hardly a democrat in the conventional Western sense, was in the best interests of the US and the region. The British empire intended to reclaim its lost colonies in Asia and to reassert its extraterritorial rights and privileges. Nowhere was this truer than in China. Britain had been the dominant European power there since 1840. Aside from the crown colony of Hong Kong, it had vast business interests and properties on the Chinese mainland, of which it had been dispossessed by the Japanese, and which it fully intended to recover. Britain's priority was commercial, not political. As long as it could preserve its commercial and economic interests, it mattered little to the British what politics China followed after the war. But Britain was also acutely aware of the changed ground realities and reluctantly ceded the dominant position to the Americans in Northeast Asia in return for Washington letting London take the lead in Southeast Asia.

The foreign policies of both these principal Western powers were, however, upended when a new political force, the Communist Party of China, began to make rapid inroads on the Chinese mainland, eventually overthrowing Chiang Kai-shek and establishing the People's Republic of China (PRC) in October 1949. A gulf opened up between the United States and the British empire on how they should handle the communist rulers of a country that had been an important Asian ally during the Second World War. From America's perspective, a China that was communist multiplied the threat from Soviet expansionism to US interests in the Asia-Pacific. Containment of the communist threat became America's priority in the Cold War. The British empire also wished to contain communism, which was threatening British colonies in Malaya and Borneo as well as British commercial interests in Southeast Asia, but it favoured compromise, not confrontation, with the new rulers of China. The stage was set for Anglo-American competition in China and the Far East, and this had far-reaching repercussions on the region's other nations, one of which was newly independent India.

India, under the leadership of Prime Minister Jawaharlal Nehru, was finding its feet as a nation, and defining its own priorities and interests. India's leadership was fiercely nationalist and anti-colonialist, and strongly supported Asian national movements against European imperialists. It wished to craft an independent foreign policy dedicated to peace and development in a world divided by the Cold War, in which it was being forced to choose sides. It saw China as a natural partner in that endeavour to shape a new post-war Asian order. But the Government of India also had to contend with the Anglo-American competition for China. On the one hand, India had ties with the British empire, and its leadership had personal relations with those of Britain. On the other hand, in order to develop, India needed economic and other assistance from the US, the world's most influential country after 1945. As Anglo-American competition over China grew in the first decade of independent India's existence, both the US and Britain desired that India follow their respective cues, and tried to convince India about the legitimacy and reasonableness of their China policies. This book is an account of how the dynamics between America, Britain and China, as well as their individual relations with India, shaped India's policy towards China between 1949 and 1959. It is based on the parsing of original documents and reports that are available in the Indian, British and American archives as well as with other resource holders.

This book covers four specific events: the question of recognition of the new communist government of China in 1949; the diplomatic resolution of the Indochina crisis at the Geneva Conference in 1954; and the two Taiwan Strait crises in 1954–55 and in 1958. In each of these events, India had interests and sought to play its part in order to defend these interests. This brought India into close interaction with the United States, Britain and the PRC. Each of them, in turn, looked at and dealt with India through the unique prism of their own strategic requirements. Their perceptions about India evolved during the course of each event. India's relationship with China was viewed in different ways by the two Western powers, which led to differences in the way they engaged with India. China's view of India's relations with America and Britain also shaped how it dealt with India.

This is also the story of the personalities who were involved in crafting the policies of their respective countries on China during this period. The book looks at the personal and political relationships between Presidents Harry S. Truman and Dwight D. Eisenhower of the United States, British Prime Ministers Clement Attlee, Winston Churchill, Anthony Eden and Harold Macmillan, Chinese Premier Zhou Enlai, and Indian Prime Minister Jawaharlal Nehru, as well as between their principal deputies—American Secretaries of State Dean Acheson and John Foster Dulles, Nehru's principal diplomats Sardar K.M. Panikkar and V.K. Krishna Menon and the three British Foreign Secretaries, Anthony Eden, Harold Macmillan and John Selwyn Lloyd. It brings out the dynamics of how the China policy was crafted in the four capitals, how diplomacy was conducted between the four countries, and, importantly, how they practised deception to secure their different national objectives in the same geographical theatre.

The book is not intended to be a detailed narration of India–China relations between 1949 and 1959. Its purpose is to understand how India acted in the four situations relating to China, and how the three other countries impacted the ways in which India acted. Although this is a historical account, the diplomatic lessons that may be drawn from it could be relevant to this century. The United States and China are again, as they were in the 1950s, bitter adversaries. Britain, again as an ally of the Americans, is seeking to re-enter the Far East through AUKUS (the Australia–United Kingdom [UK]–United States alliance) after it effectively withdrew from the western Pacific since the handover of Hong Kong in 1997. Taiwan and the South China Sea have resurfaced as the primary danger points in the Indo-Pacific region. India has expanding interests in this region that are threatened by the current dynamics between China and the Western powers. No two situations are identical, but hindsight might be a useful guide to avoid some of the errors that India made in the early years, so that its geopolitical and geo-economic interests are not compromised in this new strategic competition. The book's final chapter reflects upon some of these lessons.

The book is written in popular style with a view to engaging readers who enjoy reading about international politics and diplomacy and are curious about how the interaction between people and situations shapes national policy.

Chapter 1

Setting the Stage in the Pacific Theatre

In 1944, the world had already been at war for five years, but the tide was turning. The United States of America, the most powerful nation on earth, was fighting against Japan almost entirely on its own. The utter destruction of Japan's military power, which was the American objective, however, also presaged a new problem. Britain, which had dominated Far East affairs for a century since 1843, was exhausted from two World Wars. It would struggle to hold on to its colonial and imperial possessions, and it was unlikely to have the military and economic capacities to underwrite post-war peace in the Pacific. A vacuum was not desirable, and so, Washington came to look upon China as a possible partner in post-war Pacific Asia and a counterpoise to communist expansionism. At the Moscow Conference in October 1943, President Franklin D. Roosevelt had pushed for China's recognition as one of the 'Big Four' (comprising the US, UK, USSR and China) in the war against Germany and Japan, over Britain's objections.* At the subsequent Cairo Summit, Chiang

---

* According to British Prime Minister Harold Macmillan, 'Indeed during the Second World War many of us felt that President Roosevelt had made himself something of a nuisance about the Chinese ... The President insisted on elevating China, then largely in the hands of Chiang Kai-shek and his supporters, into a

Kai-shek joined Roosevelt and Churchill for the first time. In 1944, Roosevelt sent Major General Patrick J. Hurley as his special representative to China with two objectives: to sustain the Chinese war effort against Japan and to promote domestic political unity. Both were essential for US policy in organizing the peace and establishing the machinery of post-war international cooperation in support of America's interests.

Hurley's latter objective of promoting unity was necessitated by the intractable differences between the National Government of the Republic of China led by President Chiang Kai-shek and his Kuo Min Tang (KMT) party on the one hand and, on the other, the Communist Party of China (CPC) led by Mao Zedong. The war effort was being adversely impacted so long as they remained at loggerheads. Hurley's task was to unite both political forces in driving the Japanese away from the mainland of China while American forces focused on defeating Japan on the high seas. The Americans had been in contact with Mao and the communists in Yan'an since 1943. Hence, it was not difficult for Hurley to meet Mao in Yan'an in early November 1944. Mao welcomed him warmly. For three months thereafter Hurley carried proposals back and forth between Mao and Chiang Kai-shek. Neither was willing to sufficiently compromise. Mao wrote to Hurley in early January 1945 to say that 'all secret negotiations of the past eight years have proved that there is not the least sincerity on the part of the National Government'.[1] US Secretary of State Edward Stettinius told Roosevelt that the gap between Chiang and the Communists was 'wide and fundamental'.[2]

According to Hurley, the KMT and the CPC were not the only ones sabotaging Roosevelt's initiative on China. Hurley claimed that American military officers were bypassing the National

---

world power.' Harold Macmillan, 'Chinese Puzzle', Chapter 17, *Riding the Storm, 1956–1959* (Harper and Row Publishers), p. 540.

Government and Hurley, and talking directly to the communists about a combined guerilla force against Japan in north China (which was under communist control), led and supplied by the US Army. 'If the communists, who are an armed party, could succeed in making such an arrangement with the US Army,' he wrote to Roosevelt, 'it would be futile for us to save the National Government in China.'[3]

He also believed that Mao and Zhou Enlai were secretly trying to secure a visit to Washington to meet Roosevelt without Hurley's knowledge. 'The proposed action was in conflict with the policy of the government,' he wrote to Secretary of State Stettinius. 'It would have defeated the US policy of sustaining the National Government of China. I was of the opinion that the recognition of the communist party as an armed belligerent through our army would immediately cause chaos and civil war and a defeat of America's policy in China.'[4] Hurley was not entirely wrong in his assumption that there were two lines of thinking within the State Department in Washington. Foreign service officials felt that as a contingency in case Hurley's efforts at unity failed, the US should be prepared to provide military assistance to the Chinese communists in order to defeat the Japanese, but without also giving them the capacity to overthrow the National Government.[5] John Service, a Second Secretary at the American Embassy in Chungking (the wartime capital of China), travelled to Yan'an to meet Mao in March 1945, and reported Mao's opinion that America's policy seemed to be wavering after a good start.[6]

Concerned about the lack of progress in building unity within China when the Second World War was reaching its decisive phase in early 1945, Roosevelt took the unusual step of directly writing Mao Zedong to 'hope that you and President Chiang Kai-shek will work together harmoniously to achieve internal unity'.[7] Roosevelt's death in April and Hurley's determination to ensure that the Chinese communists could not use the US in its efforts to supplant the National Government sowed the seeds for the failure of Hurley's mission, eventually leading to his resignation in November 1945. The first American attempt at building political unity in China had floundered.

The communists had been keen to reach an accommodation with the Americans after the USSR and the US made common cause against Germany and Japan. In December 1941 the central committee of the communist party issued a directive calling for sincere cooperation with the US in order to raise resistance to the Japanese occupying force in China.[8] Two years later, after China was included as part of the Big Four in the meeting between Roosevelt, Churchill and Stalin in November 1943 in Moscow, Mao felt confident that 'cooperation among the four nations during the war will be continued after the war'.[9] The communists had reason to believe that Hurley's outreach heralded an opportunity for it to get American support to come to power. It is not unlikely, as Hurley believed, that they also conspired with the US Army to secure military assistance and to establish direct contact with Washington, keeping Hurley in the dark. This led to mutual distrust and eventually to mutual disappointment.

By then the war with Japan was over but the American policy on brokering a deal between Chiang Kai-shek and the communists did not change. The new American President, Harry S. Truman, sent General George C. Marshall as the new mediator. To strengthen his hand, Truman issued a presidential statement that a strong, united and democratic China was important to world peace. He pledged that there would be no American military intervention to influence the domestic situation, and that all major political elements would find fair and effective representation in government.[10] However, the US also threw its weight behind Chiang Kai-shek by stating that his National Government was the only legal government in China and the proper instrument to achieve the objective of a unified China. It pledged to supply military material to the national army to re-establish control over Manchuria (northeastern China) after the Japanese withdrawal, and declared the existence of autonomous armies such as the communist armies (the title of the People's Liberation Army [PLA] was adopted in 1948) as inconsistent with the aim of unity.

The Chinese communists may have been disappointed, but still hoped that American mediation would bring them to power. Hence, when Zhou Enlai met Marshall on 23 December 1945, he reaffirmed communist support for the late President Roosevelt's approach and hoped that a coalition government might be formed in China. He told Marshall the communists were only advocating the American form of government and spirit of freedom.[11] Marshall was able to register early success in January 1946 when the CPC and the KMT agreed to the termination of hostilities and the setting up of an Executive Headquarters of the Committee of Three (the third being the United States) to oversee the armistice. But the arrangements failed the Manchurian test. Both the National Government and the communists, which was in control of northern China, wanted to replace the Japanese in Manchuria.

Although Mao personally assured Marshall that the ceasefire would also apply to Manchuria,[12] conflict broke out between the Red Army and the National Army. Marshall informed Truman that it was threatening to lead to 'utter chaos in north China'.[13] The communists sharply criticized Marshall's decision to keep American troops in China (they were originally slated to leave by early 1946) as well as the China Aid Bill passed by US Congress in June 1946, as American efforts to bolster Chiang's military capabilities. 'The Chinese people deeply feel that the ammunition shipped by America to China is excessive, that the American forces stationed in China are too large and that they have created a tremendous threat to the peace and security of China,' declared a statement issued from Yan'an.[14] They demanded the immediate

withdrawal of all US troops from China. Marshall appeared
unable to capitalize on his early success at mediation in order to
bring about political unity between Mao and Chiang.

As 1946 drew to a close, statements from the CPC became more
and more anti-American in tone and sentiment. In September,
Mao described US mediation attempts as a 'smokescreen' to
strengthen Chiang Kai-shek and reduce China 'virtually to a US
colony'.[15] By the end of the year, CPC propaganda was routinely
describing Chiang Kai-shek as America's running dog or lackey.
Marshall pressed on Chiang more than once to make him realize
that the communists were too large a military and civil force to
be ignored, and that it was imperative for them to be brought
into government,[16] but to little avail. Like Hurley, Marshall's
mission also failed, and he left China in early January 1947,
declaring that the greatest obstacle to peace in China was the
almost overwhelming suspicion with which the KMT and the
CPC regarded each other. After Marshall's departure, the US
abandoned mediation. It became American policy, instead, to
assist the National Government to establish its authority over
as wide a swathe as possible. American policy was tethered to
Chiang Kai-shek.

As a result, from 1947 onwards, the antagonism between
the Chinese communists and the Americans steadily grew. Zhou
described American policy as 'reactionary' and blamed it for
inspiring civil strife.[17] In February, Zhou told Western media
that they did not require mediation to work out their problems.
Through the course of 1947 the communist armies continued to
make steady gains. By the beginning of 1948 they were threatening
to seize Manchuria and north China. The Americans threw their
full political weight behind Chiang although they realized that
he was compromising their interests in a united and peaceful
post-war China, but by then what had seemed possible in 1945
and 1946—coalition government—was no longer acceptable

to the US. Those who had advocated accommodation with the communists were silenced. Official Washington looked at Chinese communists through the prism of the Cold War. 'The communist leaders have foresworn their Chinese heritage and have publicly announced their subservience to a foreign power, Russia . . .' was how senior American cabinet official Dean Acheson would later characterize the American view of China in the White Paper issued in 1949. Marshall, who became Truman's Secretary of State upon his return from China, gave explicit instructions to Ambassador John Leighton Stuart that 'the US government must not, directly or indirectly, give any implication of support, encouragement and acceptability of coalition government in China with communist participation; the US has no intention of again offering its good offices as mediator in China; you should, of course, overlook no suitable opportunity to emphasize the pattern of engulfment which has resulted from coalition governments in eastern Europe'.[18] Cold War politics and US–Soviet global competition had removed any possibility of a pragmatic and median American approach to the Chinese communists.

As the tide decisively shifted against Chiang Kai-shek, and with no alternative in sight, American policy became defensive and reactive. It had lost hope in Chiang's ability to restore the writ of the National Government across north China even though by then the US had given it aid worth $2 billion since 1945.* Despite this enormous sum of money, Marshall admitted

---

* The White Paper on China stated that this amount was equivalent in value to more than 50 per cent of monetary expenditure of the Chinese government, and of proportionately greater magnitude in budgetary terms than the US had provided to any nation of western Europe. 'The China White Paper August 1949', originally issued as Department of State publication 3573, 'United States Relations with China with Special Reference to Period 1944–1949', *Far Eastern Series 30* (California: Stanford University Press, 1967).

that 'present developments make it unlikely that any amount of US military or economic aid could make the present Chinese government capable of re-establishing and then maintaining its control throughout all China'.[19] The Truman administration was more concerned about the US being sucked into the whirlpool of civil war rather than extricating Chiang from it. Marshall telegraphed Stuart in October 1948 to categorically state that the 'United States must not become directly involved in China's civil war and must not assume responsibility for underwriting the Chinese government, militarily and economically'.[20] But instead of finding an alternative policy, Washington instead chose inaction on the plea that it would permit the Truman administration to preserve maximum freedom of action in the fluid situation in China. Thus, as 1949 dawned, America's relations with the Chinese communists, now the dominant political and military force in China, were stressed and tense.

This was not the only American relationship that was stressed by 1948. The US also seemed increasingly at odds with Britain, its principal ally. Great Britain had been the dominant Western power in the Asia-Pacific before the Second World War, deriving this status from both its commercial pre-eminence and its colonial possessions. Aside from its trade with China, it had significant investments in shipping, banking, insurance, public utilities and services. The great British corporations such as Hongkong & Shanghai Banking Corporation, Jardine Matheson, Butterfield & Swire, Hutchison Whampoa and British-American Tobacco underwrote British power. During the war, however, Britain had been defeated by the Japanese and came to depend on the United States to restore its colonial and imperial possessions. In a short span of five years, British pre-eminence was, thus, eclipsed by American power, and the British government was deeply conscious of this fact.

In April 1945, even before the war ended, Britain suggested 'informal conversations on Far Eastern matters that might extend to China and Japan' with the US.[21] This was not a casual feeler. Hurley was in London at about the same time, on Roosevelt's orders, to obtain Britain's support for the National Government in China. He met both Prime Minister Winston Churchill and Foreign Secretary Anthony Eden. The discussion with Churchill was heated. Churchill probed Hurley about the possibilities of British reoccupation of all colonial and imperial territories with American men and financing (lend-lease options). The sharp differences between the American and the British approaches to the Far East became evident over the course of that talk.

Hurley was of the view that Britain, being committed to the Atlantic Charter signed in August 1941 which set out common Anglo-American goals in a post-war world, should restore self-government to the colonies. The new priority in the Far East was stopping communist expansionism. Hurley said that if Britain made demands on Hong Kong, the Soviets would make similar demands on north China. Churchill insisted that he would fight for Hong Kong. He branded the American policy towards China as 'the great American illusion'. In his message to the new American President Truman, Hurley wrote to say Churchill had used the expression 'Hongkong will be eliminated from the British Empire only over my dead body'.[22] Conversations between the British Foreign Office and the State Department in early 1945 also reflected similar differences in approach. In one instance, John Carter Vincent, the Director of the State Department's Far Eastern Affairs Department, went so far as to tell Britain that it was not being cooperative in US efforts to build political unity in China, and wanted to keep it weak and disunited.[23] Even in these early conversations before the end of the Second World War, the tension between the two Western allies in the Far East was clear.

After Churchill lost the general election in early July 1945, and a Labour government led by Prime Minister Clement Attlee came to power, the British Foreign Office prepared a memorandum on the situation in the Far East. The new government was informed that a striking feature of the present situation was the ascendancy of the United States in China, and that its long-term effects 'obviously cannot be a matter of indifference to Great Britain in view of our great stake in China'.*[24] Its primary concern was not so much the political situation in China as the possibility that American businesses would push British enterprises out of a market they had dominated for a century. Hugh Trevelyan, a British diplomat posted in Washington, put it bluntly: 'Now that the mantle of Britannia is giving way, at least in the Pacific, to the business-suit of Uncle Sam, the open door will remain open only for citizens of the United States.'[25] To that end, the memorandum on the China policy urged the new British government to adopt a more active policy in regard to China and for closer contact with the US government in relation to China.[26] Nonetheless, deep suspicions would remain that America was colluding with the National Government of China on a new trade treaty in a manner so as to freeze the British out of the post-war Chinese economy.[27]

Since the focus of British policy in China after 1945 was not on seeking greater influence among the Chinese protagonists so much as ensuring that American policy did not exclude Britain from commercial prospects in China, Britain was content to let the Americans take the political lead. In any case, its financial situation after the war did not permit economic aid and military supplies in the quantities needed to support Chiang Kai-shek. But it felt that the American approach was unrealistic from the beginning and thought that the US would not succeed in

---

* The memorandum estimated that 6 per cent of all British foreign investments were in China.

its efforts at mediation.[28] By the second half of 1946, Lord Inverchapel, the British Ambassador in Washington, was telling London that American policy simply appeared to be marking time for want of a clear direction.[29] When, by the end of 1946, both attempts at mediation by Hurley and Marshall had collapsed, the British were left with no clear indication of what the official American policy might be.

Britain realized that the US might not, after all, have any clear strategy to deal with the situation. A.L. Scott, who was on the China desk at the British Foreign Office in London, sardonically noted in a file, 'All this amounts to letting the Chinese stew in their own juice. The danger is that for American relish there may be substituted Russian seasoning.'[30] It became anxious that Marshall's withdrawal from China presaged the possible pulling out of the US from the Chinese theatre. At the beginning of 1947, therefore, Lord Inverchapel was instructed by London to enquire whether the abandonment of mediation was likely to lead to any fundamental change in United States policy towards China.[31] The State Department official in charge of the China policy, John Carter Vincent, assured Britain that this was not the case.[32] But British efforts to secure reassurances at the political level from Marshall, now the US Secretary of State, never fructified. The Attlee government still decided that Great Britain should continue to keep in step with its ally's policy, keeping in mind the larger picture in the Far East.

From Washington's perspective, Britain's political goals in China were to keep China weak and divided and to re-erect the pre-war balance of power in the Pacific—the opposite of the American plan. Therefore, even when in November 1946 the new British Ambassador in China, Sir Ralph Stevenson, informed his American counterpart John Leighton Stuart that Britain accepted America's lead on the China policy, the latter did not believe it. When Marshall, still in China, informed Truman about it, saying the 'British now recognize the fact that the United States has taken over the position in China previously held by the British',[33] Acting Secretary of State Dean Acheson, in turn, told him that 'there are reasons to take with a grain of salt a statement that the British are completely resigned to our having taken over the position they previously occupied in China'. His advice to Marshall was to reassure Britain that there was a broad congruence of interests but to keep it out of Chinese politics.[34] The British, therefore, watched from the sidelines with increasing despondency through 1947, as American policy failed to stem the rising tide of communism in China, leading a senior British diplomat posted in Washington, Sir John Balfour, to wryly tell Foreign Secretary Ernest Bevin that the United States had no China policy worth the name.[35]

By early 1948 doubts about the effectiveness of American policy were being openly aired in London and serious discussions about China's political future had begun in the British government. By then the British had concluded, based on reports from their embassies in Washington and Nanking, that American policy was faltering and there was little prospect for the survival of the National Government. William Walton Butterworth, the United State's new head of the Far Eastern Affairs Department of the State Department, admitted that its economic and military assistance to the National Government were akin to 'shots of cocaine administered to a patient who responds to a treatment he finds comforting'.[36] Ralph Stevenson, the British Ambassador to China, broached with London the possibility that the communists could take control of the whole of China and, for the first time, of the need to find accommodation with them. 'While doing our best to combat communism as a creed,' wrote Stevenson, 'we think it would be prudent not to provoke gratuitously the enmity or resentment of the Chinese communists . . .' He recommended that Britain 'recognize the practical necessity of dealing with them *de facto* in areas under their control, whether now or later', adding that, 'if there should happen to be a chance to promote British trade etc. we should surely not fail to take it up through over squeamishness about reddening hands.'[37] The Foreign Secretary sent down a memorandum to his officials saying he 'thought it was time that the Americans told us something about their views on developments in China and the Far East generally. We wish to cooperate with them there, but can hardly do so effectively if we are kept in the dark'.[38] From the Americans all they received were evasive replies. The feeling grew that, far from trying to create a joint Anglo-American policy on China, the US was paying scant attention to British interests when crafting its China policy. As 1948 rolled on and the communists gained territory in Manchuria and north China, the British Foreign Office came to accept Stevenson's assessment.

By the end of 1948 the British government, in a memorandum circulated by Foreign Secretary Bevin to his cabinet colleagues, made it clear that it was 'merely a matter of time' before the communists gained control over China, and that any American counteraction was unlikely to be effective.[39] Bevin's memorandum assessed that a communist victory in China would encourage communist movements in British colonies in Southeast Asia and would harden India's attitude of 'neutrality' as between the communist states and the Western democracies. Unlike its American partners, the British government felt that no firm conclusions could be yet reached on the relationship between the Chinese communists and the Soviet Union. 'It would be unwise,' Bevin's memorandum said, 'to pursue a policy that might have the effect of gratuitously driving a Chinese communist government into the arms of the Soviet Union, and it is therefore important that the interested powers should reach an agreement as soon as possible on their attitude to a Chinese communist government.' Bevin proposed to start consultation with the Americans and the Commonwealth countries with a view to protecting Britain's interests in Asia. Writing to his counterpart at the British embassy in Washington, E.M. Dening, the head of the Far Eastern Affairs Department of the British Foreign Office, opined that 'unless there is a concerted Far Eastern policy soon the future can only develop to our [US and UK] common detriment'.[40] As 1949 dawned, therefore, Britain and the US were moving on divergent paths, as the former began to consult Commonwealth and other partners in an effort to build a new British approach to China that was not tied down to America.

It was in this tense situation between the United States and the Chinese communists on the one hand, and the divergence between the US and Britain on the other that India had to find a way to develop relations with the communists in 1949. It is not as if there had been no previous contact. During India's struggle for independence, Nehru had built relationships with leaders on both sides. He made a personal visit to China in August 1939, telling Rabindranath Tagore that he was going because 'the present will pass and merge into the future, and India will remain and China will remain and the two will work together for their own good and the good of the world'.[41] He established contact with President Chiang Kai-shek. During Chiang's visit to India in February 1942, his public support for India's freedom was welcomed by Nehru and the Congress. Before his own visit to China in 1939, Nehru had also written to Mao Zedong saying he was looking forward to seeing him,[42] but the outbreak of the Second World War ended such a possibility. 'I was particularly sorry that I could not visit the north-west front in Yenan . . . to meet some of the leaders of the eighth route army [Mao's army],' he was to tell *The Hindu*[43] newspaper upon his return to India. Nehru, however, was able to meet with General (later Marshal) Zhu De and other communists in the wartime capital of Chungking (Chongqing). During the Second World War, Nehru, on more than one occasion, mentioned his dream of India and China marching together in the present and in the future[44] and that he could 'hardly conceive of a future in which these two great and ancient countries, so unlike and yet so fundamentally like each other, will not cooperate for their mutual and the world's good'.[45]

After the war India got busy with securing independence and Nehru focused on broader foreign policy for the new government as the Cold War blanketed the world. On the eve of Independence, he told the *New Republic*, a New York–based magazine, that 'in the present context of international rivalries and suspicion it is difficult to maintain a balance and not be swept away by fear or dislike . . . but that is the only correct policy which can lead out of the vicious cycle in which the world moves today'.[46] Speaking in the Constituent Assembly on foreign policy, Nehru said India must avoid entanglements or 'attaching ourselves to any particular group'.[47] He affirmed that India would be friends with the US, and presciently predicted in February 1946 the 'gradual decline of British political influence in Asia and the growth of American economic influence'.[48]

But the fact remained that India tended to judge events in the Far East from the prism of Cold War power politics, and from this perspective the US looked more to be part of the problem than the solution. This approach was also mirrored in Washington where India, until 1949, figured very low on its list of priorities, and most American policymakers lacked the time, expertise and interest to work on India. M.K. Rasgotra, who served in Washington in the early 1950s, has, in his memoirs, talked of how Nehru's views on the Cold War, and later on Mao's China, caused dismay and irritation in the Truman administration, and prevented a meeting of minds to find common ground and explore joint action between the world's most powerful country and the Third World's most influential country.[49] As a result, Britain, by default, became both the chief interpreter of Washington's China policy for India, and the interpreter of Indian policy for the Americans.[50]

In 1947–48, as Anglo-American relations with the Soviet Union deteriorated and the Cold War policy took shape in the West, the gap between India and the US over China also seemed to widen. Newly independent India felt that nationalism, not communist ideology, drove the Chinese communists, and that it would adopt a more or less pragmatic approach. Nehru's frequent assertion that communism was alien to China did not find receptive audiences in the Truman administration. The American view by then was tending towards the possibility of a Sino-Soviet condominium that could threaten American supremacy in the Pacific. This made it harder for either side to have an open discussion on the situation in China, which ought to have been a shared concern for both.

So far as China was concerned, addressing the Sino-Indian Cultural Society at Santiniketan, West Bengal, in December 1945, Nehru described China as 'undoubtedly one of the principal powers of the world today'. He felt that when China and India came together, 'their amity and friendship will not only lead to their mutual benefit but will also benefit the world at large'. Mutual contact and agreement for their self-preservation would, he felt, make the two natural partners.[51]

After independence, ambassadors were exchanged, but the personal relationship between Nehru and Chiang soured over the invitation that India extended to delegates from Tibet to attend the Asian Relations Conference in New Delhi in February 1947, and the KMT government's suspicions about India's position over the status of Tibet.[52] The National Government's attitude towards newly independent India also irked the latter. Indian Ambassador K.M. Panikkar felt that Chiang Kai-shek was patronizing in the manner of an elder, more successful brother towards a younger sibling who was still finding his feet. China expected India to acknowledge it as the recognized great power in the East after the war.[53] In any case, India was busy with post-Independence matters, including Partition, Kashmir and Hyderabad. Even on the foreign policy front, Indonesia, Palestine and the Cold War took precedence. China barely found serious mention in government statements between 1946 and late 1948.

It was only in November–December 1948, when the rapidly progressing civil war in China was tilting decisively in Mao's favour, that India refocused on China. Nehru's note to Indian Foreign Secretary K.P.S. Menon proposed the establishment of unofficial contacts with the communist leaders without making any sort of commitment, so that they might be induced not to be hostile to India. In this context he recalled his earlier contacts with Mao and other leaders ten years earlier, suggesting to the Ministry of External Affairs that India might build upon them. His assessment about both the inevitability of a communist victory and that communist China 'will just not be a hanger-on of the Soviets'[54] would later be proved correct. His instruction to Menon to stay 'wide awake and not merely hang on to Chiang Kai-shek and his fading authority, nor [should we] just follow what the United Kingdom and the United States might do in China' would also reveal a more sophisticated understanding of what was happening in comparison to the US. His analysis that 'the United Kingdom government will not break with it [communist China] and will maintain a distant cooperative attitude'[55] was also on the mark. But, neither the Government of India nor any Indian leader had had direct contact with the Chinese communist leadership in a decade. Mao Zedong, Zhou Enlai and the military leaders who were fighting their way to power against the US-backed Chiang regime had fundamentally changed. Nehru still clung to his pre-war understanding about China and the communists.

In November 1948 in Paris, Hector O'Neill's (the British Minister of State in the Foreign Office) discussions with Marshall reaffirmed British feelings that America's China policy was wobbly.[56] Bevin found it difficult to understand Marshall's insistence that the US would support Chiang to the bitter end when, by Marshall's own admission, the National Government was failing. Bevin got cabinet approval to begin consultations with others besides the United States, including the Commonwealth countries.[57] One of the first governments it consulted was that of India. K.P.S. Menon, India's Foreign Secretary, responded to the British overture. In his conversation with British High Commissioner Sir Archibald Nye, Menon agreed that Chiang's days were numbered but felt that the new government might be a coalition. 'It seems doubtful,' Menon felt, 'whether Russia will be able to stroll in and 'take over' China as she has done in the countries in eastern Europe.' India, he felt, was not in any direct serious danger in the near future. His concluding observation to Nye was that 'any hostility toward a communist-controlled China by other countries will tend to throw it more in the Soviet orbit. A realist policy should therefore lead to contacts being maintained with the new government [that might supplant the National Government of President Chiang Kai-shek] without any commitments.'[58]

When the new year was rung in on 1 January 1949, the four principal players in the drama were poised to act. Mao and the Chinese communists were focused on making the revolution, Truman and America were intent on opposing them, Attlee and Britain wanted accommodation to preserve their colonial and commercial interests, and Nehru and India stood in anticipation that it might herald a new era in Asian geopolitics. The stage was set. This is the story of how the interaction between the four nations and their principal actors shaped India's China policy from 1949 to 1959.

Chapter 2

Recognizing the Chinese Communists

Nehru was interested in foreign policy and considered it important for proper governance of independent India. In his first broadcast to the nation as the Vice President of the interim government on 7 September 1946, he referred to China as 'our friend through the ages', and expressed his hope that the 'friendship will endure and grow'.[1] However, after Independence in August 1947, domestic preoccupations as well as the civil war that had begun in China meant that the new government of India had little scope to craft a proper China policy. Moreover, the relationship between the National Government in China and the government of independent India began to sour over India's position on the status of Tibet.[2] In October 1947, the Tibetan government wrote to Prime Minister Nehru demanding that India return forthwith such territories, including modern-day Arunachal Pradesh, Sikkim, Bhutan and Darjeeling, that, according to them, had been annexed by the British-Indian government in the nineteenth century.[3] In the same month, the Vice Foreign Minister of the National Government of China (Republic of China), George Yeh, also proposed the abrogation or modification of all agreements that the British-Indian government had entered into with the Chinese empire and the successor governments (described as 'Unequal Treaties'). This included the Shimla Convention of

1914 (in which the McMahon Line was designated as the frontier between Outer Tibet and India). Yeh reminded the Indian government that the Chinese government had refused to ratify the Shimla Convention.[4] India, in response, also made it clear to the National Government that it had replaced the former government of British India in regard to all treaty rights and obligations previously existing between British India and Tibet,[5] implying that under international law these treaties remained valid.

Hardly had the two governments got around to identifying such problems when the civil war in China took a turn. In November 1948, Panikkar reported to New Delhi that President Chiang's position had become 'untenable' after a series of military defeats.[6] His conversations with high-ranking KMT leaders confirmed his view of the developments. Dr Wong Wen-hao, a former prime minister, told Panikkar that the time for negotiation with the CPC had already passed and that the KMT was 'dead', adding that 'continued resistance today is only for the purpose of safeguarding the dead body of the party [and it is] in the personal interest of certain groups.'[7] He described the National Government as a 'phantom' and predicted that it would imminently collapse.[8] From then on, the topic of China began to figure regularly in Prime Minister Nehru's letters to his chief ministers. In early December, Nehru wrote them to say that a communist victory in China would have far-reaching consequences, and that 'we have to watch this rapidly developing situation in China with great care and attention'.[9] He asked the Indian Foreign Secretary to 'give thought to this changing China',[*10] and, moreover, not to get involved too much with the 'expiring government' of Chiang Kai-shek.[11] It had also crossed

---

* Nehru directed the Ministry of External Affairs to establish some form of unofficial contacts with the communists as well.

Nehru's mind that if China became communist, this would enhance India's role and importance in Asia.[12]

The British government was also paying close attention to the situation. In very early January 1949, it asked its Ambassador in Washington to begin consultations with the United States government on the basis of the memorandum that had been approved by the cabinet for dealing with the developing situation in China. This memorandum acknowledged that the Chiang Kai-shek government had lost all control of the area north of the Yangtze (Chang Jiang) River, and surmised that it was merely a matter of time before the communists prevailed. The British government had considered, and ruled out as doubtful, all prospects of preserving its many interests through the creation of an anti-communist bloc on its own and, instead, the memorandum recommended that Great Britain consult with the US and Britain's other partners as to the best means to contain the communist threat in the Far East.[13] It was not optimistic about reaching an Anglo-American understanding but still hopeful that its memorandum (which outlined in considerable detail the implications of a communist victory in China on the rest of Asia) might spur the Americans on to reconsider their policy. In the meantime, within the British Foreign Office, a paper was prepared specifically on the recognition question. The legal advice to the Foreign Office was that since the Chinese communists controlled a large portion of the territory, it must be recognized as 'something'. But it was also acknowledged that, politically, the US might be outraged if recognition was accorded without consulting with it. The note particularly emphasized the need to avoid giving the impression 'that when British interests are at stake, we are perfectly prepared to swallow our principles'.[14]

In early March 1949, Britain was still not confident that it had been able to line up other Western powers or Commonwealth governments behind its thinking. Bevin reported to the cabinet that 'the consultations with friendly powers as to the best means of containing the communist threat to all our interests have not yet proved productive'.[15] Three countries found specific mention in this paper—the United States, which was yet to respond to the British memorandum given to it in January, France and India. The Indian response was only partially helpful. It concurred with the British government on the need to maintain contacts with the communists without any commitments, but India also felt that a communist government in China would be absorbed in its own internal problems, and might not pose a threat to the broader region. India's suggestion that communism might be contained more effectively if other countries did more to support national movements in Southeast Asia was contrary to the British policy of holding on to its colonial possessions, and therefore not helpful. For all these reasons, for the time being, the British stayed their hand. However, any hope of a change in the China policy of its principal ally, the Americans, was belied when, in mid-March, it reverted on the British memorandum and called it 'conjectural in nature'. 'Waiting until the dust had settled,' as Acheson put it to Sir Oliver Franks, the British Ambassador in Washington,[16] was baffling to the British government, which could not understand why America was unwilling to see the situation in China clearly and realistically.

Till this point of time, aside from a single consultation with India in early 1949 on the possible implications of a communist government in China, there had been no discussion between the governments of India and Great Britain. But, in April, an incident involving the British warship *Amethyst* brought India to the forefront of Britain's China policy. On 21 April, the *Amethyst*, which had been ordered to sail up the Yangtze River from Shanghai to Nanking to supply—and if required, to evacuate—the British embassy and community if the communists crossed the Yangtze, came under heavy fire from the communist army 60 miles downstream of Nanking. Three other British ships were damaged in the shelling (*Consor, Black Swan* and *London*), but the *Amethyst* was disabled and unable to sail. As a result of this incident, the British began to seriously consider the possibility of a communist attack on Hong Kong. Orders were given by the British cabinet to reinforce the military garrison, but the cabinet also felt it important to seek diplomatic and moral support, especially from the Commonwealth countries of Asia. 'The United Kingdom government must,' so the cabinet minute read, 'make every effort to carry other commonwealth governments with them in their policy in respect of Hongkong . . .'[17]

India's response was of particular value for 'the powerful effect on public opinion throughout Asia',[18] a reflection of India's stature and influence at the time. In subsequent cabinet meetings on the Hong Kong question, India's position began to matter to a greater degree than that of any other country save the United States. P.J. Noel-Baker, the Secretary of State for the Commonwealth, emphasized that the 'most valuable moral support that can be obtained would be some statement from Pandit Nehru', and was worried about not getting it because of his anticolonial stand.[19] 'Our first concern must be to make sure there is no danger of his adopting an attitude of open opposition to our policy,' Noel-Baker informed the China and Southeast Asia Committee of the cabinet later in the same month. It was relieved when, in June, the British High Commissioner in Delhi reported that Nehru's reaction was, on the whole, more favourable than expected. 'Pandit Nehru while admitting that aggression must, of course, be resisted, suggests that "our policies may be so framed as to avoid the possibility of such a situation arising". He personally doubts whether the Chinese communists would wish to take action that would mean war with a great power.'[20] The *Amethyst* incident ended on 30 July when the ship quietly slipped through communist lines and into open waters, and the threat to Hong Kong did not materialize either.

But the incident served to underscore how great an importance the British attached to securing the support of India (and other Asian Commonwealth members) especially when it was on divergent paths with the US on the question of China.

Even while Britain was preoccupied with the *Amethyst* incident, it pursued consultations with key Commonwealth and Atlantic Pact countries on the question of recognition of the Chinese communist government. The fall of Nanking, the National Government's capital, on 23 April, convinced it that there was no other alternative. Another attempt was made by the British embassy in light of the situation to talk to the Americans. The British proposed that a possible solution might be to recognize the Chinese communist government as the de facto government of the areas under its effective jurisdiction, while also continuing to recognize the National Government as being the de jure government of the whole of China.[21] But the Americans ignored this British proposal. Instead, in early May 1949, John Leighton Stuart, the American ambassador to the National Government in Nanking (who, like other diplomatic representatives, including Indian Ambassador K.M. Panikkar and British Ambassador Ralph Stevenson, had been derecognized by the communists and confined to his residence) telegraphed the US State Department recommending that it would be unwise to initiate any move towards recognizing the communist regime. 'Our tactics should be one of reserve,' he said, 'waiting for the new regime to make the first approach.'[22] Stuart's advice to the State Department seemed to have been prompted by his conversation with the British ambassador in Nanking, Sir Ralph Stevenson. Stevenson had approached Stuart wanting to discuss the desirability of extending de facto recognition to the Chinese communists. Stuart felt that he might be speaking on the basis of some policy guidance from London. This finally prompted the Americans to act. They decided to consult their Western partners in order to build consensus on a two-point agenda: namely, not initiating any move towards recognition or giving the impression to the communists that its seeking recognition would be welcomed; and the desirability of building a common policy on the question of recognition.[23] After replies were received from the Western allies, US Secretary of State Dean Acheson realized that 'London was non-committal'. Acheson, therefore, told Stuart in Nanking that all efforts should be made by him to obtain full agreement from the US's Western partners, and especially Great Britain, for a common policy against the communists.[24] From this point on, their divergence on the developing situation in China would grow and become public. As the imperial power with a long-established presence in the Indo-Pacific, Great Britain's principal focus with respect to China was on how the new communist government might impact its commercial interests in China and its colonial possessions, including Hong Kong. American interests, on the other hand, were principally strategic in the context of the Cold War and in terms of its leadership of the democratic world against communism. This was to mark the point from which the two principal Western powers would battle to win the hearts and minds of the others. India, as the other major 'Asiatic' power, became important in this evolving Anglo-American competition.

In May 1949, the British government advised other Commonwealth governments, including the Government of India, that while they watched and waited for the communists to make the first move, any appearance of 'ganging up' against them should be avoided.[25] In the case of India, however, this was not a major concern for the British. Noel-Baker had reported to the cabinet that Nehru's tendency was to 'write down the menace from that direction [communists]'.[26] The Americans had no idea about Indian thinking because it had not made any efforts to consult with India on China. In mid-May, however, Stuart informed the State Department about rumours that were circulating in

Nanking that the Indian government intended to recognize the communist government fairly promptly after a 'decent interval'.[27] All of a sudden, official Washington woke up to the importance of India. By mid-1949, the State Department and the Central Intelligence Agency (CIA) were highlighting India's political stability as an asset, and even President Truman had noted that India was 'key to the whole Asian situation'.[28] The Americans tasked Loy W. Henderson, the ambassador in New Delhi, with advising the Government of India to consult with the Americans before taking steps for de facto or de jure recognition of the new communist regime. He was assured by Sir Girija Shankar Bajpai, the Secretary General of India's Ministry of External Affairs, that India would closely consult both the US and Great Britain on the question of recognition.[29]

The gist of the conversation between Henderson and Bajpai was also conveyed to Stuart in Nanking, who in turn shared with Panikkar the news that Washington had secured a 'promise' of full cooperation from the Government of India on this issue. Panikkar was upset. He thought that America's objective was to build pressure upon the communists in order to secure favourable terms for its trade and business interests, and that it was also putting pressure on other governments in this matter in order to prevent them from following the lead of Britain, which wanted to recognize a future Chinese communist regime without undue delay. His advice to New Delhi was that any agreement with the US on this question 'cannot fail to give the impression to the new government in China that we are allowing ourselves to be used for furtherance of American interests'.[30] Panikkar's message was read out in full to the US Ambassador in Delhi by Foreign Secretary K.P.S. Menon. Menon told him that although India did not want to push ahead in recognizing the new regime, it wished to retain a 'free hand' in the matter.[31] The US was, by now, sufficiently concerned for Ambassador Henderson to have a further conversation on the subject with Secretary General Girija Shankar Bajpai, India's chief diplomat, who assured him that all important decisions on this matter would be made in Delhi and, by implication, not by Panikkar.[32]

By the spring of 1949 the National Government was rapidly fading away. It moved its capital from Nanking to the south of the country, and asked foreign embassies to follow suit. In his telegram to the Ministry of External Affairs, Panikkar's assessment was that outright conquest of China by the communists was the most likely outcome but that the situation might continue in its unsettled state for another six months. His recommendation was that the Indian embassy 'should stay in Nanking till communists take over city either by local agreement or by military action and the question of withdrawal should be decided in the light of the communist attitude'. Prime Minister Nehru concurred.[33] As the National Government in China progressively disintegrated over the summer of 1949, Nehru's own inclination was to wait and watch. He felt the situation was so fluid that no government could be recognized till it settled down and indicated how it would act towards India.[34] Nehru began thinking about the possible implications for India, wondering what impact a communist regime in China might have on Tibet and Sinkiang (Xinjiang) with which India shared frontiers.[35] The question of recognition of the communist government was still not uppermost in the Government of India's list of foreign policy priorities, but Nehru, in his letter to the chief ministers in May 1949, laid down a guiding principle, namely that India's desire 'has always been and is to retain the friendship . . .'[36] This approach, as he wrote his sister, Vijayalakshmi Pandit, who was the Indian Ambassador in Washington, meant that India would be in no hurry to recognize the new regime, 'but we are just not going to stand up as crusaders against it'.[37] A few weeks later, Nehru also took note of the positions of the two major Western powers towards developments in China.

British Foreign Secretary Ernest Bevin had disclosed at the annual conference of the Labour Party at Blackpool on 9 June that the British government was considering the issue of recognition of the communist government in China. Nehru also noted that the US was 'a little more reluctant' to go in this direction.[38] But he did not appear to be taking sides in the emerging Anglo-American divergence on China policy.

In early August the State Department released a White Paper ('Relations with China with Special Reference to the Period 1944–1949') that finally acknowledged that the National Government of President Chiang Kai-shek was unlikely to resist the communist advance in any meaningful way. Secretary of State Dean Acheson, in his Letter of Transmittal (of the White Paper) to the US Congress, 'admitted frankly that the American position of assisting the Chinese people in resisting domination by any foreign power or powers is now confronted with the gravest difficulties. The heart of China is now in communist hands.' He concluded, '[It] is abundantly clear that we must face the situation that exists in fact. We will not help the Chinese or ourselves by basing our policy on wishful thinking.'[39] Even at this stage it seemed unwilling to sever its support to President Chiang Kai-shek and the National Government so long as they retained a foothold on the Chinese mainland (in July the Nationalists were still in control of south China, including the city of Canton). Acheson told the American Ambassador in London to convey to the British Foreign Office that he was disturbed by reports that British commercial interests (British companies in Hong Kong and China) were approaching the communists to propose some form of accommodation. He suggested that Britain and the US first have 'frank and private conversations' on this matter. Acheson also reminded the British that its request for American support in case the Chinese communists attacked Hong Kong would 'imply the need to form a common position all along the line'.[40] The Americans also suggested to the British that the two major Western powers (the US and the UK) could broaden their consultations with Asian states but avoid taking leadership of this process. In this regard, Acheson felt that the 'first steps along such lines should be taken by Asiatic states, preferably under Nehru's leadership'.[41] India was now squarely in the sights of both Western powers, and it marked the beginning of strenuous efforts by both to win it over.

When Washington proposed broader consultations with Asian countries, the British realized that the American intention was to canvass support for its own policy. It appeared to be particularly alarmed at the American idea that Nehru should lead consultations on China. Britain did not want the US to influence others, especially Commonwealth members, when it was heading for a breach in Anglo-American unity over the China policy. Foreign Secretary Bevin's instructions were, therefore, 'that we must stop the Americans from talking about—"under Nehru's leadership". This would not be acceptable to some of the other powers concerned.'[42] He informed Lewis W. Douglas, the US Ambassador in London, 'in confidence', that Nehru was increasingly concerned about the spread of communism inside India and would, thus, pay progressively less attention to foreign affairs. Bevin also told Douglas that China was primarily an American problem and, therefore, they should take the lead.[43] Bevin's comment regarding Nehru's lack of attention to foreign affairs was simply not true. Indeed, the case was precisely the opposite. Nehru was not just greatly interested in developments inside China, but was also considering what policy India might adopt. From this point on Great Britain took a more active interest in trying to influence Indian thinking on the question of recognition. Britain understood well that if the US got India's support for its China policy (which was to delay recognizing the new communist regime), Nehru's stature and capacity to influence other Asian states and the Commonwealth members could potentially jeopardize British interests in the Far East.

Meanwhile, Acheson's request in July 1949 for 'frank and private conversations' with Britain on the China question spurred the latter to craft a definitive British policy. A senior British Foreign Office official, commenting on America's policy, wrote that 'it seems merely ostrich-like to wish to go on extending recognition to the bitter end only to the Nationalist rump. But we have for some time past received plenty of indications that that was the US policy.'[44] A detailed paper was, therefore, prepared in the British Foreign Office on the question of recognizing the new regime.[45] The key question to be resolved was whether the new regime should be treated as a potentially unfriendly one or whether Britain should approach 'New China' with a view to assisting the communist government to act independently of other governments (meaning the Soviet Union) by means of offering it full participation in international affairs and full trading and diplomatic relations with the West. There was, at the time, more than one view even inside the British establishment. The view that communist China should be recognized without delay was being championed by Sir Ralph Stevenson, the British Ambassador in Nanking, who summed up the entire British policy in a single word: 'trade'.* [46] On the other hand, Sir Malcolm MacDonald, the Commissioner General for the UK in Southeast Asia, struck a cautious note. Writing to Sir William Strang, the Permanent Under Secretary of State for Foreign Affairs, MacDonald pointed

---

* In a telegram sent to the British Foreign Office, Stevenson wrote: 'I think in fact it [British policy] can be summed up in one word—trade. By sticking to that policy, we not only avoid numberless difficulties but we gain solid advantages for ourselves . . . the question of recognition of the regime must therefore be decided on practical and not on ideological grounds. And there should be no undue delay in coming to a decision.'

out that diplomatic recognition of the communist government would land Britain in 'some difficult consequences' in the colonies in Malaya, Singapore and British Borneo, because it would allow communist representatives to move freely in areas with large ethnic Chinese populations. He declared this to be 'dangerous' and urged that this be a consideration on the side of postponing diplomatic recognition for as long as possible.

The Far Eastern Affairs Department of the British Foreign Office was inclined to the view that since all countries would eventually be compelled to recognize the new government, there was nothing to be lost and perhaps something to be gained if the West took the initiative at the appropriate time in offering the resumption of commercial and diplomatic ties.[47] The Foreign Office paper also pointed out that the US was focused only on the strategic competition with communism and that it did not have the same level of commercial interest as Britain in China. If consultations with the Americans on a common policy, as proposed by Acheson, had to be undertaken, 'we consider that this [consultation] should be held on the basis of mutual recognition that both (a) our respective means of control over commercial concerns and (b) our commercial interests in China, are different'.

Once the memorandum was ready, Bevin took it to the cabinet. Laying out the argument in his memorandum to his cabinet colleagues, Bevin said that American anxiety extended only to stopping the flow of strategic raw materials to the communists with no clear policy of dealing with them, whereas Britain's policy was to do its utmost to build contacts with them. The dilemma it faced was 'we must either agree to differ [with the US] and pursue our own policy of keeping a foot in the door or abandon the whole of our interest in China in order to follow in the American wake'.[48] Given Britain's commercial interests in China, he recommended the course of action of maintaining contact with the communists.* In the end, the argument in favour of trade won out in the British Foreign Office. The British cabinet also formally approved the policy set out in the Foreign Office Memorandum of 15 August.[49] The stage was now set for Anglo-American confrontation over China, as well as for their competition to influence India's China policy.

The British Foreign Office policy paper (Memorandum) titled 'China' was shared with, among others, both Washington and New Delhi in the second half of August 1949. Its main argument was that there were no further grounds for hope that the communists would fail in their bid for complete power in China and that future policy should be made on this basic assumption. Britain was not recommending a policy of appeasing the communists, but felt that a head-on conflict should be avoided. It put forth a political argument that any display of a 'general and avowed hostility' towards the Chinese communists would drive them further into the 'arms of Moscow'. The British memorandum also clearly reflected the deep commercial considerations that were driving its policy. It wished to maintain its substantial commercial and financial interests in China for as long as possible.[†] London was concerned that if American thinking prevailed about imposing harsh trade sanctions on the Chinese communists, 'it is, of

---

* British thinking was in remarkable sync with that of Mao Zedong who, in January 1949, had given strict orders not to be hasty in halting the activities of foreign banks, shipping and insurance companies or to interfere with floating cargo. ('Guidelines of the CCP on the Question of Work in the Sphere of Foreign Policy', 19 January 1949, Wilson Center Digital Archive, RGASPI, F. 558, OP. 11, D. 328, ii. 56–62, translated by Gary Goldberg, https://digitalarchive.wilsoncenter.org/document/134158.)

† As the communist revolution progressed in China, Hong Kong became the heir to Shanghai which, until then, was the base for Britain's business interests in China. Hong Kong would be the foothold for Britain to rebuild its commercial empire after the World War.

course, practically certain that long-established and deep-rooted commercial establishments and connections, once abandoned, could never be restored'. The British policy paper was given a legal colour by quoting international law, and asserting that the withholding of recognition to a government in effective control of the entire territory would be legally objectionable and complicate the protection of Western interests.[50]

A second development in the month of August also had a bearing on India. This was an invitation from the Philippines for India to attend a conference in Manila to build an anti-communist bloc in the Far East. This effort was sponsored by the United States. They wanted India to join, but Nehru saw pacts of any sort as provocative and likely to drag India into conflict. Economic development was the main priority of the Indian government at this time, and this consideration shaped its foreign policy. Panikkar wrote to Nehru on 10 August (after his talk with a Chinese communist official), asking Nehru to make a public statement about India's determination to keep out of any bloc directed against communism.[51] Nehru wrote to Ambassador Pandit in Washington that 'its [Manila Conference] objectives might look innocuous but . . . the conference itself is sure to be regarded by many as a move against communism in general and against communist China in particular'.[52] India declined to attend. The Americans were disappointed at India's non-participation in the Manila Conference, but they persevered with India on the question of delaying recognition to the Chinese communists. The American Ambassador in New Delhi was tasked with ascertaining India's position on this question since, with the fall of Canton (Guangzhou), the last major city on the east coast still in Chiang Kai-shek's hands, their expectation was that the Chinese communists would soon invite diplomatic recognition from foreign countries.[53] The American outreach happened days after the British memorandum on China was given to the Ministry of External Affairs. This was the point at which the Government of India began to take more seriously the 'distinct—and somewhat disturbing—signs of a divergence of opinion between them [US and Britain].' A note recorded by Indian Foreign Secretary K.P.S. Menon opined that Britain was all for trade with communist China while the Americans wanted to reduce it to the minimum. His view was that British policy was realistic and 'in accord with our own'. Menon acknowledged that British policy was influenced by economic and commercial considerations and that 'we have no commercial interests of any magnitude in China, but it is wise for us to adopt more or less the same attitude as His Majesty's Government from a purely political point of view'.[54]

Bajpai, who was Menon's superior in the ministry, added his own remarks to Menon's note, stating: 'The British policy is both realistic and bold; one can only hope that the United States of America will not be led away by its anti-communist hysteria. China is too big to be either bullied or ignored; either attitude would only drive its communist masters deeper into the arms of the USSR.'[55] In building out its own position on the recognition question, it is noteworthy that the Ministry of External Affairs used some of the very arguments being used by the British. This included the one about not pushing the Chinese communists into Soviet arms by taking a hard line on recognition. By early September 1949, this line of argument did not hold water. Mao Zedong had already publicly declared his intention of 'leaning to one side',[56] that is, of aligning with the Soviet Union. This had been reported to New Delhi by the Indian embassy in Nanking. The British argument dovetailed with Nehru's thinking regarding the Cold War, non-alignment and peace and stability in Asia. The fact of the Sino-Soviet alignment was, presumably, set aside in policy considerations by the Government of India.

There was also an anti-American undercurrent in some of the notes and conversations among Indian policymakers. In this regard the attitude of Panikkar in particular cannot be ignored. He was an influential and early voice against the American policy on China. He had been quite clear even in June that 'agreement with America on this question [of recognition], if any has been reached, cannot fail to give impression to the new government in China that we are allowing ourselves to be used for furtherance of American interests'.[57] Panikkar was not happy about Ambassador Stuart's efforts to organize a common front among foreign embassies in Nanking in order to line them up behind the American policy which he felt was entirely governed by Cold War and anti-Soviet considerations without showing sympathy for the Chinese mass revolution.* Panikkar carried influence inside the Indian government and his views resonated with Nehru, who also felt that partnership with China would be beneficial to India. He attached importance to what Panikkar thought, and in his letter to the chief ministers in May 1949, he specifically talked of keeping Panikkar in China to 'help us to frame our future policy'.[58] In July, when the Americans withdrew Stuart from China, Panikkar described it as a 'decided stiffening of American attitude'.[59]

In August, Panikkar recommended that India should not participate in the Manila Conference and the Pacific Pact because his communist interlocutor Han Nianlong (later Vice Foreign Minister) had said that the Chinese view about India would favourably change if India refused to attend.[60] In early September 1949, Panikkar sent a long note to the Ministry of External Affairs titled 'Some Aspects of American Policy in China

---

* Although Chinese communist propaganda regularly carried anti-Indian pieces, Panikkar still felt that 'there are reasons to think that they are prepared to follow a course of action not unfriendly to us'. (*Doc. 0078*, 'Telegram from Panikkar to K.P.S. Menon', 10 June 1949, *India–China Relations, 1947–2000, A Documentary Study, Vol. II*, introduced and edited by A.S. Bhasin [New Delhi: Geetika Publishers], pp. 114–16.)

(So Far as It Affects Other Countries)'. It was a broad critique of American policy. In his note he listed all the American actions and statements against the Chinese communists, absolving the latter of any responsibility for the hostility with the Americans by saying that 'to a large extent, it can be said that apart from general slogans against American capitalism, Chinese actions and statements have been in reply to American actions'. The Chinese communists had indulged in violence against the US Consul in Mukden and forcibly shut down the US Information Service (USIS) office, but Panikkar proclaimed that he was 'satisfied that the anti-American incidents and statements are the result of America's own attitude'.

He directly linked American policy on China to the Cold War by saying that Washington refused to see the Chinese revolution as a major event in Asia, and only wanted to consider it as a projection of Moscow's policy. He concluded this long piece of writing by warning Delhi that the US would seek to influence India in every possible way because without Indian acquiescence its policy had little chance of success.[61] Panikkar admitted to talking to 'hard-headed British business leaders' who, he claimed, were unanimously of the same view as his about America's unrealistic policy. He also regularly conversed with Sir Ralph Stevenson, the British Ambassador to China, who convinced Panikkar that American policy was untenable. There is little doubt that Stevenson was instrumental in shaping Panikkar's view on what India's policy should be. He was au fait with what Panikkar was reporting to the government in Delhi since his messages were being passed to the Ministry of External Affairs via the British embassy in Nanking and the British Foreign Office. They knew the sort of influence that Panikkar carried with Nehru. The British were, therefore, well placed to influence India's China policy through Panikkar. The Americans got to hear of Panikkar's critical views about their policy soon enough (both the US embassy counsellor in Nanking and the American ambassador in New Delhi reported on the matter to the State Department). The British tried to throw them off the scent by claiming that Panikkar's views may not be backed up by the government in Delhi.[62]

From early September 1949, once communist victory became certain, the British government stepped up its efforts to ensure that the Americans would not secure Indian acquiescence to its policy on not recognizing communist China. Bevin finally agreed to Acheson's request (made in July) for Anglo-American consultations, but before proceeding to Washington in mid-September 1949, Bevin instructed his Foreign Office to canvass support within the Commonwealth for the British policy on the early recognition of communist China.[63] The British Deputy High Commissioner in New Delhi, Frank Roberts, in carrying out Bevin's instructions, wrote to the Ministry of External Affairs 'very much hop(ing) that Commonwealth governments will feel able to support the line which the United Kingdom government proposed to take' with Washington on the recognition question.[64] In order to circumscribe the possibility of the US exerting pressure on India sufficiently to turn it to the American side, Britain also told the Ministry of External Affairs that in case the US suggested separate talks with India on this matter, 'we propose to confine ourselves to informing the US authorities that we intend to keep the commonwealth and other interested governments fully informed'.[65] The British felt that if the Americans were able to convince Nehru, given India's and Nehru's stature, other Asian and Commonwealth countries might follow suit, leading to the possible collapse of the British policy. India's position on recognizing China was now tied to Britain's core interests.

The British also tried to sow doubts in American minds about India's stand on the question of recognition by hinting that India might be acting unilaterally in an effort to assert itself as the principal Asiatic power.[66] During the preparatory talks between E.M. Dening and Walton Butterworth, the heads

of the Far Eastern departments in the British Foreign Office
and State Department respectively, Dening averred that 'India
seemed inclined to accord *de facto* recognition or appeared to
feel that recognition should not be delayed too long . . . Recently
there has been an indication that Pandit Nehru might be taking
a slightly more realistic view about the Chinese communists
than previously.'[67] In reality, the Government of India had not
yet taken any decision on recognizing the communist regime.
Indeed, it was the British who had taken the lead on the question
of early recognition and approached the Indian government with
its memorandum in mid-August. In hindsight, British intentions
were to deflect American attention from its own efforts to push
for early recognition by suggesting that it was simply following
the lead of others. It is difficult to escape the conclusion that
British efforts with both New Delhi and Washington from mid-
August onwards were with the clear objective of manipulating
both parties with an eye to advancing its own China policy.

Acheson and Bevin had two conversations in Washington
on 13 and 17 September 1949 (the second conversation also
included French Foreign Minister Robert Schuman). Acheson's
message to Britain was unambiguous. There should be no haste
in recognizing China, and that nobody (he clearly meant Great
Britain) should gain any favours from the Chinese communists
by ready recognition. The Atlantic Pact countries, he said, must
consult 'fully and carefully concert policies on recognition of the
Chinese communist government'. Bevin, in turn, laid the British
cards on the table, emphasizing that it had 'big commercial
interests in and trade with China and were not in the same
position as we (US) were relatively or absolutely . . .'[68] The two
principal crafters of their respective foreign policies went back and
forth, with Bevin expressing concerns that refusal to recognize
the communists would only push them into Soviet arms,[69] and
Acheson rejecting this by countering that 'they [Soviets] will be

there anyway'. Acheson's final advice to Bevin was that the division of policy between the two principal Western powers would be a serious error. The British later put the best possible interpretation on this exchange, claiming that Acheson 'quite understood that because of the much more extensive British interests in China the behaviour of His Majesty's government was bound to be somewhat different from that of the United States government. It was a difference in *situation* rather than a difference in *tactics*' (emphasis added).[70] In their second conversation on the same subject on 17 September (the French Foreign Minister was present as well), Acheson cautioned Bevin again that approaching the communists was just what they [Chinese communists] wanted the West to do.[71] At the conclusion of his meetings in Washington, Bevin assured Acheson that the British would 'proceed with great caution and remain in close consultation with the US, French and other governments concerned'.[72] Britain had reason to be satisfied with these consultations since the agreement to concert with the Americans was a general one and it was a matter of interpretation as to what this practically meant. The British Foreign Office informed Stevenson in Nanking that 'no decisions were reached and the talks consisted of an exchange of views. This exchange of views was, however, extremely useful and it can be said that the danger of a marked divergence between UK and US policy over China has been averted.'[73] It was clear from the two conversations in Washington that Britain had openly split with the US over the China policy.

Within a week of the Anglo-American consultations, and despite British assurances to the Americans that it would closely consult them beforehand, Stevenson, the British Ambassador in Nanking, established contact with a senior communist official, Chang (Zhang) Hanfu, the head of the Foreign Nationals Bureau in Shanghai, to convey that 'the general policy of His Majesty's Government towards China (which I said) was based on promotion of trade'. It was Stevenson's suggestion that 'foreign powers would expect some formal notification on the event of the new government's readiness to establish normal relations with them and that mere broadcasting of it to the world by the New China News Agency would not suffice'.[74] In other words, the British solicited an approach from the communists for diplomatic recognition, even as they were assuring Washington that they intended to act in consultation and concert on the question of recognizing the new communist state. On 1 October 1949, Mao Zedong proclaimed the establishment of the People's Republic of China from atop the Gate of Heavenly Peace (Tian An Men) in Beijing.* A day later, on 2 October, foreign diplomats in China received identically worded notes from the Ministry of Foreign Affairs inviting recognition from all countries of the world on the basis of equality, and respect for sovereignty and territorial integrity.

America and Great Britain acted immediately, but in very different ways. After receiving the Chinese note, Stevenson advised London that the British government should 'at an appropriate moment after the formation of the new government make an *official* [emphasis added] communication to the Ministry of Foreign Affairs'.[75] It was in this message that the full extent of the collaboration between Stevenson and Panikkar also became clear. Stevenson informed the Foreign Office that 'this telegram has been drafted in consultation with my Indian and Australian colleagues who are in general agreement with it and request that its contents to be communicated to their respective governments'.[76] Sir William Strang, Permanent Under Secretary of State for Foreign Affairs, discussed Stevenson's proposal with

---

* Mao declared: 'Dear compatriots, today I hereby declare the formal establishment of the People's Republic of China and its Central People's Government.'

Prime Minister Attlee on 3 October and telegraphed the British government's concurrence to Stevenson's proposed course of action on the same day. The British embassy in Nanking sent a formal response to the Chinese note on a government-to-government basis on 5 October 1949. The British note stated that 'friendly and mutually advantageous relations, both commercial and political, have existed between Britain and China for many generations. It is hoped that these will continue in the future. His Majesty's Government of the United Kingdom do, therefore, suggest that pending completion of their study of the situation, informal relations should be established between His Majesty's Consular Officers and the appropriate authorities in the territory under the control of the Chinese Peoples Government for the greater convenience of both governments and the promotion of trade between the two countries.'[77] Prior to sending this note, there was no consultation with the US or any other Atlantic Powers. In fact, *post facto*, the British Foreign Office first chose to inform the Commonwealth countries, and only later the Americans. The Foreign Office also told its envoys abroad to emphasize, when conveying this news, 'that this in no way represents a departure from His Majesty's Government's declared policy of consulting the friendly governments regarding the recognition question'.[78]

The Americans were upset. Their Ambassador in London was asked to demarche[*] the Foreign Office immediately. Initially, the British claimed that its communication with the communist regime did not imply de facto recognition, but was only a 'device to establish informal relationship with communist authorities'.[79] The US State Department commented that it was difficult to escape the conclusion that the failure by the British Foreign Office to inform the US was deliberate.[80] Acheson wrote to Bevin to

---

[*] 'Demarche' is a diplomatic term meaning to make an oral or written statement to a foreign government on a question of concern or interest.

say that such independent action by one of the Western powers would be exploited by the Chinese. In private, President Truman was reported to have said that the British had not played very squarely with the US on this matter.[81] The British Foreign Office took rearguard action to repair the damage by claiming that the failure to intimate the US in advance was due to the carelessness of a low-level Foreign Office functionary who had failed to send the information by telegram to the British embassy in Washington. It was a feeble claim.*

The position that India might take became of great importance. Nehru was slated to make a long visit to Washington in October, a mere ten days after Mao's declaration. Britain was, therefore, relieved when India (also Portugal and Burma) responded to the Chinese note in a manner similar to its own. The British establishment did note that India's phrasing was 'more restrained than ours',[†82] but its assessment was that India's stand amounted to de facto recognition.[83]

---

* This story went all around the world because it was picked up in Moscow and reported to Delhi by the counsellor of the Indian embassy (File 710 (2)—CJK—49, letter from R. Dayal, counsellor, Moscow, to K.P.S. Menon, 10 November 1949).

† The complete Indian response was as follows: 'The Government of India have taken note of the formation of the Chinese People's Government in China and are carefully considering the situation that has arisen. In this connection they have summoned their Ambassador in Nanking to Delhi for consultation. Pending the outcome of their consideration of the new situation the Government of India hope that *informal contacts* [emphasis added] would continue to be maintained as at present with our consular representatives in China as this course would be of mutually advantage. India and China have an unbroken friendship dating back many centuries and the Government of India have no doubt that this friendship will and must continue.'

Since Nehru was slated to visit Washington from 11 October, on 7 October, Donovan, the acting American Ambassador in Delhi, conveyed to the Ministry of External Affairs that 'there should be no haste in recognition [of the] regime'. More significantly, Donovan enunciated four important principles that the Americans hoped, at a minimum, the Government of India should satisfy itself would be met before India recognized China, namely (1) that the new government had effective control over the entire country; (2) that it showed by actions that it respected international obligations and intended to honour them; (3) that it would conduct international relations in conformity with established diplomatic practices; and (4) that it gave convincing evidence that such recognition would result in marked improvement in India's ability to protect its interests.[84] Donovan met Foreign Secretary Menon on 10 October to reiterate this message in the form of a written aide-mémoire to the Government of India. The handing over of the aide-mémoire was intended to lay the groundwork for President Truman and Secretary Acheson to discuss China with Nehru in Washington. Menon's comment to Donovan was that recognition was inevitable in the light of developments, but the final decision would be made by Nehru after he returned to India from his trip to the US, Canada and the UK.[85]

The four principles enunciated by the Americans were unexceptionable and deserved careful consideration. India had important political interests at stake—the boundary and Tibet among others. In his letters to the chief ministers, Nehru had observed that Tibet may become a subject of argument.[86] He also noted as another matter of interest that Sinkiang (Xinjiang) touched the Kashmir frontier.[87] In early September, when it was clear that the communists would soon establish a government in China, Nehru dictated a memo about a possible Chinese invasion of Tibet resulting in 'the Chinese or Tibetan communists right up on our Assam, Bhutan and Sikkim border'.[88] The Indian government was aware of the hostile Chinese communist propaganda against India on Tibet, and this continued even after positive statements by Nehru about the regime.[89] Just before finally leaving China, Panikkar met Zhou Enlai on 27 September. He reported to Delhi that Zhou had given an assurance that there were no differences between India and China and that he was anxious to safeguard in every way Indian interest in Tibet. Nehru told Panikkar that some indication from Zhou Enlai that the new communist regime would respond to India's 'suggestion for settling matters of common interest by diplomatic negotiation seems desirable before you leave'. [90] None was received. In light of this, it might have been prudent to heed American advice on securing some assurance from the new communist government of its willingness to accept the validity of the earlier treaties before according formal recognition.

On 12 October, on the eve of Nehru's meetings with President Truman and Secretary Acheson in Washington, Menon telegraphed Panikkar's views to Nehru. Both its timing and its contents hinted that arguments were being given to Nehru in Washington to counter the ideas in the American aide-mémoire. Panikkar re-emphasized that the Americans considered the new regime in China as a projection of Soviet expansionism, and that the British policy was more realistic in regard to the regime. In Washington, the Americans explained the reasons behind their policy on recognition to Nehru in the context of their strategic thinking about the threat posed to global peace and stability by communism, and the probability of a Sino-Soviet condominium. Nehru shared his own thinking with Truman, namely that the course of events in China would restore 'Chinese nationalism as a governing force and weaken the subservience to Moscow'.[91] It was the classic Cold War debate. Nehru's attitude, as per Acheson, was that since recognition was inevitable there was little purpose in postponing it by diplomatic manoeuvres. Nehru also conveyed that India's proximity to China placed it in a somewhat different position from other countries.[92] Acheson invited Nehru to his home after the White House dinner for a long conversation, hoping to find some common ground on China. Acheson would later aver that 'he [Nehru] talked to me, as Queen Victoria said of Mr Gladstone, as though I were a public meeting'.[93] When President Truman urged Nehru to consult and, if possible, concert India's action with the American government with regard to recognition of the new communist regime in China, Nehru agreed to consultation but avoided replying to the idea of concerting with the Americans. Since, by that time, Nehru was leaning towards an early recognition of the new regime in China, once again the Americans reminded him that the Chinese communists should be asked to make clear that they would meet their international obligations before extending recognition. There was no indication that Nehru heeded the advice.

While Nehru was on his official visit to America and Canada, Britain was leaving no stone unturned in its efforts to convince the Ministry of External Affairs in Delhi of the correctness of the British position and to persuade India to follow suit.[*] [94] In mid-October, Sir Archibald Nye, the British High Commissioner in New Delhi, informed Foreign Secretary K.P.S. Menon that the outgoing British Ambassador to China, Sir Ralph Stevenson, would visit Delhi en route to London and 'I have no doubt you would like to take this opportunity of discussing the situation in China with him'.[95] The British objective was to decisively influence the final decision of India in regard to the question

---

[*] Menon was reported to have told the Delhi correspondent of the *Chicago Tribune*, Percy Wood, that the British were hoping that India would take action consonant with and simultaneous to Britain on this question (of recognition).

of recognition. The combination of Stevenson and Panikkar in Delhi was a powerful one.

Pending Nehru's return, in October, the Ministry of External Affairs finally began full-scale internal consultations on the question of recognition. It was thoroughly examined from the historical, political and legal angles by C.S. Jha, Joint Secretary (North), the official most directly concerned with China. He recommended giving full de jure recognition to the PRC. The American aide-mémoire was also examined and Jha expressed himself not in favour of its idea of asking the new regime to furnish categorical proof that India's interests would be preserved before recognizing the PRC.[96] Foreign Secretary Menon also opined on the file, 'I doubt whether anything will be gained by seeking clarification whether the new government would be prepared to honour its international obligations vis-à-vis India flowing from treaties between China and India . . . Any attempt to have the position clarified will lead to endless controversy . . . I am of the opinion that we should give simple recognition first and ask for clarification on any points which may arise as and when occasions demand.'[97]

After Panikkar returned from Nanking to Delhi these notes were also shown to him. The prospects and utility of India making some kind of unilateral statement to the effect that it would be presumed that the new Chinese government would abide by all previous treaties was also examined. C.S. Jha felt that 'in view of the unsatisfactory position as regards the existence of treaties with China—the 1914 Convention not having been signed by China is not binding on them—it would perhaps be advisable to avoid anything like "The Government of India assume that the existing treaties between India and China will remain in force or respected etc".'[98] Panikkar added his view that 'since the new Chinese government has not denounced the earlier treaties it is perhaps unnecessary to say anything on the subject, especially as we have concluded no agreements after 1946'.[99]

Panikkar seems to have concluded, on what basis it is not clear, that the new Chinese government might only be interested in rescinding treaties signed after 1945, mostly those between the National Government and the Americans. A final attempt was made by the Americans to influence Panikkar when the acting US Ambassador, Joseph R. Donovan, met him in Delhi in early November, but he too was unsuccessful in persuading Panikkar to either delay recognition or seek assurances from the Chinese communist regime about respecting international obligations. Panikkar advanced the argument that Nehru had used in Washington, namely about India's frontier with China being the more pressing matter than economic interests or the menace of communism, and averring that India would be in a better position to protect its diplomatic interests if it first established diplomatic relations. Donovan reported to Washington that Panikkar's arguments would have a considerable effect upon Nehru since he discounted any danger to India arising from the recognition of the communist regime.[100]

In late October another memorandum from Bevin to the British cabinet recommended that 'it is obviously desirable to obtain the largest measure of agreement possible, and in particular the agreement of the commonwealth countries' for its policy.[101] Towards the end of October the British handed over a second memorandum setting forth the British government's views on recognition and sought India's reaction within two weeks.* While informing the Indian government that there was no change in the American attitude, this second British memorandum pushed two arguments favouring early recognition, arguments which the British hoped would resonate with India. The first was that because the Soviet Union and its allies had already recognized the PRC, the absence of non-socialist diplomatic representatives in Beijing would make it easier for the Soviets to take advantage of

---

* The same memorandum was also given in Washington and other capitals.

the situation. In other words, British policy said early recognition
by non-communist governments had become necessary because
the Soviets had already done so. The second argument (through a
note to Menon in early November titled 'Effects of Recognition
of the Communist Government in China') was that Britain was
already dealing with communist movements in its colonies in the
region and recognizing the PRC would not lead to the spread
of communism throughout Asia.[102] Again, the intention was to
counter possible geopolitical arguments that the US was making
about how the legitimization of the communist regime would
fuel communist insurgencies and movements in Southeast Asia
and elsewhere. Stevenson's presence in Delhi would doubtless
have bolstered these arguments favouring British policy. On
4 November 1949, Foreign Secretary Menon informed High
Commissioner Archibald Nye, for the first time, that India would
accord recognition de jure and not merely de facto, and that the
only question that remained was one of timing and the modalities
of recognition. This would be decided after Prime Minister
Nehru returned and had talked with Panikkar.[103] By the
time Nehru returned from his trip to the UK and the US, the
matter was ripe for final decision.

A final British effort to push India towards the decision to
recognize communist China de jure at any early date was the sharing
with the Government of India of the confidential proceedings of
a British conference consisting of British representatives and high-
ranking military officers based in Southeast Asia held in Bukit
Serene, Singapore, on 15 November. The main recommendation
arising from the Bukit Serene conference was that earliest possible
de jure recognition of the communist government in China was
desirable and that no formal conditions need be attached.[104] In
fact, the report on the Bukit Serene conference opined that if
early recognition was not given, the Chinese-origin populations

in Southeast Asia, which were largely in sympathy with the new regime, would foment trouble in these countries. By implication, this meant that non-recognition (and not early recognition) enhanced the dangers of communism spreading in the region. This was precisely the opposite of what Sir Malcolm MacDonald, Britain's Commissioner General in Southeast Asia, had said to his own government in September (Britain was already dealing with a communist insurgency in Malaya). Its claim to the contrary in the memorandum showed that it was prepared to twist facts to secure its policy. British advice that recognition should be given without attaching any conditions may also have persuaded officials in the Ministry of External Affairs to adopt this course of action. Any possibility of following the American advice, even on the question of seeking general assurances from the Chinese with regard to their honouring international treaties, thus effectively had no chance of success.

At the same time, the British Foreign Office also continued to make the Americans believe that it was India which was running ahead of everybody else, including Britain, in the matter of recognition. Krishna Menon, India's ambassador in London, reported on information that he had gathered from a 'well informed and reliable' source from a meeting between the foreign ministers of the US, UK and France in Paris in November at which British Foreign Secretary Bevin conveyed to Acheson that Britain was under pressure to recognize the communist regime owing to the attitude of India.[105] An almost similar message was delivered by a British diplomat to his American counterpart in Washington that India 'may act independently if general recognition is too long delayed'.[106] On the other hand, the British also misrepresented American thinking to the Commonwealth governments. When Foreign Secretary Bevin met with Commonwealth diplomatic representatives in London on 15 November, he conveyed his 'impression' that 'the US opinion showed signs of becoming less averse to the British attitude'.[*107] Since the American position was rock-solid on the question of non-recognition, Bevin's 'impression' was clearly intended to deceive. India bought the British line and concluded that although the Americans were likely to delay recognition for some time, they would eventually do so. This would have helped Nehru reach the decision on early recognition. (Nehru's message to British Prime Minister Clement Attlee read: 'We note that United States may not, for special reasons, accord recognition that this stage. But we are sure that they will.'[108]) Thus, Britain did its level best to ensure that India and America remained apart.[†]

There were voices in India which had expressed concern at the haste with which the government was proceeding on the matter of recognizing the new regime in China. Deputy Prime

---

* Note handed over by British Deputy High Commissioner Roberts to Sir Girija Shankar Bajpai on this meeting stated as follows: 'He [Bevin] also voiced his impression, and he made it clear that this was no more than a personal impression, that the US opinion showed signs of becoming less averse to the UK attitude, though the detention of the US Consul General in Mukden was clearly a most serious obstacle in way of recognition by the US.' This note was seen and initialled by Prime Minister Nehru.

† The lengths to which the British Foreign Office was prepared to go in support of its policy became evident when it even got diplomats from India, Australia and Canada, who had remained behind in Nanking after the withdrawal of the ambassadors, to draft a joint text to be passed on to the Chinese side in which all the four governments would jointly state that they considered all requirements in international law for de jure recognition had been fulfilled and that the only question was of timing. (File 710 (2)—CJK—49, letter from British Deputy High Commissioner Roberts to Foreign Secretary K.P.S. Menon, dated 24 November 1949. This was seen and initialled by Nehru. This initiative did not proceed because the Canadians objected.)

Minister and Home Minister Vallabhbhai Patel was one such voice. He invited Acting American Ambassador Donovan to his residence on 4 November to discuss this matter. Patel talked about the implications of the Chinese communist regime for Tibet, Burma and so on, and opined that there was no need to hurry in recognizing them and asked Donovan to stay in touch.[109] Several months later, Ambassador Henderson told the State Department that 'Sardar Patel told me last spring that Nehru would not have rushed so quickly into the recognition of Communist China if he had not been convinced by the retiring British Ambassador to China [Stevenson], and other Britishers who came to Delhi, that China should be recognized and that the United Kingdom expected to recognize China. Nehru, therefore, according to Sardar Patel, took the position that since under British leadership the whole Western world would eventually recognize Communist China, India should move first. In fact, the British, according to Sardar Patel, told Nehru that they had informal assurances from high American officials that just as soon as a suitable set of circumstances could be brought about, the Government of the United States would recognize Communist China.'[110] Despite the reservations of Patel, Rajagopalachari and even Bajpai (on the timing of the announcement), the Prime Minister presided over a meeting on 17 November 1949 where it was decided to accord unconditional de jure recognition to the newly established People's Republic of China.

In the note that he personally recorded on the decision to recognize the People's Republic of China, Nehru specifically made mention of two persons to whom he had spoken on the matter, namely Panikkar and Stevenson, saying that both had been 'anxious that recognition should be given as early as possible'. It is not clear whether the 17 November meeting, where the final decision to recognize the PRC was taken, had reflected upon the difficult questions relating to the boundary and other treaties and arrangements relating to Tibet that the British-Indian government had signed with the earlier Chinese governments or whether the Government of India should first satisfy itself that the new government would respect earlier treaties and agreements. A detailed record of that meeting is not available. What is clear is that no conditions were required to be fulfilled by the new Chinese regime in return for recognition by the Indian government. The only question that remained to be decided after 17 November 1949 was about the timing of the announcement.

On this point, too, Nehru accepted Panikkar's advice that India's act of recognition should precede, and not follow, the Commonwealth Foreign Ministers' Conference (which was scheduled in Colombo for mid-January 1950) so that India was seen to be acting independently of the other powers, especially Great Britain.[111] Again, this fitted in with Nehru's thinking. In the minutes of the meeting on 17 November he referred to the 'limitations' of time. It was decided that recognition should be sometime between 15–25 December. One of the primary reasons recorded in this note for the delay of one month after the decision was taken to recognize the PRC was in order to 'also show that we have not been precipitate in our action but have consulted those countries whom we normally consult in such matters. I am inclined to think that Panikkar's point about our recognizing before the Commonwealth Conference is a good one.'[112] Thus, in the matter of timing it was the optics that mattered more than substance. Secretary General Girija Shankar Bajpai's advice, recorded on file, that early recognition might jeopardize India's position on Kashmir in the UN Security Council because Chiang Kai-shek's government still held the China seat[113] was not heeded. It is not clear whether Nehru consulted the cabinet as Patel had asked him to do.[114] Declassified papers contain a brief document titled 'Meeting of the Cabinet Held on Tuesday, 27 December 1949', in which it is simply stated: 'The Prime Minister informed the Cabinet that it was proposed to recognize the new government of China before the end of this month.'[115]

The explanatory telegrams sent out by New Delhi to Indian embassies and high commissions in Washington, London, Ottawa, Canberra, Colombo and Rangoon (Yangon) after the decision on recognition was taken on 17 November used some of the reasoning from the two British memoranda. 'We are strongly advised that delay in recognition may well be injurious politically and economically and may encourage wrong tendencies in China . . . Economically it must hamper normal trade and commerce and cause loss to those foreigners who are engaged in it [India had no trade to speak of with China]. The internal situation in many countries in south-east Asia, where there are large Chinese populations, also points to the need for early recognition . . . We note that this has been realized at the recent Regional Conference in Singapore' (to which India was not invited since it was a meeting of British heads of mission and military personnel).[116] Nehru assured the chief ministers that India would not be affected in the sense of any military danger even if the communist regime spread into Tibet.[117] There were internal concerns on this account. Nehru had told Menon and Panikkar that while India would recognize communist China 'it must be made clear to all concerned that any threat to Nepal, Sikkim, Bhutan, Ladakh or the McMahon Line areas will be resisted with all our force'.[118] Yet the Government of India did not see it fit to convey this position to the new communist regime in Beijing or to seek confirmation on the boundary alignment at the time of according recognition.

The Americans made one final effort in early December to delay India's proposed recognition of the communist regime. State Department officials advised Secretary Acheson to convey to the Indian Ambassador in Washington that hasty recognition by leading democratic powers might prove an 'illusory benefit' and might have 'undesirable repercussions' in Southeast Asia.[119]

Acheson met Vijayalakshmi Pandit, the Indian Ambassador in
Washington, on 6 December. The outcome of that discussion
is not available, but Ambassador Pandit had reported to Delhi
just prior to her meeting with Acheson that 'conversations with
smaller members indicate that State Department not unwilling to
recognize new Chinese regime but strong Republican opposition
in Congress causes delay'.[120] In hindsight, this might have
been an erroneous judgement because the American policy was
well-known.

Having succeeded in securing confirmation from the
Government of India as to both recognizing the new regime in
Beijing and a date for this, the British government turned coy
about the precise timing of its own recognition. It took a month
(till 15 December 1949) to confirm its decision to recognize the
new regime. It was conscious that, as Bevin told the cabinet on
12 December, 'it would be a stab in the back' to the Americans.
It did not wish to be the first to do so, although it had been
the principal force in favour of accommodating the communists
since the end of 1948. When it learnt that Nehru was keen
to make the announcement before Britain, Britain was happy
because this would make it easier to justify to the US as to why
a concert of actions had not, after all, been possible.* Prime
Minister Attlee played to Nehru's ego by telling him that Britain
had taken the views of its Asian friends into account.[121] Nehru,
in his reply to Attlee, expressed his appreciation for 'your taking
into account views of Asian countries in regard to this problem
which is primarily Asian'.[122] The Government of India took care

---

* Foreign Secretary Bevin told US Secretary of State Acheson, 'We have
to be careful not to lose our grip of the situation in Asia and to take into
account views of our Asian friends.' (British Embassy to the Department of
State, Personal Message from Mr Bevin to Mr Acheson, *FRUS, 1949, The
Far East: China, Vol. IX*).

to keep the US informed. Nehru still hoped, perhaps based on Britain's assurances, that the US would come around soon to recognizing the new regime and, in the meantime, understand India's special position.

On 29 December 1949, the Government of India withdrew recognition from the Republic of China (Chiang Kai-shek's government now based on the island of Taiwan) and informed its ambassador in New Delhi of the decision. On 30 December, via telegram, the Indian representative who had remained in Nanking after Panikkar's departure informed Zhou Enlai of India's decision to accord recognition to the PRC, and asserted that this act by India would further strengthen the 'immemorial friendship' between the two countries and would be conducive to the stability of Asia and the peace of the world.[123] Britain followed suit on 6 January 1950. Bevin telegraphed Acheson to assure him that 'this does not lessen our determination to resist communism in south east Asia', while keeping up pretences that its hands had been forced by the 'views of our Asian friends'.[124]

Nehru's decision to recognize China was a strategic one based on his world view that India and China, as the major Asian powers, had to work together if India was to carve out an independent role in the Indo–Pacific region. His strategic instinct was sound. But the tactical planning was absent from the exercise. Recognition became an end in itself. It became a procedural matter, rather than a matter for negotiation in which bargaining would bring desirable outcomes beneficial to newly independent India's national security. Wider consultation within the Indian system might have led to greater reflection on the issue, but instead the matter was discussed and decided upon within a closely held group of advisors around Nehru, and in close consultation with Britain.

Chapter 3

Geneva and Indochina

The loss of China was a serious setback for the foreign policy of the United States. They had failed to maintain a united front with Britain on the question of recognizing China. America turned its attention thereafter to stabilizing Japan and consolidating its position in the northwestern Pacific Ocean where it had strategic interests. Britain was allowed to take the lead in Southeast Asia.

The Sino-American confrontation in the Korean War in October 1950 was a game changer. It revived the domestic narrative in the United States about the loss of China, and fed the view that the Soviets and the Chinese were united in their objective to expand communism in the rest of Asia. The Truman and—subsequently—the Eisenhower administrations were determined to stop them. Britain was pursuing different interests—the colonies, trade and influence in the region—and was fighting a communist insurgency in Malaya. The gradual decline in its global power meant that it had fewer means to maintain its empire in Asia. The British government was fully aligned to American thinking about the Soviets and the Cold War in Europe, but less convinced that the Chinese communists posed a similar threat to its own Asian interests. Anthony Eden, Britain's Foreign Secretary, described British policy as a combination of containment and compromise, not containment and confrontation.[1] Any attempt by China to extend its influence in Southeast Asia by force was to be resisted, but in other circumstances British policy was to avoid provoking China while gradually working towards normal diplomatic and commercial relations.

A situation was developing in Southeast Asia in the early 1950s that caught the attention of the US and Britain. The Japanese empire had seized French Indochina (Vietnam, Cambodia and Laos) in 1940. After Japan's defeat in August 1945, France intended to recover it. The US disliked the colonial mentality and wanted the Europeans colonists to give freedom to their colonies, but the Korean War and the anti-communist sentiment in the US altered American strategic objectives in Asia. Vietnam was effectively divided between the communists (known as the Vietminh) led by Ho Chi Minh in the north and the French which controlled the south. France reinstated Bao Dai (who was the last monarch of the Nguyen dynasty that had ruled Indochina since 1802 until he abdicated in August 1945 and went into exile in France) as the Chief of State, and the US and Britain decided to back the French in its fight against the communist Vietminh. To avoid making Bao Dai look like a Western 'puppet', Asian recognition of the new Bao Dai government was deemed essential for its credibility, and newly independent India's support was considered vital.

Nehru was close to the British, but also fiercely anticolonial and a strong proponent of the view that it was nationalism, not communism, that was the most powerful political force in post-war Asia. He also believed that the refusal of the Europeans to give the Asians their freedom was the real cause for instability and the primary threat to peace. Despite British pressure, he refused to recognize the Bao Dai regime, describing French policy as 'very unwise and completely unsuccessful'. The People's Republic of China had just been established, and Nehru presciently predicted, in a letter to Indonesian President Sukarno, that developments not favourable to the French would soon take place in Indochina

because of the effects of the Chinese revolution.[2] The civil war and
the steady advance of the Vietminh against the French in 1951 and
1952 proved that Nehru was correct. His advice to both Britain
and the US was to deal with the matter of Indochina as a political
problem, rather than one that might be resolved by use of military
force or money.[3] Nehru urged Loy Henderson, the American
Ambassador in Delhi who was a staunch anti-communist, to study
the psychology of Asian nations and take into account the state of
mind of the Asian people before contemplating 'intervention' in
Indochina.[4] British efforts to influence India's position on the Bao
Dai regime were to no avail. The issue reportedly led to a marked
confrontation between Nehru and Malcolm MacDonald, Britain's
Commissioner General for the Far East, at the Commonwealth
Conference in Colombo in January 1950.[5]

By 1953, the Vietminh was militarily gaining ground and the
mood in the French-backed Bao Dai regime in southern Vietnam
was defeatist. In June 1953, MacDonald brought this to London's
notice, but the British embassy in Saigon was sanguine. In his
annual review, Sir Hubert Graves, the British Ambassador, opined
that although the Vietminh was making headway, 'the climate
favourable to communist penetration would be absent and I think
we have far less to fear from Chinese communist manoeuvres
in Vietnam'. Indeed, Graves was more interested in American
attempts to use economic aid to secure trading benefits, and was
pleased to report to Foreign Secretary Eden that there was no
evidence to suggest this was the case.[6] The Vietminh's military
successes with China's support were also noticed by Washington.
At the end of December 1953, America's new Secretary of State,
John Foster Dulles, threatened military reprisals by the United
States if the Chinese intervened in Indochina. This ran contrary to
Eden's policy of 'containment and compromise'. Sir Oliver Harvey,
the British Ambassador to France, however, assured London that
the French government would not support such a move by the

Americans since it would involve the risk of China sending its ground forces into Indochina, something that the French were none too keen to see.[7] The overall British assessment at the end of 1953 was that France and the Bao Dai regime would eventually be forced to negotiate for peace. There was no indication that a crisis was imminent.

At the beginning of 1954, the situation in Indochina suddenly worsened. The Vietminh made significant military gains against the French in northern Vietnam, and cornered French forces at Dien Bien Phu. This alarmed Washington and London, and was also noticed in New Delhi. It was the subject of American discussion at the National Security Council (NSC) in the presence of President Eisenhower on 8 January 1954. Eisenhower was very clear that he would not permit any deployment of American ground forces,[8] but agreed to set up a group headed by General Walter Bedell-Smith, Under Secretary of State, and including high representatives from the Pentagon, the US military and the CIA, to undertake an analysis and prepare an 'action plan'.[9] Reporting to London upon the deliberations of this group, Sir Roger Makins, the British Ambassador in Washington, told Eden that the outlook in Indochina was not encouraging either from a military or political point of view. He felt that despite this, the Americans would not send troops.[10]

The Indochina situation was one of the topics for discussion at the Berlin Conference from 25 January to 18 February 1954 between the foreign ministers of the US, Britain, France and the Soviet Union. Soviet Foreign Minister Vyacheslav Molotov proposed a Five-Power conference (China being the fifth power) to resolve the Indochina question.* Dulles was not initially keen on the idea, but eventually went along out of necessity to avoid breaking with France, which had accepted Molotov's offer. The

---

* The Geneva Conference was to discuss the Korean and Indochina questions.

four countries agreed to hold the conference in Geneva at the end of April 1954. The text of their agreement explicitly said that neither the invitation to nor the holding of the conference would be deemed to imply diplomatic recognition of any state. The US did not want to let China gain back-door legitimacy. Dulles was adamant that it could not be called a 'Five-Power' conference because there was no question of promoting China's prestige and authority or of allowing China to be treated as an equal. The first cracks appeared in the Anglo-American alliance in Berlin over the question of China's participation. Dulles was to report to Eisenhower that 'Eden became a problem. He did not wish to have the resolution contain any language which appeared to impugn the good faith of the Chinese communist government.'[11]

The developing situation in Indochina also caught India's attention. In early 1953, Nehru had ruled out the idea that India might have a role to play in resolving tensions. He was not sure how China would react to such an idea. Nor did the situation seem that serious. But by early 1954 the impending military crisis was apparent. Also, the Government of India thought it had a better measure of the Chinese as the two countries were engaged in intense consultations over the question of India's extraterritorial rights and privileges in Tibet from January to April 1954. Nehru also had a favourable view of Ho Chi Minh, the leader of the Vietminh, and, moreover, was a staunch advocate of decolonization. In a speech in Parliament on 22 February 1954, Nehru declared that he deemed it desirable to have some kind of a 'ceasefire' in force between the parties concerned in advance of discussions on Indochina in Geneva.[12] Although he publicly went as far as assuring the House that 'we have no desire to interfere or to shoulder any burden or responsibility in this connection', he asked N. Raghavan, India's Ambassador in China, to find out the Chinese government's reaction to his 'ceasefire' proposal.[*] [13]

Nehru's speech set off alarms in a few capitals. Graves and Harvey, the British ambassadors in Vietnam and France, promptly reported to the British Foreign Office that the idea of the ceasefire was not acceptable to either government. Graves, from Saigon, described Nehru's proposal as 'highly dangerous and if allowed to develop at this stage, could only serve the further communist aims in this area'.[14] Eden was unhappy that Nehru had waded in on a matter that the four major powers had already decided upon in Berlin, and anxious that India's stature in Asia might lead others in the region to support the ceasefire proposal. He told B.G. Kher, India's High Commissioner in London, that he had doubts as to the wisdom of this proposal at this time and hoped that next time India would consult with the British government in advance of any ideas being made public.[15] In his memoirs, titled *Full Circle*, Eden confirmed that he was not happy that Nehru had made such a proposal just before the Geneva Conference.[16] He was also reluctant to share his thoughts with Kher on whether India would be invited to it. Kher, presumably on instructions, discreetly hinted that India 'had no desire to butt in, but at any time it was thought helpful they would be glad to do what they could'.[17] The British government at that point in time was not deeming it essential to secure India's backing for British objectives at the Geneva Conference but Nehru felt more confident about a role for India. In his replies to debates on foreign policy in Parliament on 23–24 March 1954, Nehru pushed his 'ceasefire' proposal again, and explicitly stated that 'in a climate when nations are arrayed against each other and nobody is prepared to listen to reason, then a third party's advice may be beneficial'.[18]

---

[*] A similar message was sent to Ambassador K.P.S. Menon in Moscow.

By the end of March 1954, the Vietminh had cornered the French armies at Dien Bien Phu and the Americans started to contemplate military intervention. Dulles told his cabinet colleagues that it was necessary to help the French to win the battle and that it might mean taking strong action involving risks. 'But,' he said, 'these risks will be less if we take them now rather than waiting for several years.'[19] He delivered a major policy address at the Overseas Press Club on 29 March. Dulles declared that 'under the conditions today the imposition on south-east Asia of the political system of communist Russia and its Chinese communist ally, by whatever means, would be a grave threat to the whole free community. The US feels that the possibility should not be passively accepted, but should be met by united action.' Dubbed as the 'united action' speech, it was seen as an official statement of US intention, and it set the American cat among the global pigeons. Dulles was a dominating and controversial global figure. Gaganvihari L. Mehta, India's long-serving Ambassador to the United States, wrote that 'Dulles believed that God had created him to be the Secretary of State of the United States'.[20] Nehru thought he was narrow-minded and bigoted.[*] [21] The Chinese also thought poorly of Dulles. Apparently, even both Churchill and Eden intensely disliked his appointment as Secretary of State because they thought that his mindset led to policies that would precipitate a global war.[22] And yet, whatever the views of others, Dulles was, as Mehta said of him, somebody who 'was respected and feared, disliked and distrusted, but he was not and he could not be ignored'.

On the day previous to his speech at the Overseas Press Club, Dulles had shared the contents with British Ambassador Sir Roger Makins. Using Eisenhower's phrase that Southeast Asia

---

[*] These were some of the words that Nehru used in describing Dulles to Mao Zedong in October 1954.

was of 'transcendent importance' because it sat astride the routes between South Asia and the Pacific Ocean, Dulles presumed that a communist Indochina would be as problematic to the British as to the Americans, and he hoped Britain and America could maintain an understanding on the need to act together to stave off such a possibility. The British government was jolted into action by Dulles's assumption that it would endorse his thinking. It was disturbed by two specific ideas. First, the idea of military intervention to assist the French to retrieve the situation, which Eden thought to be 'unrealistic'. He felt that conditions for this might no longer exist as a result of the French military setbacks against the Vietminh. Second, the proposal that a collective defence or security grouping be established in Southeast Asia against the Chinese communists. Eden thought the idea was workable, 'but I felt that to form and proclaim a defensive coalition before we went to the conference table would be unlikely to help us militarily and would harm us politically, by frightening off potential allies'.[23]

Eden promptly instructed Makins to inform Dulles that the British government could not support the American proposals. When Makins saw him (and Under Secretary Bedell-Smith) on 3 April, Dulles was insistent that they would not tolerate the loss of Southeast Asia to communism. Dulles handed Makins a memorandum of points. The gist of the memorandum was that France, which was militarily fading rapidly, should not be allowed to hand over any part of Indochina to the Chinese, that the United States 'remains unalterably opposed' to any idea that would give communist China a special place on par with the great powers, and there would be no American concessions in the negotiations in Geneva.* It was Makins's assessment that the policy expounded by Dulles was the 'fruit' of long deliberations at the highest levels

---

* He told Makins on another occasion 'there would be no further trading of our performances against their [Chinese] promises'.

in Washington and that 'the Americans had decided to block the communist advance in Southeast Asia'.[24] The chances of an Anglo-American split multiplied.

On 31 March, N.R. Pillai, Secretary General of India's Ministry of External Affairs, summoned American Ambassador George Allen. He conveyed to Allen that Dulles's 'united action' speech had led some (unnamed) Indian officials to believe that the Americans were calling for conflict. Pillai said he was anxious because these (unnamed) officials would present their 'interpretation' of Dulles's speech to Nehru, causing him in turn to make 'rash and unhelpful' statements.* [25] Pillai had a similar conversation with the British High Commissioner in Delhi, Alexander Clutterbuck, telling him that Nehru was 'much exercised' by Dulles's speech.[26] The Indian Ambassador in Washington, G.L. Mehta, also met Dulles on 30 March to ask what he meant by 'united action', and in turn was informed by Dulles that he had nothing specific in mind, but that military action was always the last resort. He repeated his point that they could not agree to any settlement if it meant giving Indochina away to the communists. He later instructed Ambassador Allen in Delhi that, for tactical reasons, he should not make plain the US intentions in suggesting united action.[27] He never explained the reason for this but, perhaps, he might have thought that India could share information with the Chinese.

As Pillai had correctly predicted in his talk with Ambassador Allen, Dulles's speech did lead to an 'outburst' from Nehru at a meeting of the Congress parliamentary party on 9 April. Nehru told the delegates that recent statements by Dulles 'may not be helpful for a successful outcome of the forthcoming Geneva conference'.[28]

---

* Allen told the State Department that he believed the 'troublemaker' to be V.K. Krishna Menon.

This was precisely the conclusion the British government had independently reached, but until things were clearer it did not wish to share its thinking with New Delhi. The message from the Commonwealth Relations Office to Clutterbuck read: 'Indian interpretation of situation is not far different from our own. But there is, we think, a fundamental difference in that Indians seem to be prepared to see with equanimity substantial concessions to the Vietminh, which in our view would inevitably lead to the loss of the whole of Indo-China and the development of a serious threat to south-east Asia.'[29] Clutterbuck was told not to say anything in response to Pillai's enquiries until after Eden had spoken with Dulles (who was to visit London). In a memorandum that Eden circulated to the cabinet on 7 April, in which he detailed American demands and expectations from Britain, he informed that the governments of Australia, New Zealand, Canada and France were being taken into confidence. India was not on that list. The British were not certain of what stand India might take.

The Eisenhower administration's decision to contemplate military support to the French faced opposition in the US from both the Congress and the general public. In a conference with Congressional leaders in Washington on 5 April, Dulles asked for their backing for the President's use of air and sea power in the interest of national security, but they conveyed that there would be no decision on such a request unless Dulles had first obtained commitments of a political and material nature from allies.[30] American diplomacy, in the first two weeks of April, were thus focused on achieving two objectives—persuading Britain to align its policy with America, and extending material support to France in its military campaign against the Vietminh. On the first objective, Dulles suggested that Eisenhower write to Churchill.

The thrust of Eisenhower's letter was that Britain's strategic position would also be threatened by a communist takeover in Indochina, and that the 'consequent shift in the power ratio throughout Asia and the Pacific could be disastrous' for both. The idea of 'united action', Eisenhower wrote, was to establish a new coalition comprising nations which had a vital concern in the checking of communist expansion in the area, including Britain's Commonwealth partners, Australia and New Zealand.[31] Britain's backing for American policy was regarded as an aspect of crucial importance. Dulles told the National Security Council on 6 April that 'if we can get the United Kingdom to line up with us throughout Asia in resistance to communism, and if the UK is prepared to risk the loss of Hongkong in order to save Malaya, all of this might prove to be the beginning of the creation of a real US policy in Asia'.[32] Anxiety to secure British support was not simply to satisfy the US Congress. The administration was also divided. At the NSC meeting on 6 April, Dulles and Admiral Radford, Chairman of the Joint Chiefs of Staff, had strongly argued for intervention, but Treasury Secretary George Humphrey and Governor Harold Stassen, the Director of the US Foreign Operations Mission, had apprehensions about the extent of American military commitment. Vice President Richard M. Nixon later recorded in his memoirs that Eisenhower himself 'seemed resigned to doing nothing at all unless we could get allies and the country to go along and he did not seem inclined to put much pressure on them to come along'.[33]

Even before Dulles visited London, the British government began to take a stand. Eden felt the Americans were exaggerating the seriousness of the military situation in Indochina.[34] An internal cabinet memorandum circulated by Eden on 7 April expressed 'grave misgivings' about the American idea to create an ad hoc coalition of countries as a joint warning to the Chinese to stop aiding the Vietminh. Aside from the feeling in London that such a plan would have no effect on the Chinese, and might even lead to a warlike situation, the internal memorandum also clearly recommended that British forces should not be committed.[35]

There were good reasons. British military resources were already stretched. Its reserve forces were tied up in the Suez canal zone (Egypt). They were fighting the communists in Malaya and had no reserve of ground forces that could be spared for the Indochina theatre. On the eve of Dulles's visit to London, Eisenhower referred to the situation in Indochina as the 'falling domino' (the phrase suggests that one development is likely to have a cascading impact on several connected events) and said the possible consequences of the loss of Indochina to the communists were incalculable to the free world. There were expectations on both sides that when Dulles visited London from 11–13 April, the discussions would be long and arduous.

Britain maintained that north Vietnam was lost, and it was better to concentrate efforts on attempting to hold the rest of Indochina. Joint intervention in north Vietnam would probably result in overt Chinese intervention. It would also require the commitment of substantial military forces and, importantly, it would foreclose the possibility of a successful negotiation in Geneva. Eden told Dulles that any implied commitment to involvement in the war would be intensely unpopular in Britain. Nor was Eden prepared to spell out the possible options for 'united action' until the Geneva Conference had concluded so as not to prejudice any chances of a negotiated settlement.[36] Dulles, at the very least, required a joint statement with the British in order to satisfy the demands of Congress and public opinion in the US, and so he could proceed with his plans of 'united action'. He latched upon a suggestion by Eden that they could jointly examine the possibility of establishing a system of collective defence for Southeast Asia. The joint statement issued on 13 April[37] indicated the willingness of both countries to explore this possibility, but only after the Geneva Conference. It papered over their fundamental differences on the question of taking military action before the conference ended. Dulles felt that it was adequate for his purposes.

While the diplomatic efforts were underway, the Americans were already secretly working on plans for possible military intervention. Eisenhower held an off-the-record meeting in the Oval Office on 4 April, in which a plan presented by Dulles and Admiral Radford to send American forces to Indochina under certain conditions was agreed to by Eisenhower on the strict condition that it would look like a joint action with British troops and 'Asiatic' representation.[38] Both decisions—to send military support to the French and to build a system of collective defence in Southeast Asia—would bring India into the ambit of the Anglo-American discourse and disagreement.

On the issue of military support, the American government approached India on 4 April to seek approval for landings or overflights of US Air Force planes that were transporting French troops from Europe or Africa to Indochina. Ambassador Allen met Nehru on 6 April. Nehru flatly rejected the American requests for either landings or overflights. He said that he had given commitments in Parliament he was not prepared to violate.[*] His refusal would have upset the Eisenhower administration. It was on the second issue, the idea of collective defence in Southeast Asia, that India became a serious point of difference. The Americans wanted to restrict discussion on this subject to the regional countries, including Australia and New Zealand. Eden, while agreeing to the idea of collective action, had also proposed that other countries that were not a geographical part of Southeast Asia but had interests there should be invited to the proposed discussion. India was specifically suggested by Eden as a country of importance that needed to be part of the discussion. Dulles was lukewarm to this idea. He said if the matter regarding India was pressed by the British side, he would be urged to accept participation by the Chinese nationalists in

---

[*] The American airlift was conducted by avoiding Indian territory.

Formosa.[39] This would needlessly complicate the situation for Britain in the Far East. The British knew that Taiwan's inclusion in this grouping was like waving a red flag at the Chinese and would, therefore, scuttle any prospects for peace negotiations in Geneva. Hence, there was no agreement between Dulles and Eden on the possible composition of the group that would discuss a future collective defence system when Dulles left London for Paris on 14 April.

In his memoirs Eden would later say that he did not like the balancing of India with Formosa.[40] But it seems unlikely that he was motivated out of concern at India's exclusion or the likely reaction from New Delhi if it felt left out. Eden was concerned that Britain might be isolated in any discussion on collective security within the group of countries being proposed by the US (which included its allies Thailand and the Philippines as well as Australia and New Zealand which supported the American view on the Indochina crisis). Eden needed political allies to keep Britain out of Indochina entanglements. India was an obvious candidate because it was a Commonwealth country with ties to Britain as well as an influential diplomatic force in Asia. The British government had followed India's statements on the crisis, and received briefings about Indian concerns over potential American military involvement. It had confirmed its view that India's position closely matched that of Britain. It was, thus, after the meeting with Dulles in London, when they had failed to bring the Americans around to their point of view, that India became important to the British strategy in Indochina.

Matters were precipitated when Dulles unilaterally decided to summon a group of ten countries for a meeting in Washington to discuss collective security arrangements for Indochina.*

---

* The ten countries were the US, the UK, France, Australia, New Zealand, Thailand, the Philippines, Vietnam, Laos and Cambodia. It was referred to as the 'Meeting of the Ten'.

This was despite the fact that there had been no consensus on the group's membership between Dulles and Eden. India did not receive an invitation to join. The Americans had their own reasons to exclude India. They were generally unhappy about India's stand on the Indochina crisis not only because of Nehru's speeches in Parliament, but also because India was still pushing the 'ceasefire' idea* and because it had rejected American requests for overflights and landings of US Air Force transport planes carrying French troops to Indochina.† Since 1949, in different situations—the question of recognizing China, Korea, the Peace Treaty with Japan—India was already seen in Washington as being insensitive and, by some, even unhelpful. In the circumstances, the US probably felt that India's inclusion in discussions on collective security arrangements for Southeast Asia would be counterproductive to American strategy and interests.

The American decision to convene the 'Meeting of the Ten' upset Britain. British Ambassador Roger Makins was forbidden to send British representatives to the meeting. He conveyed Eden's message that there had been no understanding on his part that a working group would go forward at once on the subject of collective defence arrangements in Southeast Asia, and no agreement between Dulles and himself on membership.[41] Britain's refusal to join the Meeting of the Ten embarrassed the Eisenhower

---

* American officials told Ambassador Mehta on 12 April that a ceasefire could, under the present circumstances, work only to the advantage of the communists. (Doc. 739, 'Memorandum of Conversation by N.G. Thacher of the Office of South Asian Affairs', 12 April 1954, FRUS, 1952–1954, Indochina, Vol. XIII, Part I).

† Ambassador Allen told Nehru on 24 April that several American senators had resented India's refusal to permit overflight and hinted that it might complicate the aid programme to India. ('Problems of Accepting American Economic Aid, Note to Secretary General et al.', 24 April 1953, SWJN, Series II, Vol. XXV, February–May 1954).

administration and compelled it to call a larger group of countries for what they described as a 'briefing' instead. To clear up any misunderstanding that had been caused by this issue, Dulles lunched with Eden on 22 April in Paris en route to the Geneva Conference. Eden justified the British about-face by claiming that when he had agreed to Dulles's idea (in London on 13 April), he had 'overlooked' the Colombo Conference of Asian Prime Ministers (on 26 April). He felt it would be most undesirable to give any public indication about the composition of any grouping that might discuss the idea of 'united action' before the end of the Colombo Conference, since criticism emanating from the Asian prime ministers would be unhelpful at Geneva.[42] Eden would further claim in his memoirs that one of the reasons for not participating in the Meeting of the Ten was because India (and Burma) had been given no opportunity to express views, and that holding such a meeting would be 'insulting' to them.[43] As a result India, unknowingly, was dragged into the Anglo-American policy fight on Indochina and the Geneva Conference.

It is true that India was critical of the London communiqué but up until that point of time there had been no in-depth discussions between the British and Indian governments on Indochina, including the Geneva Conference (where India was not an invitee). British ambassadors in Delhi, Karachi, Colombo, Jakarta and Rangoon had merely been tasked to enquire how these countries might look upon the idea of collective security in the region and they, in turn, had mostly expressed their desire to remain neutral.[44] Hence, the reasons for Eden's making a reference to India as one of the reasons for Britain's inability to go along with the US on collective security arrangements prior to the Geneva Conference deserves closer scrutiny.

In Paris, Dulles talked about the possibility of military action, and felt that if such action was on a joint Anglo-American basis, it would have a powerful moral effect in rallying anti-communist forces in Southeast Asia. The American proposals were of such importance that Eden flew back to London on the same day to consult with the cabinet. Dulles's ideas about Anglo-American military intervention alarmed the British. Eden told the cabinet that any general assurance of joint military assistance in the defence of Indochina was bound to lead to the committing of British ground forces in this theatre over a long period. His recommendation was that since French defeat was inevitable, the best hope for a lasting solution lay in the partition of Indochina and in finding a solution at the Geneva Conference. In other words, Britain did not deem it in the national interest to talk of military action or collective security until the Geneva Conference was over because it would upset the Chinese and scuttle peace efforts.

Both immediate and long-term British policy dictated the need for improving relations with China. An internal cabinet directive drafted by Eden[45] and approved by Prime Minister Churchill on 25 April laid out the policy, namely, that Britain would not undertake to give military undertakings or assistance to the French in advance of the Geneva Conference; Britain would provide no assurances to the US or others of what possible actions it might be willing to take in case the conference failed; and Britain would join in setting up a collective defence grouping in Southeast Asia only after the conference, as set out in the London communiqué in order to guarantee the settlement along with others. Nowhere, either in the record of the cabinet deliberations[46] or in the policy document, was there any consideration given by the cabinet to what others, and more particularly India, thought about the idea of collective security arrangements, or of any other Indian sensibilities and concerns. It was only after the policy had been decided in the cabinet that Eden sent personal telegrams to India, as well as Pakistan and Ceylon, enquiring whether they could contemplate being associated in any form with the collective security guarantee.[47] Eden's claim (to Dulles) in mid-April—that one of the reasons for the lack of British support was because of India's opposition—appeared intended to mislead the Americans. A seven-point memorandum that Eden gave Dulles on 30 April—which claimed that 'we [the British government] have succeeded in diverting Mr Nehru from his original intention of condemning it [collective security] root and branch. We have thus averted the danger that the Asian Prime Ministers conference at Colombo would unite in condemning our project'[48]—was also intended to push the blame on to India.

Eden, it has to be concluded, was deliberately offering extraneous justification for the British reluctance to go along with the US in order to relieve the pressure on Britain. Britain saw a use for India not only as a potential political ally, but as a convenient alibi as well. It is difficult to escape the conclusion that Britain was projecting India as the villain of the piece to cover up its own deep opposition to the US's policy. It was a game that it had played in 1949 as well, when it suggested that it was India, not Britain, that had taken the lead in pushing for early recognition of the PRC.

Eden's explanation resonated with Dulles, who already had reasons to be upset with India's position. Dulles told members of the US Congress that the British position against the US policy had 'frozen against us' partly due to pressure from Nehru.[49] A day later, he told the NSC that British 'back-pedaling' on 'united action' was due to India's position and the desirability of inducing Nehru to take a cooperative attitude.[50] American attitude hardened against any sort of an Indian role, or even the accommodation of India's interests, in the Southeast Asian theatre.

In April, meanwhile, Nehru closely followed the Indochina situation even though India was not invited to the Geneva Conference. There was bitterness on this point. Krishna Menon would blame the Americans[51] but there is no evidence either

that Britain pushed for Indian participation. This did not deter
Nehru from thinking about what role India might play. In mid-
April he wrote to Raghavan, India's Ambassador in Beijing,
urging him to quickly conclude negotiations with China on
the bilateral agreement on Tibet before the Geneva Conference,
saying that this would have a salutary effect on the 'very grave
situation [that] has arisen because of the new policy enunciated
by Dulles [on Indochina]'.[52] He saw the successful conclusion
of this agreement with China as leverage for India to play at
being some sort of an intermediary. On 24 April, he delivered
a major speech in Parliament on peace in Indochina. 'We are
not participants either in the conference or in the hostilities
that rage in Indochina,' he said. 'We are, however, interested
and deeply concerned about the problem of Indochina and,
more particularly, about the recent developments in respect of
it.' He was critical of both the American threats at instant and
massive retaliation against the Chinese if it intervened and the
idea of 'collective action', declaring this last idea to be a sort of
unilateral 'Monroe Doctrine' in Asia. He told Parliament that
India was neither seeking a special role in Asia nor championing
narrow Asian regionalism, but that Asians deserved to decide
their own fate, and build a peace area in the region.[53]

Nehru offered a six-point solution to the crisis, including, inter
alia, a ceasefire, complete independence for the three Indochina
countries and a solemn guarantee of non-intervention by the
major powers after a settlement had been reached. Krishna Menon
claimed the credit for drafting Nehru's speech. Four days later,
Nehru was successful in persuading the Colombo Conference of
Asian Prime Ministers to adopt his proposals, and thus set the
stage for India's diplomatic moves in Geneva. It is most likely
after the Colombo Conference that Eden and Nehru established
direct communication on the Indochina question, because Britain

was keen to recruit India as a political ally.* Nehru later disclosed to Zhou Enlai (during his visit to India in late June) that Eden had sent him messages (in early May) enquiring whether India would be prepared to join in collective security arrangements in Southeast Asia after the conference.[54]

Thereafter, Eden arranged for Nehru to secretly receive records of the meetings in Geneva through the British High Commissioner's office. In order to remove any doubts in Nehru's mind about a two-faced British policy, Eden sent Nehru a personal message on 16 May. 'You will no doubt have seen press reports of French–US discussions concerning possible United States intervention in the Indochina conflict in certain circumstances. I was given no advance information about any such discussion . . . We shall continue to do our utmost to ensure that this conference brings peace and a lasting settlement.'[55] Eden wanted that Nehru should harbour no doubts about Britain that might cause reluctance in Delhi to fully support the British position. On Nehru's orders, Eden's messages were also shared with Krishna Menon.

The Geneva Conference began at the end of April 1954. On 5 May Nehru sent a message to Eden (presumably in response to Eden's outreach) saying that India would be ready to assist in promoting and maintaining a settlement in Indochina. Eden said this was 'good news'.[56] Krishna Menon was in Cairo on his way to New York when he claimed he received a message from Eden to meet him in London. It is more likely that he was contemplating some form of diplomatic activity on the Indochina front. Subimal Dutt recalled that Menon had told Nehru before leaving Delhi

---

* Dr K.S. Shelvankar, the London correspondent of *The Hindu* newspaper, reported that even a conservative organ like the *Sunday Times* had noted India's 'statesman-like moderation' on the Indochina situation at the Colombo conference. (K.S. Shelvankar, 'Satisfaction Over Trend at Geneva, UK Press Welcomes Eden's Lead', *The Hindu*, 3 May 1954).

of his plan to halt in Geneva.[57] It is also clear from Nehru's letter of 3 June to his chief ministers that he (Menon) had Nehru's approval to proceed to Geneva.* Menon remained in Geneva virtually until the month's end, with a brief departure in mid-June when the conference went into a recess. He claimed 'we did not stand on dignity. We just stood on the doorstep and tried to be helpful.'[58] But Menon did not carry a government brief to Geneva, according to Subimal Dutt. Menon, he said, acted mostly on his own, keeping Nehru informed only of the brief outlines of his talks. He kept the Ministry of External Affairs out of the loop.[59] Nehru's instructions to Menon, if any, were probably oral.

Few within the system had an idea of what India's end game in Indochina was beyond broad statements by Nehru that India desired to enlarge the area of peace and non-alignment in Asia. There is no official record about Menon's work in Geneva. The news reports from Dr K.S. Shelvankar, the London-based correspondent of *The Hindu*, who had temporarily moved to Geneva to cover the conference, thus became the only means of learning about Menon's activities. Weeks before Menon arrived, there was already 'persistent curiosity' about his movements and stories of his impending arrival.[60] It is possible that either Menon or Britain could have leaked information about Menon's imminent arrival. Shelvankar called it a new diplomatic offensive by Nehru and said the question on everybody's lips was whether Indian intervention would prove to be 'the deux ex machina' reconciling Europe and Asia without, at the same time, giving offence to America.[61]

---

* The Americans thought so too. After Menon's first meeting with the chief American delegate, Walter Bedell-Smith, Smith told Washington that although Menon claimed that he was not speaking with any authority from his government, 'I knew, of course, that he would not have spoken as he did without Nehru's authority.' (Doc. 596, 'Smith–Menon Meeting, Geneva, US Delegation to Department of State', 25 May 1954, *FRUS, 1952–1954, The Geneva Conference, Vol. XVI*).

As soon as he arrived in Geneva on 22 May, Menon quickly established contact with all the principal players—Chinese Premier Zhou Enlai, British Foreign Secretary Eden, French Foreign Minister Bidault and American Under Secretary of State Walter Bedell-Smith (the chief US delegate after Dulles's departure). Since India had no locus standi inside the meetings, Menon busied himself with diplomacy in the margins of the conference. Krishanlal Shridharani, the correspondent of the *Amrita Bazaar Patrika*, wrote that Menon was 'quicker in contacting different delegations than a butterfly is in contacting flowers of varying hues'.[62] Menon's peregrinations between the villas and hotel rooms in Geneva were described as being the 'real centre of gravity' of the conference, and as a sort of general recognition by the rest of the 'indispensable and mediatory role' which India alone in the existing circumstances was in a position to fulfil.[63] A Swiss paper called the activities of Nehru's representative as 'so intense and his visits to Chou Enlai have been so frequent that one wonders whether he is not trying, even at this stage, to create a climate which would be favourable to him acting as a mediator if it should be necessary'.[64]

He pushed Nehru's proposal for a ceasefire right from the start, and suggested that after the 'standstill' had been achieved, a neutral authority should sort out the belligerents. India, Menon said, would accept this responsibility if agreed to by all and requested to do so.[65] Menon's idea was discussed on 26 May at the tripartite meeting between Bedell-Smith, Eden and Jean Chauvel (France), with Eden favouring Menon's proposal for the creation of an international supervision authority to oversee the end of hostilities in Indochina.[66] At the end of May, the Indochina conference saw initial success when the armed belligerents agreed to an armistice. However, differences arose on how its implementation would be supervised (there were significant differences between the major powers on the composition and procedures of the International Supervisory Commission). Menon again did the rounds to reconcile the differences between the Chinese, the Vietminh and the French. It might be said, with good reason, that India, and Menon, played a helpful role in carrying messages between the different parties during this initial phase of the Geneva Conference.

During the second phase of the Geneva Conference, from the end of June until the signing of the Geneva Accords on 21 July 1954, Menon's role became less critical. The principal actors, especially Eden and Zhou, had by that time developed a rapport through regular meetings. They exerted great effort on the other participants, including the US, into agreeing on the framework for resolving the Indochina crisis. Eden and Zhou could both claim the lion's share of the credit for the successful outcome of the Geneva Conference on Indochina. Both acknowledged Menon's contribution. Shelvankar's description of Menon as an intermediary trusted by both sides, and a 'link between the East and the West to combat by her [India] very presence the cold war mentality'[67] was, however, exaggerated.

Menon's activities in Geneva were viewed in very different ways by the principal players. Some used him for achieving their objectives. The Americans had no liking for Menon and thought he was a communist Chinese sympathizer. Since he was the only Indian present in Geneva and also a close confidante of Nehru, the Americans assumed that he was reflecting the Indian position. Dulles told Eisenhower in mid-May that 'we are obviously subjected to the United Kingdom veto, which in turn was in Asian matters largely subject to the Indian veto, which in turn was largely subjected to Chinese communist veto. Thereby,' said Dulles, 'a chain is formed which tended to make us impotent.'[68] America felt isolated in Geneva and, possibly, held Menon partially responsible for it. Menon felt the Americans were obsessed with stopping communism, were against the Soviets and the Chinese, and jealous of India.[69] Menon could establish no meeting ground with the Americans in Geneva.

By the time Menon arrived in Geneva, Anglo-American relations were highly strained. Eden told Richard Casey, Australia's Foreign Minister, 'unfortunately, I fear there is a fundamental difference of approach on this question [Indochina and the Geneva Conference] between the Americans and ourselves. Our purpose is to reach an agreed settlement at Geneva on the Indochina problem, and then to institute measures for the collective defence of south-east Asia in the light of that settlement. Theirs, I suspect, is to secure support for intervention in Indochina. The latter in our view would involve the risk of war with China and possibly with the Soviet Union as well.'[70]

Eden needed to work with the Chinese (and the Soviets) to achieve their objective. Menon had developed a rapport with Zhou (they had nine personal meetings in Geneva). Eden found it convenient to utilize Menon to pass messages between himself and the Chinese in order to find compromises. This was a perfect way to satisfy a key British objective, namely to give the Geneva Conference a chance of success without doing grave damage to Anglo-American relations.[71] It helped Eden to deflect American pressure and anger away from him. He admitted later that he succeeded in his peace efforts in Geneva because 'in this I had an ally, India'.[72] Menon also helped build understanding between Britain and China which led to bilateral discussion on resumption of trade and business, and opened the road to Britain to pursue its commercial interests in the hope that it could reclaim lost ground (and assets) on the Chinese mainland.* [73]

As for China, this was its first major outing on the world stage. It wanted to make sure that the Geneva Conference

---

* Shelvankar reported that Britain was faced with the choice between keeping in step with India or with the US, and she had shown no tendency to move too far away from India. (*The Hindu*, 'Settlement in Indochina, Menon's Mission', 25 May 1954).

would not end without a result. Its objectives were to break out of international isolation by building direct ties with Western powers. Menon unquestionably facilitated this. In the final days of the Geneva Conference, when an agreement seemed to be tantalizingly close and yet so far, Menon met Zhou on at least four occasions. During these meetings he would share valuable insights with Zhou about Anglo–American thinking. When Zhou was concerned about whether the Americans would boycott the closing sessions and oppose the Geneva agreement, it was Menon who told him that the Americans would send Bedell-Smith, and the only thing left for the US to decide were the tactics for bringing him back to the conference. Menon also offered his services to Zhou, at one point saying that 'you can ask me to do anything with other delegations'.[74] A day later Menon told Zhou that India could propose 'concessions' that the Chinese side might be thinking of offering so that it did not appear as if the Chinese side was compromising.[75] India's (and Menon's) friendship was used by Zhou to raise China's, and his own, prestige in the world, and to ensure a favourable outcome in Geneva. It was Zhou who pushed the idea that India should play a key role in the international supervision of a ceasefire.[76] China also tried to capitalize on America's isolation in Geneva to build an anti-American bloc. One of Zhou's objectives in visiting India in late June was for the purpose of 'conduct(ing) preparation work for signing some form of Asian peace treaty and to strike a blow at the United States' conspiracy to organize a southeast Asian invasive bloc'.* [77]

---

* In an exclusive interview that Zhou gave Shelvankar on the eve of his visit to India, he alluded in a thinly disguised manner to how America's 'aggressive policy of splitting the Asian countries into opposing military blocs is increasingly threatening peace and security of all Asian countries'

India's approach to Indochina was guided by two fundamental pillars of its foreign policy after 1947—the desire to be independent of bloc politics and the belief that Asians needed to be consulted by the great powers in deciding questions of peace and security in the region. When asked about the reason for India's involvement in the Indochina situation, Menon would tell Michael Brecher that it was 'because it's Asia, it is peace'.[78] Beyond this sweeping statement of intent, there is no detailed policy. India was not a formal participant and he was not a government representative, and there was no need for him to report anything to the government.

Undeniably, Menon's work and Nehru's ceasefire proposal contributed to the final outcome of the Geneva Conference on Indochina. India's diplomatic influence and Nehru's personal stature also helped India secure a post-conference role in Indochina. India became the chairman of the three commissions that were established under the Geneva accords to supervise their implementation in Vietnam, Cambodia and Laos. But there was no basis for Krishna Menon to claim in his letter to Nehru on 21 June that 'World War III has once again been staved off for the time-being' because of India's efforts.[79] Nehru would amplify such claims as if he believed that it was his (Krishna Menon's) efforts, not those of Eden, Zhou, Molotov, Pham Van Dong and Mendes-France, that had made the greatest difference in reaching the Indochina accords at Geneva. Menon and Nehru engaged in mutual admiration. Menon heaped praise on Nehru's foreign policy in Asia and, in turn, Nehru said that without Menon's efforts he doubted if any settlement could have been reached in Geneva.[80] Menon's work in Geneva was favourably presented to the Indian public by the media, but some, like Krishnalal Shridharani of the *Amrita Bazaar Patrika*, were more critical.

(Shelvankar, 'India's Work for Peace, Mr Chou En-lai's Tribute', *The Hindu*, 24 June 1954).

He questioned the popular impression that Menon was carrying proposals to resolve the deadlock. 'Actually, I learnt upon my return to Delhi,' Shridharani wrote, 'Mr. Menon intended to give an inside picture of the Colombo Conference to his friends like Eden, describe Nehru's latest thoughts and report the reactions thereto to his boss in Delhi.'[81]

Menon's efforts in Geneva helped to build his international credentials and, to some degree, also helped India build its image as a global influencer, but it also deepened the mutual mistrust between Washington and New Delhi. Writing to Ambassador G.L. Mehta in Washington, Nehru described the American attitude on the Indochina question as 'not only wrong but wholly lacking in realism'.[82] The anti–Cold War mentality was deeply embedded in Nehru's thinking, and the conviction that China would play a positive and beneficial role in Asia had also set in with the concluding of the agreement between India and China on trade and intercourse with the Tibet region, in which were embedded the Five Principles of Peaceful Co-existence that, Nehru believed, were the new principles to organize international relations.

On the US side there was a mirror-imaging of Indian policy. Ambassador G.L. Mehta reported Dulles as telling him that while America respected India and its policy even if they did not agree on all the points, there was more misunderstanding and misrepresentation in India about the US than it was here. According to Mehta's version of their meeting, Dulles claimed 'India seemed to believe that the US was a war-monger and out to throw atom bombs. If they had such a policy they could have easily welcomed a war in Korea or Indochina. But they wanted peace. He [Dulles] did not understand why India represented them as war-mongers and so on and so forth.'[83]

After accomplishing the Geneva Accords, Eden was keen India should join the Southeast Asian collective security arrangement that he had agreed to with Dulles in April. Nehru's view was that

Indian participation or support would mean abandoning India's established policies and extending the Cold War to South Asia. He told Krishna Menon that he would oppose any arrangement that meant India had to line up with one group against another.[84] In Washington, Ambassador Mehta asked Under Secretary of State Bedell-Smith whether talk of collective security arrangements did not undermine the spirit of conciliation which had set in at Geneva. Bedell-Smith's reply was a 'definite no'.[85]

Despite India's opposition, the US and Britain went ahead by holding the Manila Conference in September 1954 during which they established a collective security arrangement—South East Asia Defence Organization (SEADO, later SEATO).* Zhou had suspected as much and voiced his concern to Menon in Geneva over reports of a US-led collective defence treaty (SEATO) which Britain and France had agreed to be parties to, adding, 'If all this is true, agreement at Geneva [is] merely a scrap of paper.'[86] Zhou's hunch was to prove accurate. The outcome of the Geneva Conference may have raised India's stature but the long-term objective of expanding the area of peace and non-alignment received a setback. India's expectation that the Geneva Accords would lead to lasting peace and alleviate Cold War tensions in the region were belied. The United States began a multi-year military commitment that led to prolonged conflict in Indochina. More immediately, the Manila Pact aggravated tensions between China and the United States, and led almost immediately to the first crisis in the Taiwan Strait. India's victory in Geneva was pyrrhic.

---

* Dulles had told the National Security Council that the British 'seemed now willing to go ahead to make plans for the defence of south-east Asia despite India'. Doc. 1080, Memorandum of Discussion at 207th Meeting of NSC, 22 July 1954, *FRUS, 1952–1954, Indochina, Vol. XIII, Part II.*

Chapter 4

The First Taiwan Strait Crisis

In January 1953, President-elect Dwight Eisenhower met British Prime Minister Winston Churchill in Washington. They had an old friendship going back to the Second World War when Churchill was the wartime Prime Minister and General Eisenhower was the Supreme Commander of the Allied Forces in Europe. Eisenhower was accompanied by his Secretary of State–designate John Foster Dulles. Dulles informed Churchill that the incoming Eisenhower administration (Eisenhower was to be sworn in two weeks later as the President of the United States) intended to change the mission of the US Seventh Fleet so as to remove the prohibition against launching an attack on the People's Republic of China in case it attacked the Republic of China (Formosa/Taiwan) or US forces who were doing their duty in that area.[1] Churchill suggested that both governments might talk further about this subject after Eisenhower had settled into office, but Dulles made it clear to Churchill that he might regard their discussion as an official intimation of change in US policy.

This change was significant. The Korean War of 1950–53 had marked a turning point for the US in its Far East policy. Beating the communists across the globe became the American priority. In June 1950, after the Chinese military action in Korea, President Harry S. Truman (Eisenhower's predecessor) had outlined a new American policy for the Taiwan Strait. It was known as the 'neutralization' policy. Truman declared that the occupation of Formosa (Taiwan) by communist forces would be a direct threat to the security of the Pacific region and to the American military forces that were performing their duties and functions in that region. 'Accordingly,' he said, 'I have ordered the Seventh Fleet to prevent any attack on Formosa.'[2] Truman also postponed a final decision on the status of Taiwan (which under the Cairo and Potsdam Declarations was to revert to China after the defeat of Japan but still remained under American control). Truman's neutralization policy was also, however, intended to ensure that Chiang Kai-shek could not attack the mainland.

Eisenhower's decision to change Truman's policy, by removing that responsibility from the Seventh Fleet to restrain Chiang Kai-shek from attacking the mainland, deeply worried the British. They were certain it would, inevitably, result in a hostile Chinese response and, therefore, once more endanger British interests in the Far East. British policy had been to accommodate the Chinese while remaining allied to the Americans.[*] Immediately, as the Eisenhower administration settled into office, the British government asked its embassy in Washington to convey to the State Department that the abandonment or modification of the neutralization policy 'would have great international political repercussions'.[3] Britain felt that any such change in policy should first be mutually discussed among the interested parties. The furthest the Americans would go, however, was to inform the

---

[*] After recognizing the PRC on 6 January 1950, relations between Britain and China were affected by the Korean War as well as the treatment meted out to British businesses in China. The British were unable to persuade the Americans to consider any compromise over China. As for British businesses inside the PRC, the taxes and regulations eventually compelled them to leave in May 1952. Subsequent losses were estimated at Sterling 200 million. But the British still remained hopeful of returning.

British that Eisenhower would clarify matters in his first State of the Union address to the US Congress, and the only assurance they made was that the new policy implied no aggressive intent on the part of the United States.

In his State of the Union address on 2 February 1953, the President described China as the 'aggressor' in Korea, Indochina and Malaya, and reminded Congress that Truman's policy, announced in June 1950, giving the US Seventh Fleet the dual task of preventing an attack by the Chinese communists on Formosa (Taiwan) as well as ensuring that Formosa would not become a base for Chiang Kai-shek to launch a military operation against the PRC, meant, in effect, 'that the United States Navy was required to serve as the defensive arm of Communist China'. Eisenhower conveyed that since China was not being cooperative on the Korean question, 'consequently there is no longer any logic or sense in a condition that required the United States Navy to assume defensive responsibilities on behalf of the Chinese communists'.[4] As promised to his British allies, he did say that the new policy implied no aggressive intent on the part of the US. So far as Britain was concerned, however, the policy change complicated its own Far East policy and relationship with the PRC. Therefore, British Foreign Secretary Anthony Eden conveyed to the Americans on the same day that it had been the British government's hope that the neutralization doctrine would be maintained without modification, and that 'Her Majesty's Government regret this decision which they consider will have unfortunate political repercussions, especially in the United Nations'.[5]

The British response troubled the new American administration because it indicated a gap between their respective China policies. At the end of July 1953, Dulles instructed US ambassadors in the Western powers to ensure that American allies remained in lockstep with them on maintaining political and economic pressure on China. Dulles was concerned that the existing differences over the China policy might otherwise intensify and lead to 'a serious breach between the United States and its major allies in the Far East'.[6] But no particular effort was made by Washington to engage with its British ally, and American policy on the Taiwan Strait continued to harden during the course of the first year (1953) of the Eisenhower administration, making it more and more difficult for the Americans and the British to concert their actions. By the end of 1953, the US National Security Council (NSC) concluded that the Chinese would continue to maintain a basic hostility to the West in general and the US in particular[7] and recommended to the US government that the US should defend Formosa (Taiwan) and the Pescadores (Peng Hu Islands) in case China attacked. Besides these main islands, the Chiang Kai-shek government was also in control of several offshore or coastal islands. These were the Quemoy (Jinmen) and Matsu (Mazu) islands, which were less than 12 nautical miles off the coast of mainland China and within easy striking distance of the PRC. The Americans were ambivalent about committing forces if these islands came under attack from the PRC, but the NSC concluded that, in the circumstances of a Chinese military attempt to seize Formosa, it might also become necessary to help the Chiang Kai-shek government defend these small offshore islands, albeit without committing American ground forces.[8] This position that the US took with regard to these small islands (Quemoy and Matsu) off mainland China's coast (hereinafter collectively referred to as the 'offshore islands') meant that a serious difference over the China policy between the two principal Western powers became more likely as the year 1954 dawned.

In February 1954, President Chiang Kai-shek's government proposed a bilateral defence treaty with the Americans. At this point in time the United States was preoccupied with the Korean crisis and the worsening situation in Indochina. Although the

PRC had, from time to time, declared its intention to take Taiwan back, the Americans did not expect any imminent Chinese action. The primary US concern was, in fact, that Chiang should not be allowed to drag the Americans into a conflict with China, since he still harboured dreams of regaining the mainland through military means.[9] Within the State Department, the bureau in charge of South Asia observed that such a treaty might drive India closer to China, but the Far East department felt that any possible Indian reaction could not be an overriding consideration.[10] Since the US chose not to pursue the security treaty at that time, these internal debates were of little immediate consequence. The Americans were busy with the Geneva Conference on Korea and Indochina, which was from late April to July 1954. This has been discussed in detail in the previous chapter, but it does bear repeating that both Britain and China felt they had come out on top as compared with the United States. Humphrey Trevelyan, the British representative in Beijing who had also participated in the Geneva Conference, summed it up thus in a letter to Anthony Eden: 'In spite of the United States government's reservations, the Chinese communists were treated in Geneva as representative of the only real Chinese government . . .'[11] After the Geneva Conference, Britain prepared to use its new relationship with China to consolidate ties and, therefore, on 17 June 1954, announced its intention to formalize its diplomatic representation in Beijing. It viewed it as a possible new beginning to advance British commercial interests. The Chinese too hoped that better Anglo-Chinese relations might lead to normalization of relations with other Western countries.

At the end of July 1954, as the situation in Indochina was easing off, a new situation began to develop in the Taiwan Strait. Eisenhower and his closest advisors were discussing intelligence reports indicating that the Chinese were amassing forces along the coast with the intention, possibly, of seizing the small offshore islands that were under Taiwanese control.[12] They were not entirely wrong in their assessment. In late June 1954, the Central Committee of the Chinese Communist Party had instructed Zhou Enlai to prepare for a struggle against the United States and Chiang Kai-shek after the Geneva Conference. The Chinese felt that the US was unlikely to passively accept the diplomatic setback at the Geneva Conference on Indochina, and would create tensions by using Taiwan to blockade China. They also had information on the proposed US–Taiwan (Republic of China) defence treaty. They, consequently, decided that their struggle against the Americans should take the form of both a political campaign to emphasize their determination to 'liberate' Taiwan and also in the form of military action by enhancing naval and air attacks against Chiang's forces in the coastal areas.[13] The Soviet Union (Premier Georgy Malenkov) was briefed about these plans.[14]

The festering differences between the US and Britain over China came to a head when, on 23 July 1954, China shot down a Cathay Pacific passenger airliner near Hainan Island (China admitted that it was shot down by mistake and offered to pay the compensation claim of Sterling 3,67,000). Three of the dead were Americans. The US took this attack as a sign of aggressive Chinese intent and was unhappy at the way in which Britain handled this matter. Eisenhower asked Dulles to send a 'stiff note' to Foreign Secretary Eden, making it clear that the US would take a tough line since American citizens had been killed, and that it expected the British government to follow suit.[15] The British government, far from stiffening its attitude towards China, was actively engaged in building the relationship in the hopes of securing commercial advantage. Hence, when the first Taiwan Strait crisis started a month later, Anglo-American relations were already under some degree of stress over the China policy.

The crisis started on 3 September 1954. China initiated heavy artillery bombardment against the island of Quemoy (Jinmen).

The Eisenhower administration discussed how the US should respond, and the President's first concern was to enquire of his officials whether an American response might drive a wedge between the US and its principal allies, especially Britain.[16] After the British and French had visibly broken ranks at Geneva, leaving the Americans isolated, he wanted to ensure that the West maintained a united front in this crisis. He thought to ask Churchill as to where the United Kingdom would stand if the Americans engaged in military action against China over the offshore islands. Dulles and Eden met in London on 17 September. Eden told Dulles that Britain was worried about the crisis escalating into a war. He emphasized that, so far as Britain was concerned, war over the defence of Formosa was one thing, but conflict over Quemoy (Jinmen) and the other offshore islands was an entirely different matter. The British Joint Chiefs of Staff, according to Eden, were of the view that Quemoy was neither defensible nor essential to the defence of Formosa itself. Dulles told Eden in turn that the Americans held the opposite view.[17]

Dulles subsequently telephoned Eisenhower to say that Britain was being noncommittal. The two foreign ministers had a further talk on 27 September, at which Eden clarified that, so far as Britain was concerned, it considered the status of the offshore islands to be different from those of Formosa (Taiwan) and the Pescadores (Penghu Islands), in as much as Britain regarded the offshore islands as belonging to the PRC. With such a fundamental divergence between them on the ownership as well as the military significance of the offshore islands, Dulles and Eden realized they needed to find common ground. Dulles suggested that the Taiwan Strait crisis should be taken to the UN,[18] and eventually both agreed to this idea with the objective of getting the two parties (the PRC and Chiang Kai-shek) to cease fire. If the UN succeeding in doing so, it would solidify the status quo in the Taiwan Strait, with Chinese consent, such that there would de facto be two

Chinas. This suited both, the British, because it eased tensions in the Far East, and the Americans, because it preserved their control over the entire island chain from Japan to the Philippines which, in their strategic view, was essential for the containment of the communists. Eden proposed to bring it to the UN with the help of New Zealand, which was a non-permanent member of the United Nations Security Council (UNSC), in order to give it greater credence, and to make it more acceptable for the Chinese. Eden thought that the plan's only chance of success was if China was invited to present its own case to the UN. The final decision to go ahead was taken on 29 September in Eden's apartment in London.[19] It was called Operation 'ORACLE'. The differences between the two Western allies over the actual status of the offshore islands still remained unresolved, but at least they had a common action plan. The British representatives in Beijing and Moscow were asked to brief their hosts and underscore that ORACLE (this was a secret code name and was never used when the British talked with Moscow and Beijing) was a serious and sincere attempt to stop a larger conflict in the Taiwan Strait.

With ORACLE set into motion, the Americans also, however, decided to simultaneously fast-track the defence treaty with Taiwan which had been, more or less, in cold storage for seven months. Dulles still had reservations on the proposed treaty because of the possibility that it might involve American forces in defending the offshore islands.[20] But, anticipating that Chiang Kai-shek might consider ORACLE as yet another secret bargain being made behind his back, the offer of the treaty was intended to demonstrate to Chiang that the US was watching out for his interests. The Americans also framed the provisions of the treaty in ways that would restrain Chiang from adventurism that could drag America into a general war with China. Further, it was also intended as a signal to the Chinese that they should not misinterpret Western efforts to negotiate in the UNSC as a sign of

American weakness. The treaty would signal that it was prepared
to deter any Chinese attack on Taiwan. The draft treaty was given
to Chiang Kai-shek on 2 November with President Eisenhower's
approval, and the British government was informed that this treaty
was a 'very definite possibility'.[21] Britain was caught by surprise.
Eden informed the cabinet that Britain's credibility in Moscow
and Beijing would be undermined if they thought that the British
had deliberately withheld knowledge of the proposed US–Taiwan
Defence Treaty while speaking to them about ORACLE. The
cabinet agreed with Eden that Britain should not proceed with
ORACLE until it had got complete knowledge of the treaty.[22]
Dulles explained to Eden that the treaty with Taiwan was necessary
because they had information that the Chinese were preparing to
attack the offshore islands and that a 'serious situation' might be
developing in the strait.[23]

But Eden did not agree, and said that according to Britain's
information the situation in the area of the offshore islands was
not as immediately menacing as claimed, and that it would
be 'most dangerous if [the] Americans should as a result of
Nationalist pressure go ahead with the Treaty'.[24] A day later, Eden
asked Sir Roger Makins, the British Ambassador in Washington,
to make this point clear to Dulles. Makins reiterated that the
status of the offshore islands was substantially different from that
of Formosa (Taiwan) and the Pescadores (Penghu). The British
government would, therefore, find it difficult, on legal grounds,
to support America's position that the Chinese communists were
guilty of aggression in trying to capture the offshore islands that
the British government already regarded as Chinese territory. For
the first time, Eden also underscored through his Ambassador in
Washington the strain that this would place on Anglo-American
relations and asked Dulles to 'bear these hard facts constantly in
mind'.[25] It was at this stage, when Britain grew concerned about
the widening divide with the Americans over their proposed

confrontation with China in the offshore islands, that it decided to enlist India's efforts in salvaging the situation.

Eden told Makins to make it clear to the Americans that it was not simply British public opinion that the Americans should take into consideration, but also what other countries, and in particular India, thought about the Taiwan Strait crisis and the proposed treaty. Makins suggested the United States might share some details with the British government as well as consider the possibility of taking Indian Prime Minister Nehru into confidence before proceeding further.[26] Livingston Merchant, the US Assistant Secretary of State for European Affairs, also told Dulles that Eden desired to 'carry India along with the action in the Security Council (ORACLE) by informing them in advance'.[27] The Americans had a different opinion. The US State Department told the British Ambassador that it was 'not clear as to the purpose of your proposed consultation with Nehru'. It feared that any information shared with India might lead to premature disclosure either to the press or to the Chinese communists. The US Assistant Secretary of State for Far Eastern Affairs (Robertson) even told Makins that confiding in India might be tantamount to giving New Delhi, and perhaps even Beijing, a veto.[28]

The differences that the Americans and the British had over India's involvement in efforts to resolve tensions in the Taiwan Strait stemmed from their individual experiences with India after 1947. From the British perspective, India and Britain had been on the same page since 1949 when they had closely consulted each other on the question of recognizing the People's Republic of China. Though their interests in China were different, they had continued to cooperate and coordinate on Far Eastern matters thereafter, including at the Geneva Conference. Britain's relationship with the PRC was still strained despite the personal relations that Eden and Zhou had built in Geneva, but Nehru had good personal relations with both, and, in the circumstances, the British government felt that India might act as a useful interlocutor with China. Nehru obliged them by passing messages back and forth between London and Beijing. In June 1954, after Premier Zhou Enlai's visit to India, Nehru confidentially shared information with Eden about his discussions with Zhou. He told Eden that Zhou had given him to understand that he was 'anxious to have better relations with the United Kingdom'.[29] During that same visit he similarly told Zhou that some talk between the Chinese government and the United Kingdom was 'highly desirable' because while Washington may be more powerful, London was more important, especially for Europe.[30] Nehru again pressed the British case with Mao and Zhou during his visit to China in October 1954. 'Not long ago,' he told Mao Zedong, 'I received a short message from Churchill in which he said that he was anxious to curb the tendencies towards war, and he was trying his best to work on some [people] in America.' Nehru said that Churchill was hoping that China would soon be admitted to the United Nations.[31] Britain saw good value in these exchanges with the Chinese communists through the Indian channel.

India's relations with the US in general, and specifically on matters relating to China and the Far East, had evolved differently than with Britain. The Americans were disappointed by India's early recognition of the PRC. Since then, the gap between them on China had continued to widen. The US had expected more robust support from India for its stand-off against communist China in Korea but Sir Girija Shankar Bajpai, the Secretary General of India's Ministry of External Affairs, told the acting American Ambassador in India that although Nehru understood the totalitarian nature of communism, India would continue to talk softly to China because of the long common boundary and fear of Chinese aggression in Southeast Asia.[32] India's position on the Korean question had irritated the Americans, and Eisenhower's decision to change the mission of the Seventh Fleet in the Taiwan Strait had, in turn, disappointed the Indians.[33]

Dulles visited India in May 1953 hoping to salvage the relationship. M.K. Rasgotra (later India's Foreign Secretary), who was posted in Washington as a junior diplomat at the time, recalled that Dulles was intolerant of dissent and utterly ignorant about Asian sensitivities. Driven by the zeal to destroy communism, there was little common ground between him and Nehru on any topic related to Asia.[34] Soon after Dulles returned to Washington, relations took a turn for the worse over an unrelated matter. The US learnt that a consignment of thorium nitrate from Indian Rare Earths Limited was bound for China. The American Ambassador raised the matter with Nehru since exports of strategic raw materials to China were banned by the West. Nehru told Ambassador Allen that he had no means of stopping the shipment without there being a fallout on India–China relations. When he was reminded that such exports were not permitted per the terms and conditions for American technical assistance to Indian Rare Earths Limited (under the Battle Act),[35] Nehru was incensed. 'While we gladly cooperate with the United States we cannot,' he stated in a subsequent note to Foreign Secretary K.P.S. Menon, 'consider ourselves bound by the provisions of the Battle Act.'[36] Dulles at one stage even contemplated terminating aid to India because of this shipment.[37] Towards the end of 1954 the Americans felt that India was not sufficiently sensitive to American concerns about China. One US National Intelligence Estimate virtually wrote India off, saying it was becoming the focus of increasing Chinese attention.[38]

On the Indian side, too, the antipathy to the US grew within the context of the Cold War. In July 1950 Nehru wrote to the chief ministers to say that India faced two rival camps—the vast and powerful Soviet group of nations that was expansionist, and the Western group of nations which encouraged reactionary and military elements, especially in Asia. 'We have to follow a line which may not completely fit in with the two prevailing tendencies of the age.'[39] Nehru felt the Americans did not understand the situation in Asia. He believed that nationalism, not communism, was driving the political changes in Asia, and felt that if the Americans supported nationalist movements there, communism would not take root in the region. Added to this was Nehru's belief that Asian problems could only be settled in consultation with Asian nations, which was not being done in his view. When Premier Zhou Enlai visited India in June 1954, Nehru ventured to share his concerns that the US was building bases around the Soviet Union and China and thus creating a 'vicious cycle of fear' in Asia.[40] He also talked to Zhou about the growing gap in Anglo-American relations, and of how important it was for China and India to support Britain's policy on Asia so that they did not feel isolated. There was also his personal bias towards the American leadership. He told Mao in October 1954 that Eisenhower was 'weak'. He was harshly critical of Dulles, describing him to Mao as a 'big threat', as 'narrow-minded' and as 'dangerous'.[41] Views about Nehru in the American leadership mirrored his own about them.

So far as the Taiwan Strait was concerned, as far back as August 1950, Nehru had described it as a 'danger point' and was worried that it might become conflict-prone.[42] He acknowledged that China and America held strong opposing views about Taiwan. In early 1951 he had predicted that the situation would grow progressively worse[43] and counselled moderation for all parties. So far as the US was concerned, however, India was not relevant in the context of Taiwan other than marginally, by way of the department in charge of India raising concerns that the proposed defence treaty with Taiwan might further antagonize India and 'drive it closer to communist China'.[44] Nehru's public pronouncements on US policy towards China added to American disillusionment about India. Speaking in the Lok Sabha in September 1954, Nehru said that 'a great part of our present-day difficulties, certainly in the Far East, is due to this extraordinary shutting of one's eyes to the fact of China'.[45] He did not name the US, but it was quite clear which country he was alluding to. A similar comment was made by him in Parliament in early October when Nehru described it as 'rather unfortunate that some western countries were so obsessed with communism and anti-communism that they completely failed to see any other force at work in the world'.[46] As a result, at the beginning of the Taiwan Strait crisis, India was not on the list of American allies and partners with whom it might consult and take advice from.

In October 1954, Nehru made his first visit to China at the invitation of Premier Zhou Enlai, in the early days of the Taiwan Strait crisis. Both London and Washington closely followed his visit. His talks with Mao and Zhou covered every possible topic of mutual interest, including the situation in the Taiwan Strait. The two Chinese leaders told him how intolerable the American presence in Taiwan was to them. They made Nehru aware of their concerns about the use of the offshore islands in particular by the American-backed Chiang Kai-shek to threaten Chinese shipping and the coastal regions. Zhou had come armed with maps of the Taiwan Strait in order to show Nehru the location of the offshore islands and to convince him that the problem would be resolved only if the US ceased to help Chiang Kai-shek in occupying these islands close to the Chinese mainland. Even prior to his visit to China, Nehru had referred to the offshore islands in a way that showed sympathy for the Chinese position.[47] He returned from China not only convinced about China's legitimate claim to these islands but, more importantly, that the American refusal to accommodate the reasonable Chinese demands for the evacuation of the offshore islands (Quemoy and Matsu) by Chiang Kai-shek was the cause of the crisis in the Taiwan Strait. In a note that he recorded immediately after his visit, Nehru opined that '. . . it was made clear to me that great importance was attached by the Chinese government to this issue of Taiwan and even more so to the islands off the mainland, and the interference with normal coastal trade and attacks of the mainland'.[48] Nehru had no intention, at this point, of getting involved, and told Zhou that he did not wish to 'mediate', but it was also from this point on that India started taking an active interest in the developments.

Britain and the US drew different conclusions from Nehru's visit to China. N.R. Pillai, Secretary General of the External Affairs Ministry, briefed the British government on the visit, in person, in November 1954. The briefing included his reply to a question about whether China had expansionist ambitions, to which Pillai said that 'he and Mr Nehru did not know the answer, but the government of India was prepared to give the Chinese the benefit of the doubt until there was evidence to the contrary'.[49] This, as well as India's view that a resolution of the status of the offshore islands would de-escalate the tension, matched with British thinking on this question. A conversation that Nehru had upon his return to India with Desmond Donnelly, a British Member of Parliament who lunched with him on 20 November 1954, reinforced the view in London that Nehru's thinking was aligned with that of the British government on the question of the offshore islands. Nehru told Donnelly that his talks with the Chinese leaders had 'confirmed the impression that there was a distinction between the Chinese attitude to Formosa (Taiwan) and to the groups of islands near the coast because the latter were the most important bases for raids on shipping and the mainland'. Nehru told Donnelly that 'he felt that if he [Mao] got the islands and the raiding on the mainland stopped, they [Chinese] would not be likely to invade Formosa itself'.[50] Donnelly had promptly passed Nehru's assessment to the British Foreign Office. The British considered it an affirmation of its own position, and resolved to rope India into their efforts to dampen tension in the Taiwan Strait. They could work on the Americans and, they hoped, India could work on the Chinese since Nehru enjoyed excellent personal relations with the Chinese leaders.

The Americans saw the outcome of Nehru's visit to China rather differently. Nehru's briefing to Sir Alexander Clutterbuck, the British High Commissioner in New Delhi, to the effect that the Taiwan Strait situation had turned critical because of American intransigence on the question of the offshore islands,[51] was promptly shared with Dulles on an 'eyes only' basis. It seemed to confirm American thinking that Nehru was pushing the Chinese case. Nehru's public statements, such as his interview to the *Manchester Guardian* in December 1954, did not help matters either. 'There can be no solution for Formosa until it is returned to the mainland. For one thing it is part of China . . .' said Nehru. 'The Chinese live in perpetual fear. Even if America does not help Chiang, the fact that he is supported by them was bound to perpetuate tension with China.'[52] Such statements did not encourage American confidence in Nehru's role or place in its China policy. A National Intelligence Estimate by the NSC surmised that India would almost certainly condemn any US action (a naval blockade in the Taiwan Strait, for example) and would, in the UN, attempt to bring about a solution in favour of China.[53]

From November 1954 it became the objective of the British government to draw India into the Taiwan Strait crisis on its side. Alexander Clutterbuck was instructed to brief Nehru on various sensitive matters relating to the Taiwan Strait crisis, including the proposed US–Taiwan Defence Treaty, and to 'stress to Nehru the prime importance of stopping the fighting and preventing further outbreaks, and [to] ask him to urge on the Chinese the dangers of making such attacks'.[54] During Secretary General Pillai's visit to London, the British Foreign Office acquainted him in general terms with ORACLE. It wanted India to reassure China that America's

real purpose in concluding the defence treaty with Taiwan was to
put legal restraints on further adventurism by Chiang Kai-shek
against the mainland, and that such a treaty would be helpful,
not harmful, to China's security.[55] A similar message was also
passed to G.L. Mehta, India's Ambassador to the US, through the
British embassy in Washington. Mehta reported this to Nehru,
saying 'the British ambassador [Roger Makins] observed that you
[Nehru] were exercising a moderating and restraining influence on
China. He, therefore, hoped that the Peking government would
listen to your advice and not precipitate matters which would
only make the adoption of a more conciliatory policy by the US
even more difficult.'[56] Such unilateral British efforts to get India
to adopt a more direct role in the Taiwan Strait crisis did not have
American endorsement. The level of disappointment with India
in Washington was such that at higher levels a proposal from the
State Department's senior official handling Indian affairs to invite
Nehru for a state visit to Washington in 1955 was 'not on balance
considered desirable' by Dulles and turned down.[57]

British pressure on India to work in tandem on the Taiwan
Strait crisis increased further after the formal signing of the
US–Taiwan (Republic of China) Mutual Defence Treaty on
2 December 1954. The Chinese, as anticipated, sharply criticized
the signing of this treaty. Zhou described it as a 'serious war
provocation' aimed at converting Taiwan into an American
military base to extend aggression to the Chinese mainland.[58]
What concerned the British to a greater degree, however, was that
China was not only upset that the British government publicly
welcomed the treaty, but angered that it had referred to the
Chiang Kai-shek government as the 'Nationalist Government of
China'. At the National Day Reception in the Finland embassy on
7 December, Zhou told the British charge d'affaires (the senior-
most diplomatic representative who officiates when there is no
Ambassador), Humphrey Trevelyan, that London appeared to have

changed its position on Chiang Kai-shek by acknowledging his government by its official title[59] (Foreign Secretary Eden became upset at this lapse on part of the Foreign Office).* Anglo-Chinese relations worsened still further when Britain's Minister of State for Foreign Affairs, Sir Anthony Nutting, who was leading the UK delegation to the United Nations in New York, was reported by the American media as saying that Britain would join the US in action if 'Red China' attacked Formosa.† (Eden asked the Foreign Office to send a stern warning to Nutting. Nutting would later resign from the government during the Suez crisis in 1956 over differences with Eden who, by that time, had become Prime Minister.) The Americans were delighted at Nutting's statement.‡

---

* File 371/110241, Folder 11, Note by C.T. Crowe, 15 December 1954: 'Secretary of State has minuted on Peking telegram No. 1026 that it is unfortunate that the alleged use by a foreign office spokesman of the phrase "Chinese Nationalist Government" has been taken very seriously in Peking.' Secretary of State refers to Eden, since his formal title is the Secretary of State for Foreign Affairs (popularly known as Foreign Secretary).

† Zhou Enlai told Trevelyan that 'Even worse, Under Secretary for Foreign Affairs Nutting said publicly while in America that, if China were to move to liberate Taiwan, then the UK would take action, together with the United Nations . . . This is a totally hostile attitude towards China (Transcript of Conversation between Zhou Enlai and Humphrey Trevelyan, 5 January 1955, Wilson Center Digital Archive, *Zhou Enlai Waijiao Wenxuan* (Selected Diplomatic Papers of Zhou Enlai) (Beijing: Zhongyang Wenxian, 1990), pp. 94–105, translated by Simon Schuchat, https://digitalarchive.wilsoncenter.org/document/260506.

‡ Ambassador Henry Cabot Lodge Jr, the US Ambassador to the UN, wrote to President Eisenhower to say that 'Nutting is the best thing that I have seen in the political field for a very long time . . . For the first time there is someone here from a major power who helps actively in rebuttal (*FRUS, 1952–1954, China and Japan, Vol. XIV, Part I*, Doc. No. 438, 'The United States Representative at the UN (Lodge) to the President', 11 December 1954.

The British felt that between American stubbornness and Chinese peevishness, their entire Far Eastern policy was falling apart.

Their attempts to mollify the Chinese were unsuccessful. Trevelyan tried repairing the damage when he met Zhou on 5 January 1955 to convey an oral message from Eden to the effect that there had, in fact, been no change in the British policy towards China. Eden wanted Zhou to know that Britain, unlike the US, had no relationship with the Chiang Kai-shek regime in Taiwan and was not a party to the US–Taiwan security treaty. Zhou appeared unconvinced. He said that he had hoped, after the Geneva Accords on Indochina in mid-1954, that Sino-British relations could improve but, to the contrary, the British government had colluded with the Americans in formalizing the Manila Pact. This, he said, showed that Britain had a 'hostile attitude' to China. He made it clear that the Americans wanted China to accept the creation of two Chinas, which China would never accept. If Eden wanted to ease tensions, said Zhou, then the British government should encourage the Americans to withdraw all their troops from Taiwan. Trevelyan attempted to retrieve the situation by asking Zhou not to shoot the messenger, saying that 'when a third person [Britain] steps in to mediate he usually ends up being beaten himself'. To which Zhou retorted, 'right now, the third person [Britain] is not getting beaten himself, he is just accusing and cursing the second person [China] who is being beaten instead of asking the first person [US] to stop.'[60]

This worsening of the Anglo-Chinese relationship at the turn of 1954–55 was more than matched by rapidly deteriorating Anglo-American relations over the issue of the Taiwan Strait. Two developments brought political tensions between the US and Britain to fever pitch. First, the US government decided that the developing situation in the Taiwan Strait was critical enough for Eisenhower to seek authorization from Congress to commit military forces in the event of a Chinese attack on

Taiwan. This did not mean that the US was committed to defending the offshore islands, but it was not denying it publicly either.[61] The British considered Eisenhower's efforts to secure the Congressional resolution as a further provocation to the Chinese. They remonstrated with the Americans. Makins told Dulles that his government was 'disturbed' because the British thought that it was 'our common objective [US and UK] to work in a situation under which the Chinese communists accepted a separation of Formosa from the mainland (ORACLE) and the Chinese Nationalists abandoned the Offshore Islands.' Makins said the Chinese could never be brought to accept a ceasefire agreement in the UN (ORACLE) under the new conditions, and held out the warning that the British government would reconsider the entire question of proceeding with ORACLE in these circumstances.[62] The Americans went ahead despite the British objections. Eisenhower's formal request, on 24 January 1955, asking Congress to authorize the use of military force if required, stated that 'in the western Pacific a situation is developing in the Formosa straits that seriously impairs peace and security', and that China's actions have established a 'pattern of aggressive purpose . . . that they proclaim is the conquest of Formosa'.[63] Eisenhower urged Churchill to recognize that the psychological effect in the Far East of deserting their friends on Formosa would risk the collapse of Asiatic resistance to the communists, and that this was almost as important to Britain in the long term as it was to America.[64] The message was clear: Britain's short-term commercial and colonial interests must not blind them to the bigger strategic picture. But the British government, already deeply worried at the impact of Sino-American tensions on British interests in Hong Kong and elsewhere, grew more anxious after hearing the Chinese response to Eisenhower's action. In a tense interview between Zhou and Trevelyan in Beijing on 28 January 1955, Zhou described the

President's message to Congress as a 'war message'.[65] According to Trevelyan, Zhou was 'tense and absolutely uncompromising'.

As if the aggravation caused by the Congressional resolution and the rising Chinese rhetoric wasn't enough to cause alarm in London, China also rejected the idea of discussing a ceasefire in the United Nations. As long as the possibility of a ceasefire being negotiated was alive, Britain still had hopes for easing tensions. But, the British government became more certain that a war was brewing when, on 24 January 1955, Zhou publicly declared that the Americans were 'engineering a conspiracy for a so-called ceasefire through the United Nations to intervene in the Chinese peoples' liberation of Taiwan'[66] and added that China would never separate the question of the offshore islands from that of Taiwan (then known as Formosa) and liberate them all.[67] The British government concluded that in light of Zhou's uncompromising statement, the pursuit of ORACLE was more likely to do harm than good,[68] causing Dulles some days later to comment, rather dryly, to Makins, that 'there was no reason why the UN's action should collapse at the first blast from Chou Enlai'.[69] Once the Chinese rejected ORACLE, the chances of an open split between the Americans and the British increased.

In the circumstances, Britain felt it necessary to take two important steps. First, it made its position on the offshore islands explicit to the US. Makins told Dulles over dinner on 28 January that Britain stood firmly behind the US insofar as it related to Formosa and the Pescadores, but that the offshore islands of Quemoy and Matsu were entirely another matter. War was being risked over the offshore islands that Britain had already recognized as being Chinese territory.[70] Secondly, the British decided to mount pressure on India to actively intervene on its side. Eden met Vijayalakshmi Pandit, India's High Commissioner in London, on 25 January 1955, to convey that the British government was seriously concerned over the situation in the Taiwan Strait.

He specifically wanted India to intercede with China in order to persuade it to attend the Security Council discussions on a ceasefire in the expectation that it would damp down the crisis. 'We very much hope,' Eden told Pandit, 'that Mr Nehru will be prepared to do what he can to help us convincing Chou Enlai that the interests of peace demand Chinese attendance.' His views were also subsequently given in writing to the Indian High Commission in London in order to reinforce the gravity of Eden's request.[71] Up until then, despite hints and appeals by Britain, Nehru was still undecided about whether anything could be usefully done by India in the Taiwan Strait crisis. It was in this undecided frame of mind that he travelled to London for the Commonwealth Prime Ministers' Conference. Eden did not give up. Still in pursuit of the idea of a UN-brokered ceasefire, he sent Nehru a personal message on 2 February. 'It might be of decisive importance,' Eden said, 'if you [Nehru] could see your way to use your great personal influence with the Chinese in order both to confirm them in this inclination and also to persuade them to send a representative to New York, briefed to play a constructive role in the Security Council's debates.'[72] He continued working on Nehru during the Commonwealth Prime Ministers' Conference. The British government was keen to align the Commonwealth countries to the British position on the offshore islands issue, and Nehru's position in this regard was deemed to be crucial.

The US also tried to gauge Nehru's thinking through a conversation that the American Ambassador in London held with Nehru on 3 February. Nehru was in a reflective mood. He felt that history had indeed already passed Chiang Kai-shek by. He told Ambassador Winthrop Aldrich that Chiang's raids against the mainland from the offshore islands were like continuous pinpricks to the Chinese communists. A 'running sore' is how Nehru characterized the status of the offshore islands in the Taiwan Strait. He also told Aldrich that Mao Zedong was not an unreasonable man with whom the US could talk.[73] Eden, meanwhile, was telling the US that the Commonwealth member countries fully shared the British view on the legal status of the offshore islands as belonging to China.[74] In reality, though, the Commonwealth Prime Ministers' Conference had reached no such agreement, a fact that Nehru confirmed in his telegram of 10 February to N. Raghavan, India's Ambassador in Beijing.[75] One senior American official later summed up the British effort in the following terms: 'what they [the British] are trying to tell us without putting it into words is that they [Britain] can swing all of the Commonwealth, including a reluctant and sobered Nehru, behind our policy if we can indicate we are prepared to have the Chinese Nationalists withdraw from the offshore islands'.[76] It was a tantalizing offer, but the Americans refused to budge. Instead, Washington upped the ante. US Ambassador Aldrich was instructed to convey, on the President's behalf, that if the Commonwealth countries lent an appearance of surrender on Quemoy and Matsu at this time, this would have a most serious effect throughout the Far Eastern area.[77] Eisenhower reiterated this message, telling Churchill that if international communism penetrated the island barrier in the western Pacific Ocean, it would be in a position to threaten the Philippines and Indonesia directly, and everybody would be in far worse trouble. 'Certainly, the whole region would soon go,' wrote Eisenhower, in a clear indication that he thought the British policy to be short-sighted.[78]

As the Americans built their pressure on Britain, the British became more keen to find ways to bring Nehru on board with Britain's position on the status of the offshore islands and their idea that Chiang's withdrawal from the offshore islands was the only way of resolving the crisis peacefully. An opportunity arose when the Soviets made a proposal for Britain, India and the Soviet Union to chair consultations on resolving the tense situation in the Taiwan Strait. Moscow's proposal was that the three countries would sponsor a conference in New Delhi with the participation of all interested parties, but not including Chiang Kai-shek. Britain felt that the Soviet proposal held promise because it also had Chinese support.[79] The Americans considered the Soviet effort as an attempt to win over the Asians, particularly India, and to cause a split between the US and Britain.[80] Nehru was undecided. He wanted the Moscow proposal to be endorsed by the United Nations before proceeding further.[81] America poured cold water over it before the idea gained any traction. Dulles told Ambassador Makins that he did not think that a group of this composition (the UK, the USSR and India), all of whom recognized the PRC, could be unbiased. Dulles was also concerned that the three countries might insert themselves as intermediaries.[82] He finally buried this idea in a further conversation with Makins during which he said that 'the British could take it as definite that their informal proposal for establishment by the Security Council of a group comprised of the UK, USSR and India to examine into the Formosa question was not agreeable to the United States'.[83]

Concerned that the opportunity to build solid support for the British position among the members of the Commonwealth was slipping away, Eden reportedly told the Commonwealth leaders that the US government would welcome a return to Truman's policy, and would be glad to encourage Chiang Kai-shek to leave the offshore islands, including Quemoy, but was unable to state this position in public.[84] This was not what the Americans were actually telling the British. It is difficult to escape the conclusion that Eden was intentionally misleading Nehru and other Commonwealth leaders. The steady pressure mounted by the British led Nehru, at least in part, to have the first tentative thoughts on greater Indian involvement in the Taiwan Strait crisis. From London, on 1 February 1955, he acknowledged the gravity of the unfolding crisis in a message to Indira Gandhi, saying that 'the situation in the Far East is a difficult and a dangerous one because two great countries with high ideas of their own prestige and "face" and with a good deal of passion are at logger heads'.[85] In a separate message also from London, to Raghavan, India's Ambassador in China, Nehru shared that he was thinking of taking some steps but had no definite proposals to make as yet. He was hoping for some indication from Zhou, and he asked Raghavan to meet him to 'get some private indication of his present reactions'.[86] Raghavan met Zhou on 8 February, but nothing much emerged that could help Nehru to determine the future course of action that India might adopt.

After the Commonwealth Prime Ministers' Conference ended, Nehru again wrote to Raghavan and outlined India's approach for the first time since the crisis erupted. 'We must lead up to negotiations and in the meanwhile (a) secure coastal islands for China (about which there is less difficulty), (b) bring about some steps which in some form at least bring issue into at least first stages of negotiation, direct or indirect, (c) prevent United States from committing herself more and more, (d) press for recognition of Peking as the government of China.'[87] But Nehru was still unsure on how to proceed. He was not comfortable with Eden's suggestion that Nehru try to convince Zhou that the Americans were prepared to be flexible on the offshore islands if China, in turn, agreed to a ceasefire.[88] He thought any outreach to the Chinese would stand a better chance of success if he could tell Beijing that what Eden was telling him was the American policy.[89]

While Nehru continued to remain in two minds on whether to involve India more directly in mediating the crisis, Anglo-American relations continued their downward spiral through February and March 1955. On 10 February, perhaps concerned over a possible united Commonwealth position on the offshore islands that went against American policy, Eisenhower again wrote Churchill to emphasize the importance of the offshore islands, as part of the bigger island chain (stretching from Japan to the Philippines) built by the Western powers to contain the communists. He said that withdrawal from the offshore islands would mean the almost immediate conversion of that asset into a deadly danger because the communists would seize the islands.[90] Churchill reiterated Britain's position that the offshore islands were legally Chinese territory and that 'nobody here considers it a just cause of war'. Eden and Churchill made statements to that effect in the British Parliament on 15 and 23 February 1955.[91] Dulles responded sharply, telling Eden that 'there comes a point where constantly giving in only encourages further belligerency', and warned him not to cross that point with the Chinese because 'in such a case further retreat becomes worse than a Munich'. His drawing a parallel with Britain's policy of appeasing Adolf Hitler at Munich in 1938 highlighted the extent to which the two principal Western powers now differed in their approaches.[92] Anglo-American differences on the China policy were now in the open and between the highest levels of government.

It was in these gloomy circumstances that Eden and Dulles met in Bangkok on 25 February 1955 for a two-hour post-dinner talk about the Taiwan Strait crisis. Eden enquired how the Americans would defend the offshore islands, which were so close to the mainland's coast, against a Chinese attack. Admiral Felix Stump, Commander of the US Pacific Fleet, who was accompanying Dulles, apparently said 'by means of deep bombing of communist bases on the mainland'. Eden was alarmed. He reported to Churchill his impression that this could include the use of atomic weapons. Worried that war was imminent (Eden personally thought that the US navy was itching to pull the trigger), he broached with Dulles the possibility of a direct approach by the British to the Chinese government to see if there was any chance that war might be averted. Dulles did not object to the idea.[93] Trevelyan, Britain's charge d'affaires in Beijing, was now asked by London to talk to Zhou Enlai. Zhou met with him twice, on 25 and 28 February.

The discussion was testy and polemical. Zhou was still displeased with Britain's support for American policy since the beginning of the crisis, and unwilling to accept Eden's assurance that the British government was neither hostile to China nor favouring the US.[94] Zhou said that the Americans wanted to trade their intervention in the offshore islands against the Chinese acceptance of the existence of two Chinas. 'This was,' he told Trevelyan, 'a dirty deal and the Chinese would have nothing to do with it.'[95] Zhou said he would welcome a visit by Eden to China, provided their discussion would be confined to the ending of American aggression against China and the complete withdrawal of American forces from Taiwan. These preconditions made it impossible for Eden to go to China. In his letter to Zhou, Eden regretted that 'a common basis does not yet exist on which discussion could take place for a peaceful settlement of serious issues at stake. Please therefore consider that a meeting between us at this stage would not achieve our purpose.'[96]

But what was significant was that with this exchange between Zhou Enlai and Anthony Eden, the British felt that for the first time since the beginning of the crisis in September 1954, they might be back in the game. It was of even greater significance that the British government took particular care to ensure that the Indian side was not informed until much later about this direct British outreach to Zhou Enlai. The Americans were explicitly requested not to make the details of the exchanges between Eden and Zhou publicly known.[97] There were explicit instructions from the British Foreign Office to their High Commissioner in Delhi not to share any information with the Government of India.* It was only after the exchanges between Eden and Zhou were over that,

---

* This was not so with the members of the 'Old Commonwealth' (Australia, New Zealand, Canada and South Africa) who were regularly briefed on the developments.

Mao Zedong, chairman of the Communist Party of China, with Patrick Hurley, President Roosevelt's special representative to China, 1945

John Leighton Stuart, US ambassador to Nationalist China

US President Harry S. Truman (third from left) shaking hands with the prime minister of India Jawaharlal Nehru upon the latter's arrival in Washington, 11 October 1949

Nehru (left) with US Secretary of State Dean Acheson during his visit to the United States, 12 October 1949

Mao Zedong with Indian ambassador K.M. Panikkar, Beijing,
26 January 1951

French foreign minister Georges Bidault (right), British foreign secretary
Anthony Eden (centre) and US Secretary of State John Foster Dulles,
Geneva Conference, 1954

Anthony Eden and V.K. Krishna Menon

Mao Zedong and Jawaharlal Nehru during the latter's visit to China,
Beijing, 23 October 1954

Nehru with Premier Zhou Enlai and Madam Song Qingling,
widow of Sun Yat-sen, Beijing, October 1954

Krishna Menon with President Eisenhower (left) and John Foster
Dulles (centre) at the White House during the first Taiwan Strait
crisis, June 1955

Jairam Ramesh, *A Chequered Brilliance*

Krishna Menon with Henry Cabot Lodge, US representative to the
United Nations, during the second Taiwan Strait crisis,
New York, 1958

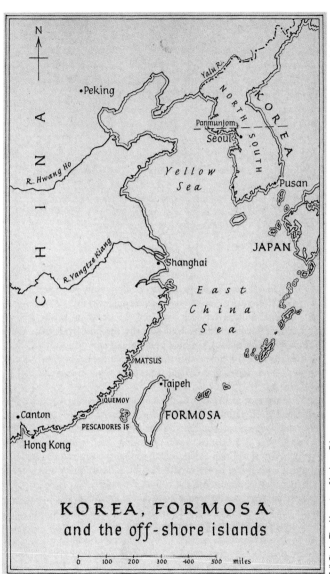

The geography of the Taiwan Strait: The map shows the island
of Taiwan, the Penghu (Pescadores) islands and the islands off
the coast of China, collectively known as the Offshore Islands
(Quemoy or Jinmen, and the Matsu or Mazu islands)

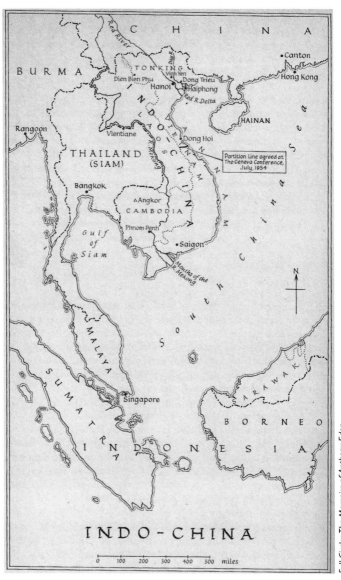

Within the map:

CHINA

BURMA

Red River

•Canton

TONKING
Dien Bien Phu •Vinh Yen
•Dong Trieu Hong Kong
Hanoi •Haiphong
Red R.Delta

Rangoon Vientiane

HAINAN

Dong Hoi

THAILAND
(SIAM)

Partition line agreed at
The Geneva Conference,
July, 1954

Bangkok

•Angkor
CAMBODIA

Phnom Penh

Gulf
of
Siam

•Saigon

Mouths of the
R.Mekong

N

South China Sea

MALAYA

SUMATRA

Singapore

SARAWAK

BORNEO

INDONESIA

INDO-CHINA

0   100   200   300   400   500   miles

The geography of Indochina: The map shows North Vietnam (Democratic Republic of Vietnam) and South Vietnam (Republic of Vietnam), the 17th Parallel, which separated the two Vietnams, and the remaining two Indochina nations of Cambodia and Laos in mid-March, the Foreign Office finally permitted the British High Commissioner in Delhi to brief the Indian government. This was done more out of the concern that the credibility of the British as a reliable partner of India might be compromised if the Chinese or the Soviets shared this information with Delhi,[98] than out of any particular concern to keep India in the loop. This deliberate disingenuity on the part of the British Foreign Office meant that when Nehru was, finally, actively considering the prospect of 'mediation' (mostly at the British behest), he was denied a vital piece of information that would have been helpful, namely that the Chinese had categorically rejected the proposal of a ceasefire. Nehru continued to believe that pressing for a ceasefire in the Taiwan Strait was the way ahead in resolving the problem.

Nehru decided that the presence of Premier Zhou Enlai and the Chinese delegation at the forthcoming African–Asian Conference to be held in Bandung, Indonesia, from late April 1955, would be an opportunity to play a role. India had lobbied for China to be invited to Bandung and Nehru felt he had developed a good equation with Zhou during his visit to China. He decided to sound out the Americans about this possibility. V.K. Krishna Menon, Nehru's advisor and confidante on foreign affairs, therefore, travelled to Washington for meetings with President Eisenhower and Secretary Dulles. At the meeting with Eisenhower on 15 March 1955, nothing of consequence resulted so far as the Taiwan question was concerned. Indian Ambassador G.L. Mehta later recorded, 'It seemed to me, & Mr Menon subsequently told me that he had the same impression—that the President and Dulles had decided not to raise any issue of controversy nor to refer to the situation in the Far East.'[99] When Mehta told the President that he might be interested to know that Menon was going for the Bandung Conference, Eisenhower feigned disinterest. Mehta's observation was that Eisenhower asked him 'one or two casual questions about it'. It did not lead to any serious exploration of possibilities. A week later, Menon also met Dulles in Washington for a longer talk. On this occasion, Menon expressed his hopes that talks could be initiated between the Americans and the Chinese. In order to make progress, Menon suggested that direct but informal contact would have to be established between the US and the PRC, and he commented that a 'third party' might be useful for this purpose but without specifically offering India's good offices. Dulles informed Menon that in his latest speech at the Advertising Club of New York, on 21 March, he had already publicly said that the US would not use force in an aggressive manner. But Dulles also made it clear that the 'choice of war or peace rested with Peking'. Dulles told Menon that the 'Chinese Reds' constituted a greater danger to world peace than the Soviet Union[*] while Menon said that his government felt 'absolutely confident' that Beijing had no expansionist ambitions.[100] There was no indication that Dulles responded in any manner to Menon's suggestion about 'third party' involvement for resolving the issue, nor did the Americans confirm what the British had been telling Nehru, namely that the Americans were prepared to facilitate a quiet withdrawal of Chiang's forces from the offshore islands in return for a ceasefire by all parties in the Taiwan Strait. Yet, according to the American account, after his meeting with Dulles, Krishna Menon 'expressed his satisfaction' at the talks and said he felt optimistic that tensions in the Far East would be relaxed if 'people could be brought together and [would] start talking'.[101] Krishna Menon, quite possibly, gave this optimistic picture to Nehru, and they both went to Bandung with the intention of playing a role.

---

[*] Menon shared Dulles's view with Zhou Enlai in Bandung ('Mr Krishna Menon's Interview with Premier Chou Enlai on Thursday, 12 May 1955 in Beijing', File 347, Part II, Nehru Memorial Museum and Library, New Delhi).

The Americans tried to unilaterally push ORACLE at the United Nations in March even though the Chinese had categorically rejected the idea in January. The British objected. Eden felt that 'instead of improving our position before the Afro-Asian conference, [ORACLE] might worsen it by alienating the Indians, Burmese and others whose views may not be without influence in Peking'.[102] Anglo-American relations faced a crisis of confidence. Eisenhower told Churchill that 'our attitudes towards problems in the Orient are frequently so dissimilar as to be almost mutually antagonistic', adding '. . . your own government seems to regard communist aggression in Asia of little significance to the free world future'.[103] Anglo-American relations appeared to reach a breaking point over the China policy. Both recognized that the Western alliance faced a crisis. The British Foreign Office gave the State Department a memorandum urging the US to exercise restraint 'lest we frighten the Asians into China's arms', and expressing concern that the Bandung Conference might otherwise be used by China to isolate the US again (as in Geneva).[104]

The American President had meanwhile begun rethinking the crisis. A US National Intelligence Estimate in mid-March had assessed that the Chinese had accumulated adequate capabilities near the coast to be able to seize Quemoy and Matsu from Chiang Kai-shek, and that the Soviets might also intervene if the US got militarily involved.[105] Eisenhower was concerned enough about the US drifting into what looked like a bad situation to send a memorandum to Dulles in early April about his reluctance on committing military forces to the defence of the offshore islands. 'To do so would commit United States military prestige to a campaign under conditions favorable to the attacker. Because the world generally regards the coastal islands as part of the mainland, our active participation would forfeit the good opinion of much of the Western world, with consequent damage to our interests in Europe and elsewhere. There is much opposition in our own country to becoming involved militarily in defense of the offshore islands, and in the event of such involvement our people would be seriously divided at the very time when increased risk of global war would underline the need for unity. Finally, even a successful defensive campaign would not stabilize the situation; a new attack could be expected at any time. But with American prestige committed to the success of the defense, a disproportionate amount of our disposable, mobile, reserves would be tied down indefinitely to this one spot.'[106] This represented a significant shift in American policy prior to the Bandung Conference. They became interested in exploring what prospects the forthcoming conference in Bandung held to get the Chinese to back down in the Taiwan Strait. Dulles decided to approach 'certain friendly countries' to work towards persuading China at Bandung about the advantages of negotiating with the Americans. But this list of countries did not include India. Nehru's recent speeches in Parliament criticizing the Manila Pact, NATO and Western 'meddling' in the Middle East had irritated Dulles. The US turned to Pakistan, the Philippines, Thailand, Turkey and Lebanon, among others.[107] Once it had decided on a policy of accommodation rather than confrontation with China, its relationship with Britain also began to return to the cooperative track. It made it possible once more for Britain to collaborate with the US without a reversal of the entire British Far Eastern policy since 1949 that was fundamentally designed to achieve modus vivendi with the Chinese.

The Chinese too were looking for a way out of the impasse. They told the Indonesians (who told the US Ambassador in Jakarta) that Zhou was willing to directly negotiate with the US on easing tension in the Taiwan Strait.[108] On 23 April, Zhou had lunch with seven leaders, including Nehru, at the residence of the Indonesian Prime Minister. He said: 'The Chinese people are friendly to the American people. The Chinese people too do not want to have war with the United States of America. The Chinese government is willing to sit down and enter into negotiations with the US government to discuss the question of relaxing tension in the Far East and especially the question of relaxing tension in the Taiwan area.'[109] It set the stage for India's full-blown 'mediation' in the crisis.

Krishna Menon was well acquainted with Zhou Enlai. They had spent many hours together in Geneva and, he thought, they had a good rapport. Menon also believed that he had been instrumental in helping the Chinese in the Geneva Accords, and the Chinese would, therefore, willingly accept his mediation. They had several hours of discussion at Bandung. According to Chinese accounts of these meetings, Menon conveyed to Zhou that the Americans would be willing to have direct talks with the Chinese provided some preparatory work was done in advance. It was a thinly disguised attempt to insert himself as a go-between for this purpose. The Americans had made only a conditional response to Zhou's offer of talks. Dulles told American media on 26 April that the Chinese communists had been compelled to negotiate because at Bandung they had found no backing for their announced programme of seizing Taiwan by force. 'Whether or not this is a sincere proposal remains to be seen,' he said.[110] Despite Dulles's conditional response to his offer for direct talks with America, Zhou thought it was sufficient to explore the possibilities. Zhou invited Menon to visit China for further discussion. Neither the United States nor China, however, fully trusted him. The Americans thought that the Chinese had relented at Bandung as a result of their own efforts and pressure.* Dulles did not consider it necessary to have intermediaries. In that respect he

---

* Dulles told the US Cabinet that Nehru had suffered a great loss of prestige at Bandung, and that Zhou had gained ground ('Anglo American Tensions over the Chinese Offshore Islands', Tracie Lee Steele, London School of Economics, September 1991, published by ProQuest LLC [2014], p. 102).

singled out Krishna Menon. In telegrams that he sent to American Ambassadors in several countries, Dulles stated that 'the United States is not utilizing services [of] any intermediary at present and specifically Krishna Menon's prospective trip [to] Peiping [is] not undertaken at our request or with our knowledge'.[111] The Chinese, too, had their doubts about Menon. In the report that Zhou's delegation in Bandung submitted to the Chinese government, they recorded their views on Menon. 'We can see from Menon's words that India's idea is that Jinmen and Mazu will be returned to China and Taiwan will be an autonomous province on the condition that the USA recognizes China's unity and China peacefully liberates Taiwan. We believe that Menon's words also represent part of the UK's idea. For this, we didn't make any definite comment, but agreed for Menon to come to Beijing in the middle of May to continue the discussion on China–US talks.'[112] They thought Menon was doing the bidding of the West. But Zhou also felt that Menon had his uses. Hence the invitation to him to visit China.

On his return from Bandung, Nehru apprised the chief ministers on India's plans to explore avenues for peace and Zhou's invitation to Menon. 'The most practicable course,' said Nehru, 'is to proceed as informally as possible through private talks with the parties concerned.'[113] Nehru maintained that Menon 'did not go there as a mediator but because he was invited by Zhou Enlai'.* [114]

---

* Senior officers of the Ministry of External Affairs were also sceptical about Menon. Y.D. Gundevia, India's Deputy High Commissioner in London, when asked by Sir G. Laithwaite, a senior British Foreign Office official, about Krishna Menon's forthcoming trip to Beijing, 'replied, with a smile, that no one ever knew what Mr Krishna Menon was going to do or say, still less did they know his motives. He could not see any particular reason for the visit so shortly after the discussions at Bandung—but then nor could he see any reason for most of Mr Menon's international tours' (FO

Before leaving for China, Menon had a long talk with John Sherman Cooper, the American Ambassador in New Delhi. He said that China was not an expansionist power. India did not fear communist China. Zhou had spoken many times with Menon. Menon said that Zhou's offer to negotiate with America was made in good faith. Menon said that India was ready to offer its good offices to facilitate further contacts. But Menon also told Ambassador Cooper that whether the Americans agreed or not to this idea, he still intended to explore possibilities for negotiation on the Taiwan Strait crisis. He would go to Beijing even if the Americans did not need India's help. Menon broadly spoke about a three-stage process to ease tension, beginning with an exploration as to the willingness of both to enter into negotiations, followed by the second step of relaxing tensions, and moving on to actual negotiations regarding the status of Taiwan as the final stage. Cooper thought that Menon 'was vague as to channels for bringing US–China understanding, as to subject matter [for talks] and as to limits on various stages of negotiation'.[115] Washington promptly sent a directive to Ambassador Cooper to avoid giving Menon any impression that he had a mandate to speak for the Americans when visiting Beijing.[116] Cooper may not have been able to communicate this to Menon in time.

In Beijing, Krishna Menon had five separate meetings between 12–20 May with Premier Zhou Enlai, each spanning three or more hours, during which there was an extensive enquiry by Zhou on each and every aspect of American thinking relating to US–China relations, to the point where Menon finally retorted, 'Mr Prime Minister, you must not put me in the position of the US and expect me to answer these questions.'[117] In his very first meeting, Menon made clear to Zhou that he was neither carrying

371/117291, 'Political Relations between India and the UK' [Government Papers, National Archives, Kew, 1955], accessed on 30 January 2023).

any message from the Americans, nor was he offering to mediate. He had come to Beijing, he said, 'to see if there is any way of common exploration. If you [Zhou] say there is nothing I can only see the sights and go home!'[118] Menon claimed he had been told, in strict confidence, when visiting Washington in March, that the Americans were prepared to explore matters without the Chinese having to give up their moral or political position or the question of principle on the Taiwan issue. Menon hoped the Chinese would see this as progress in American thinking. On more than one occasion, Menon underscored that there were differences between the American and the British positions, especially with regard to the offshore islands. At this point Zhou disclosed that the British government had also been reaching out to him through Trevelyan, and that the 'British government would like very much to play a part in bringing about peace'.[119]

At the subsequent meetings with Zhou Enlai, Menon outlined his three-step process—lowering tensions as the first stage; maintaining the lowered tensions as the second stage; and negotiations on Taiwan as the final stage. Zhou told him that China had already taken the first step by making the statement in Bandung that it was ready for direct talks with the US. Menon pushed the ceasefire proposal as a first step by way of maintaining lowered tensions. 'If it is possible within the standstill period [he meant the ceasefire] to establish the position of the coastal [offshore] islands becoming united to China . . . then we have a situation where the only problem to be negotiated is Taiwan. It appears to me that if this is the position, China does not stand to lose anything because she would have established her position over the coastal islands without forsaking her claims on Taiwan.' Zhou listened, but did not reveal his thinking (he had already categorically rejected the ceasefire idea when Eden had suggested it in February) during several rounds of talks with Menon, merely saying that China's view was 'utterly far from it [Menon's proposals]'.[120] In hindsight, Zhou was testing Menon, and also goading him by, from time to time, mentioning that the British, Indonesians, Burmese and others were also interested in mediating. He had correctly guessed that this would get under Menon's skin. At one point, Menon irritably retorted that Nehru had the capability to approach Eisenhower directly whereas other intermediaries did not, and that India should be given 'a certain amount of time' before the Chinese government took the help of others, leading Zhou to comment that there was no need for Menon to become 'too nervous'.[121] He was playing a cat-and-mouse game with Menon.*

After Zhou had fully extracted all the information from Menon, he finally disclosed China's position. First, China would talk to the US only about relaxation of tension in the Taiwan area, but not about the status of Taiwan. Second, it could be a three-stage process—namely, the relaxation of tensions, followed by direct negotiations between China and the US on the question of American withdrawal and maintenance of peace in the Taiwan Strait and, finally, the reunification of Taiwan with the mainland which, Zhou said, was an entirely internal affair of China's. Evacuation of the offshore islands by Chiang's forces should be part of the relaxation of tensions and not a matter for negotiations. If this plan was agreeable to the Americans, China would guarantee not to attack Chiang Kai-shek's forces during the evacuation process. Third, the Americans also needed to take other steps to relax tensions, including the lifting of the trade embargo, allowing

---

* Menon may have been too self-absorbed to see through Zhou's tactics. He had a supercilious attitude to Zhou. In his interviews to Michael Brecher, Menon claimed he had introduced Zhou Enlai to everyone in Bandung. 'I don't say Zhou was a kind of younger brother to us but he cooperated. We found him useful' (Michael Brecher, 'Bandung 1955', Chapter 5, *India and World Politics: Krishna Menon's View of the World* [London: Oxford University Press, 1968], p. 58).

American citizens and the American media to visit China, as well as permitting Chinese citizens in the US to return to China.

China offered, in exchange, to release several American prisoners of war (China had captured a number of US airmen who had flown secret missions over the mainland in 1953). In order to give Menon credibility with Washington, Zhou said that Menon could inform the Americans that four of their imprisoned airmen would be released immediately as a gesture by the Chinese. Finally, Zhou proposed direct contact with the Americans in friendly capitals such as Moscow, London or Delhi. Playing to Menon's ego, Zhou added, 'even with those contacts you yourself will have to remain to be the go-between because although you have said you are not the negotiator, you cannot as well shake the responsibility of a go-between'.[122] Then, as if to put added pressure on him, Zhou informed Menon that he was also planning to talk with others, including the British, to explore what sort of role they might be able to play. This was Zhou's way of ensuring that Menon remained faithful to the Chinese argument when acting as go-between. Zhou's ultimate goal was to establish direct contact with Washington, and at this point in time he still regarded India to be the most likely intermediary through which this might be initiated. He would tell Trevelyan immediately after Menon had left China that 'in the case of India Mr Menon is coming to Beijing but he will also visit Washington. This is mediation'.[123]

The Americans were very interested in receiving a report on Menon's visit to China, but did not wish to see Menon himself. They asked Ambassador Cooper to get the feedback.[124] Menon probably convinced Nehru that he was in possession of first-hand knowledge about Chinese thinking which was best shared in person in Washington. He got Nehru to write a letter to Eisenhower expressing his hope that the President would find it possible 'without delay to engage in informal conversations [with Menon] in Washington'.[125] Dulles finally, and with the utmost reluctance, agreed to see Menon after it became clear that Menon was planning to take all the credit for securing the release of the four captured American airmen.*

As always, the Government of India had dutifully briefed the British about Menon's talks with Zhou. Ever since the Eden–Zhou exchanges in February, the British government had been quietly engaging in its own direct contacts with the Chinese. On 9 May, Humphrey Trevelyan, British charge d'affaires to China, had sought a meeting with Premier Zhou Enlai to transmit a message from new Foreign Secretary Harold Macmillan (who had succeeded Eden after he became Prime Minister on 6 April 1955). According to Vice Foreign Minister Han Nianlong, Macmillan's message to Zhou was as follows: 'London views Premier Zhou Enlai's statement at the Bandung Conference with great interest and hope and wishes to know if China has any message for Britain to convey to the United States.' Mr Trevelyan added that the Foreign Secretary was anxious that Britain should lose no opportunity to play a role. Premier Zhou Enlai replied promptly that he would make a formal response after consideration.'[126]

Within days of Menon's departure from China, Trevelyan met Zhou Enlai again on 26 May. Zhou conveyed the same position that he had conveyed to Menon a few days previously, and because the British had received a detailed readout of the Menon–Zhou

---

* There was a race between him and UN Secretary General Dag Hammarskjöld to claim credit. Eisenhower wryly observed that Hammarskjöld would be 'quite burned up' at Menon for moving into his act (Doc. 261, 'Memorandum from Acting Secretary of State to Secretary of State', 28 May 1955, FRUS, 1955–1957, China, Part II). Eden called it an 'undignified scramble' that would amuse Zhou Enlai (FO 371/115181, FCI 1691/110 Eden Minute to Dixon Telegram, 3 June 1955, in footnote, 'Anglo American Tensions over the Chinese Offshore Islands', Tracie Lee Steele, London School of Economics, September 1991, published by ProQuest LLC [2014].

talks, they realized that the Chinese were also treating them as a potential interlocutor with the US. Menon visited London in early June to brief the British government about his talks with Zhou and met with Eden and Macmillan. The new Foreign Secretary was not impressed with Menon's 'very involved subtleties', and felt that Menon's hopes of getting the Chinese and the Americans to begin talks were misplaced.[127] The British government likely concluded at this point that there was no longer the same requirement for India to act as a go-between since the UK had established direct contact with Zhou. With the Anglo-American rivalry over the Taiwan Strait crisis abating significantly once Eisenhower had decided that conflict was not an option, the urgency of getting India on the British side had also disappeared. It is doubtful if India was aware of this change in the situation because, by this time, Krishna Menon was in the thick of the mediation.

The Americans already had prior knowledge of Menon's talks with Zhou before he arrived in Washington because the British government had apprised them of it.[128] Menon's first meeting was with Eisenhower, in the White House, on 19 June 1955. In some ways it was to presage the longer conversations that Menon subsequently had with Dulles. He began on the wrong foot by observing that there was a better atmosphere and basis for direct negotiations between the United States and China, that talks could begin, and that the 'relatively smaller question of prisoners and other American nationals in China' might be easily resolved later.[129] Menon's description of American prisoners in China as 'lesser' problems did not sit well with either Eisenhower or Dulles. Both pointed out that these were not minor issues but a vital matter that involved an important principle. America would not deal with a country that treated prisoners as bargaining chips.[130] Ambassador Mehta noted that Dulles used strong words like 'hostages' and 'kidnapping' in this context, and 'flared up' at Menon's description.[131] Menon's suggestions to allow American

citizens and the media to visit China if it lifted the travel ban, as a
goodwill gesture to the Chinese, was also not favourably received.
Dulles told Menon that American citizens might be apprehended
or imprisoned by the Chinese if they travelled to China. Menon's
response was that this was 'hardly conceivable', and that India was
prepared to intervene if it came to that. Menon told Eisenhower
that he was not trying to judge between the US and China on
specific issues nor did he want to produce any formulas. All that
he was proposing was that in order to avert the risk of war or loss
of prestige, it would be desirable for both sides to take advantage
of the lull in hostilities to open negotiations. The Americans felt
that at this point Menon became 'rather rambling'.[132] Eisenhower
said that as a matter of principle they would not impose a solution
on Chiang Kai-shek against his will or settle Taiwan's fate without
its consent. They were not going to compel Chiang Kai-shek to
withdraw from the offshore islands and hand them over to China.
Despite there being no visible common ground, Mehta recorded
in his subsequent note that the Indian side thought the interview
went well. When Menon suggested another round of discussions
with Eisenhower, he was noncommittal and asked Menon to talk
with Dulles.

Dulles and Menon had four meetings (including one private
meeting) between 14 June and 6 July 1955, each one progressively
more contentious than the preceding one. At the first meeting on
14 June, immediately after Menon had met Eisenhower, it became
apparent that there was no common ground between the two
sides. Dulles said that the US had no desire for war with China
and had taken several steps to contribute to easing of tensions.
He was interested in hearing what the Chinese might be willing
to do in this regard in the light of Menon's discussions in Beijing.
Menon clarified that it was not his intention to discuss the status
of disposition of Taiwan, but to get direct negotiations started.
But then Menon, rather tactlessly, told Dulles that the Chinese

could seize the offshore islands if they wanted, and it was better to try to settle this issue through negotiations. This prompted Dulles to say that some issues, and he meant the question of Taiwan in particular, should not be forced prematurely into negotiations, because they might lead to undesirable results.[133] This was contrary to what Menon was hoping to hear from the Americans. On the various other ideas that Menon had broached with Eisenhower on steps that America might take to ease tensions, Dulles similarly prevaricated. He said that permitting American citizens to visit China when they still held American prisoners-of-war was 'like sending another child to the kidnappers of one's baby'. The same held true for American media. Menon's tactlessness was again on display when he told the Secretary of State of the world's leading power that Nehru and he were making all these efforts to 'help increase and promote the prestige of the United States throughout Asia'. Towards the end of the meeting, Menon said that he had come from China with some hope that it would be possible to work something out, to which Dulles responded that he hoped Menon's hope was justified. Dulles gave no indication at this meeting that the US desired Menon to be an intermediary. Foreign Secretary Macmillan, who was in New York at the same time as Menon, recorded in his diary of 17 June that 'the Americans could not understand Menon's plan, and didn't like it, as far as they did understand it'.[134] Dulles subsequently reported to Eisenhower that 'Menon was troublesome because he was mixing up the channels of communication'.[135] More importantly, it was during this discussion that Eisenhower and Dulles took the decision to have direct dealings with China as an alternative to using representatives of third powers. Following Dulles's talk with the President, it was in New York, on 20 and 21 June, that Dulles and Macmillan also had long discussions on China that would ultimately lead to the British helping the Americans to establish direct contact.[136] Menon's subsequent meetings with Dulles were fated to fail because he wanted the Americans to acknowledge him as the intermediary, and Dulles was equally determined to deny him that role.

In the next talk that Menon had with Dulles on 1 July 1955, the latter questioned Menon's credentials as intermediary, and said that several others were also offering to interpret Chinese views to the American government, thus making it difficult to discern who was the authoritative intermediary. Menon enquired whether Dulles was telling him in polite terms 'Thank you for nothing!'[137] On the question of the offshore islands, Menon said that they were the crux of the problem and their status had to be settled for peace to prevail. Dulles was adamant the US could not contemplate withdrawal of Chiang Kai-shek from Quemoy and Matsu. When Menon interjected that 'everybody agreed to these islands being part of China including the British', Dulles dryly enquired whether the British would also be prepared in that case to relinquish Hong Kong since it was also geographically, ethnically and economically closer to China in similar fashion to the Quemoy and Matsu islands.[138]

Menon almost certainly made things worse by suggesting to Dulles that India was only making these efforts since a Chinese attack on the offshore islands might create a very awkward situation, because 'either the US may have to withdraw and lose face or there would be the risk of a third world war, neither of which contingency was desirable'.[139] This was not the sort of conversation designed to endear him to the high representative of a superpower. Dulles retorted by saying that there was no need to force the issue. If Germany, Vietnam and Korea could be partitioned, then why not China, he said. 'A quick solution [through early negotiations] to the entire problem could be very dangerous,' according to Dulles, 'because they would be more likely to end in war than in peace.'[140] Dulles also criticized Menon's efforts to interfere in the United Nations' efforts to secure the release of remaining American prisoners-of-war, causing Menon to petulantly say if that was the case, he would 'drop the whole matter'.[141] Menon progressively went on the back foot as he saw the opportunity to play the role of mediator slipping away. By now, it was clear that the Americans had no intention of allowing Menon, or India, to play this role, but he was a man obsessed. When the meeting ended, he requested another one with Dulles. In his report to Nehru on this meeting, Menon claimed, with little basis, that Dulles 'thought better of things and of us towards the end'.[142] It seemed a total misreading of the mood of this meeting and the overall attitude of Dulles.*

The final meeting between Menon and Dulles on 6 July was acrimonious and ended possibilities for any kind of role for India. Dulles refused to consider any of Zhou's suggestions about how tensions might be relaxed, and questioned Menon's intentions in asking the US to take unilateral actions. Dulles said that the Chinese were the threat since they wanted to take the offshore islands by force. Menon said that the existence of Formosa and Chiang Kai-shek's regime constituted the real threat because it was supported by the US. There followed a discussion on which country was more principled in its behaviour—India or the US. Menon, tried more than once, to say that he was not speaking for China or justifying their actions.[143] Their final exchanges revealed

---

* Indian Ambassador Mehta sent a secret and personal note to Nehru after Krishna Menon's visit to convey that 'if I may state frankly, Mr Menon has still to get over some part of the previous prejudice against him. This prejudice has to some extent been due to his rather curt treatment because he is undoubtedly temperamental and sometimes rather difficult to get along with. It is also felt by some people that he has in the past been unnecessarily critical and harsh about the United States while he never offers any criticism about the Soviet bloc' (No. 129-A/55, 'Secret and Personal, Mehta to Nehru', 7 July 1955, File 360, Part II, Krishna Menon Papers, Nehru Memorial Museum and Library, New Delhi).

the depth of the true antipathy towards each other. Dulles told Menon that he had spent more time with him than with any other foreign diplomat and, when Menon said he was not a diplomat, Dulles smilingly added, 'Well, whatever you call yourself.' After Menon had left the room he turned to George Allen, assistant secretary of state for Northeast Asia, bitterly saying, 'Your Secretary [Dulles] has said to me in so many words: "Go away, you are not serving any useful purpose."'[144] There was nothing more left to be said. So deep was the bitterness between the two of them that, even many years after both had retired from politics, Menon would say 'he [Dulles] was the man who prevented the negotiations with China when I came back from Peking in 1955 and there was hope of bringing China to talk to the US'.[145]

Menon's final meeting with Eisenhower on 6 July was simply a courtesy. He told Eisenhower he had little to report to Nehru in positive terms. Eisenhower assured him that everything he had said in Washington would be carefully weighed by the administration. Dulles's comment about Menon having interfered in the UN's work on the American prisoners still rankled with the latter. He told the President that the bona fides of the Government of India should not be suspected and Eisenhower assured him this was not the case.[146] Eisenhower later recorded his own views about Menon. 'Krishna Menon is a menace and a bore. He is a bore because he conceives himself to be intellectually superior and rather coyly pretends to cover this under a cloak of excessive humility and modesty. He is a menace because he is a master at twisting words and meanings of others and is governed by an ambition to prove himself the master international manipulator and politician of the age. He has visited me twice (in company of Secretary Dulles) to talk about some basis of mediation between Red China and ourselves. I have bluntly told him, both times, that the American people will not consider using the lives and freedom of their own citizens as a bargaining material.'* [147] Eisenhower moved to close down the 'Indian channel' by writing to Nehru soon after his meeting with Krishna Menon, to say that the visit by Menon to Washington had served a useful purpose, and to inform Nehru that the US had decided on holding direct talks with the Chinese at the ambassadorial level which, they hoped Nehru would consider as advancing the cause of peace in Asia.[148] He acknowledged India's role and efforts in this matter, but there was no reference to seeking further assistance from India.[149]

In the meantime the British government had, for some time, indicated its desire to be helpful, and conveyed to Dulles that while it did not wish to engage in 'back-seat driving', it was anxious to do anything to help.[150] After Trevelyan's talks with Zhou in May (both prior to and after Menon's visit), the British developed confidence in directly dealing with the Chinese. Even as Menon was speaking with the Americans in Washington, Dulles was also speaking to Harold Macmillan, the new British Foreign Secretary, about China. Macmillan said that Menon was 'messing things up'. Dulles agreed that the 'situation had slipped backwards as a result of Menon's meddling'.[151] Dulles shared his wish to begin some sort of direct contact with the Chinese. It was Macmillan who suggested that 'anything we did along those lines could be better done through the British than through the Indians'. Macmillan said that the Indians were not very reliable and that they talked a great deal without accomplishing anything. The British government apparently kept the Government of India in the dark about these side-bar exchanges taking place in San Francisco in the third week of June.

---

* MacMillan recorded almost identical thoughts about Menon in his diary, describing him as 'vain and a bore' (*The MacMillan Diaries: The Cabinet Years, 1950–1957*, edited by Peter Catterall (MacMillan, 2003), p. 447.

On 8 July, two days after Dulles's acrimonious meeting with Menon, he messaged Macmillan to say that the United States was 'ready to request your government as representing US interests in Peiping [Beijing] to make suggestion to Zhou Enlai along lines of President's message to Nehru'. He also explicitly asked his Ambassador in London to tell the British Foreign Office that 'I do not, however, want to get Nehru in the position to being our intermediary in this matter'.[152] The two exchanged drafts on the precise nature of the communication that the British would deliver to the Chinese in Beijing. The new British charge d'affaires in Beijing, Con O'Neill (who had replaced Trevelyan), conveyed the American proposal directly to Zhou Enlai when he presented his credentials to the Chinese government on 13 July. Two days later, the British embassy in Beijing received a positive response from the Chinese Foreign Ministry. Although Krishna Menon was visiting London on 11 July and had met with Foreign Secretary Macmillan, the latter did not share the text of the American message that was delivered by the British in Beijing with him.[153] It was only shared in New Delhi with Nehru on 14 July, after it had been delivered by O'Neill to Zhou in Beijing. They thought the Chinese might consult Nehru. Hence, this was done in order to thwart any Indian involvement in the exercise.

After Nehru received the text of the American message to the Chinese from the acting British High Commissioner in Delhi, Nehru wrote to Zhou implying that this change in the American attitude towards China was the result of Menon's discussions in Beijing and Washington, and that India was 'continuing to try our utmost'.[154] He also expressed his scepticism that the US offer of ambassadorial talks could make much progress. In his opinion, expressed in a message to Zhou Enlai, 'this is only a preliminary move on part of the US government and can hardly take us far'.[155] Krishna Menon could not believe that the British had taken over his role as the interlocutor; he felt confident that the Chinese would wish to talk through him. 'He is, of course, very much offended,' Macmillan recorded in his diary, 'that the Americans have sent their message to Chou En-lai through us, instead of through the Indians. He says that he is not at all offended—so it is clear that he must be deeply injured.'[156]

The Chinese had also realized that Krishna Menon was not acceptable to the US. In a top-secret document outlining their plans for talks with the Americans, they acknowledged that the US wanted to exclude Menon, and India, from the mediation process.[157] Hence, Zhou started to deal directly with the British government. The extent to which India was out of touch with developments became evident a few days later after Raghavan, the Indian Ambassador in China, telegrammed Menon to say that Zhou, over lunch, had told him the 'British government thinks this [US] proposal is most useful. We are prepared to agree to this proposal'.[158] Direct contacts between the US and China began less than two weeks later, on 1 August 1955, in Warsaw, Poland. It became popularly known as the Warsaw Channel. Britain took full credit for it. India's role was not formally acknowledged by any of the three parties. With the beginning of the Warsaw talks, the first Taiwan Strait crisis gradually abated with no further Indian involvement in this process.

Although the West had no further use for India, China still felt that India had some utility and that it might be useful in helping it secure full American recognition of the PRC. In the initial rounds of talks in Warsaw, the Chinese nominated India to handle the affairs of their nationals and students in the US. The US consented that India could aid in the return of Chinese nationals. China felt that if this arrangement could be formalized, 'it is equal to the recognition of the People's Republic of China'.[159] However, the US government did not recognize the PRC either directly or indirectly until 1972. The repatriation of nationals was the only tangible outcome of the Warsaw talks. The talks continued for two years until they were finally suspended at the end of 1957. No steps were taken to address the roots of the Taiwan Strait crisis. It was a matter of time before it would flare up again.

Chapter 5

The Second Taiwan Strait Crisis

After the first Taiwan Strait crisis ended in July 1955, the United States was locked in global confrontation with the Soviet Union. Communism everywhere was the challenge, and the Eisenhower administration did not differentiate between the Soviets and the Chinese. In June 1957 in San Francisco, Dulles delivered a major policy speech on the Eisenhower administration's China policy. It portended a hardening of their position. Alluding to the intrinsically violent nature of the Chinese communist party, Dulles said that 'it is bitterly hateful of the United States which it considers a principal obstacle in the way of its path to conquest'.[1] He also made it clear why America would still not recognize the People's Republic of China. Unlike in the case of the Soviet Union in 1933 (President Roosevelt had recognized the USSR sixteen years after its founding in November 1933), he said, China's record was one of armed aggression and violation of international agreements. 'The political purposes of communist China clash everywhere with our own.'

President Eisenhower had cleared Dulles' speech, so this was now the official American policy. The Chinese reacted fiercely to the speech, characterizing it as hostile and aggressive.[2] The ambassadorial level talks in Warsaw that had begun on 1 August 1955 as a consequence of mutual efforts to defuse the first Taiwan Strait crisis also petered out at the end of 1957 after the transfer of U. Alexis Johnson, the American Ambassador in Warsaw, who was also their principal negotiator. The Americans proposed that talks could continue at lower levels but the Chinese suspended the dialogue. Frustration built up on both sides. The National Security Council, with the US President in the chair, met in early October 1957 and felt it should preserve the status quo on the Taiwanese-controlled offshore islands by providing training and weapons to Chiang Kai-shek's army, and to commit military support in case Eisenhower determined this was appropriate in assuring the defence of Taiwan and Penghu.[3] In Beijing, Premier Zhou Enlai told the diplomatic corps that America was intent on pursuing a two-China policy in the hope of obtaining wider recognition for the Chiang Kai-shek regime, which the PRC could never accept.[4] An uneasy stalemate seemed to prevail on the surface, but underfoot developments were taking place that would lead to a second crisis in the Taiwan Strait.

In the first half of 1958, various instances were noticed of a Chinese military build-up on the mainland opposite the offshore islands. This included repairs to the coastal airfields. In the middle of July, Chiang Kai-shek held a review. He concluded that some sort of military action by the communists was in the offing. Taiwan's Joint Chiefs of Staff issued orders cancelling all leave for its armed forces and placing the army in full combat readiness. This was the first action of its kind since 1949.[5] At the beginning of August 1958, Chiang Kai-shek raised the alarm with the Americans, but the US Joint Chiefs of Staff concluded that there was, as yet, no evidence of such Chinese build-up as might lead to offensive action by China in the general area of the offshore islands. Accordingly, the US State Department in Washington advised its Ambassador in Taipei to allay Chiang's concerns, and 'dampen [the] crisis atmosphere'.[6]

In fact, Chiang had good reason for concern. Mao was, most likely, planning some sort of military action in mid-July although, for reasons not clear, he subsequently rescinded his orders.[7] Soviet General Secretary Nikita Khrushchev suddenly visited China for talks with Mao (31 July–3 August). Khrushchev's visit convinced Chiang that the Chinese communists intended to attack with Soviet support. Admiral Roland Smoot, the Commander of the US–Taiwan Defence Command, passed Chiang's concerns on to Admiral Felix Stump, Commander-in-Chief of the Pacific Command, who, in turn, passed the information on to Washington.[8] The Americans began to look more closely at the situation in the Taiwan Strait, and some days later CIA Chief Allen Dulles confirmed that the situation was indeed 'heating up'. The President, however, strongly advocated caution, telling the NSC on 7 August that there was no excuse for American intervention to defend the offshore islands unless a Chinese attack on them was a prelude to an invasion of Taiwan.[9]

Evidence of a possible military attack by China began to pile up in Washington. The British Consul in Tamsui (Taiwan) reported to London on 9 August that US intelligence officers had evidence that the Chinese might institute a possible air and naval blockade of the offshore islands.[10] Walter S. Robertson, the Assistant Secretary for Far Eastern Affairs at the US State Department, wrote to Dulles that Beijing was readying for some sort of military action.[11] Dulles, in turn, told Eisenhower that the US 'should consider an attack on the offshore islands constitutes attack on Formosa [Taiwan]'.[12] The President was sceptical. The State Department issued a guarded statement to the effect that it was closely watching the situation, but no further action was taken, possibly because of Eisenhower's doubts about the extent to which the US should commit itself to the defence of the offshore islands.

Eisenhower personally had never been convinced that the offshore islands should be given the same importance as Taiwan and Penghu when it came to the question of committing US military forces. In fact, the Mutual Defence Treaty concluded with Taiwan in December 1954 had excluded these offshore islands from their purview. Eisenhower felt that they had little strategic or military significance of their own, but recognized that if they fell to the Chinese communists it might have a devastating impact on the morale of the Taiwanese military and on Chiang Kai-shek personally. He thought the problem was more psychological than purely military in its nature. At the meeting of the NSC on 14 August, Eisenhower told his military not to take 'instantaneous action' such that it would speed up hostilities if the Chinese made any move against the offshore islands.[13] The Americans were on the horns of a dilemma. If they involved themselves militarily in the defence of the offshore islands they might risk a broader conflict with China, but if the offshore islands fell to China because the US had not come to Taiwan's assistance, the psychological demoralization might lead to the collapse of the so-called Republic of China in Taiwan and endanger the security cordon (the first and second island chains) that the Americans had built to contain the communist threat to Southeast Asia. As a result, the Americans had no clear strategy to deal with the emerging crisis. Robertson continually pressed upon Dulles to make a decision on whether or not to defend the offshore islands under all circumstances,[14] but doubts at the very top meant that the United States officially adopted a wait-and-watch stance through the month of August.

On 23 August 1958, the Chinese began heavy bombardment of Quemoy, forcing the Americans to finally take a stand. Eisenhower convened a meeting at the White House on 25 August to review the situation. His reticence at getting sucked into conflict was evident in his categoric instructions that American 'involvement with these islands would be for one reason and one alone, namely to sustain the morale of the government of the Republic of China which had deliberately committed major forces to their defence contrary to our 1954 military advice'.[15] The findings of a national intelligence estimate suggested that the principal purpose of the Chinese bombardment of the offshore islands was to test the resolve of the Taiwanese and the US to defend them. The Chinese were not looking for a military showdown with the US.[16] In retrospect, the American intelligence assessment was surprisingly accurate. Mao's intention in bombarding Quemoy was indeed to test the American resolve. He had instructed the Defence Minister, Peng Dehuai, to bombard Quemoy with artillery from the coastal batteries in order to put pressure on Chiang Kai-shek and his American allies. He was explicit that the Chinese air force must not cross into Taiwanese airspace over the offshore islands under any circumstances. He had no intention of providing any pretext that might lead to greater American involvement in the defence of the offshore islands.[17] At a meeting of the Politburo in the seaside resort at Beidaihe, to which the Chinese leadership annually retreated en masse in August when Beijing became unbearably hot, Mao said that his intention was to 'create international tension for a purpose'. He wanted to seize the initiative to test whether the US defence perimeter extended to the offshore islands. Whether it was Mao's eventual intention to seize the offshore islands, or to merely see if the Americans 'wanted to carry these two burdens [Quemoy and Matsu] on their backs',[18] was unclear, but the opening gambit, as the US intelligence estimate correctly surmised, was to probe the Americans.

The first decision the US took was to give orders to the US Pacific Command to provide US naval escorts for Taiwanese ships that were carrying supplies to sustain Taiwanese military forces on the offshore islands. Eisenhower did so with great reluctance and after long discussion. He feared that the US might be crossing a bridge to war if any untoward incident involved an American warship that was performing close-in escort duty. He was persuaded only after being assured that American naval escorts would remain in international waters and not enter the 3-nautical-mile limit of Chinese territorial waters.[19]

The eruption of the crisis caused alarm in London. Samuel Viscount Hood, the Minister at the British embassy in Washington, enquired of London whether they wished him to approach the Americans and, if so, what answer he might give in case the US asked for British support for their actions in the Taiwan Strait.[20] On London's instructions, Hood told Acting Secretary of State Christian Herter on 30 August that the UK had recognized the PRC's legal right to the offshore islands, as set out in Eden's statement in the House of Commons on 15 February 1955, that there was no change in that position, and that the 'British government would greatly deplore a war that developed from an effort to hold the islands'. Hood added that it would be difficult for the British to defend the American stand, and also that any British outreach to Beijing might be useless in view of their strained relations with the PRC.[21] Hood was prescient in his remarks. A day later, the British representative in Beijing (Wilson) telegraphed London saying that the Chinese were likely to totally disregard any restraining advice given to them and, in fact, suggesting to London that they might be more amenable to listening to advice from the Indians.[22] Herter told Hood that the Americans were under pressure from Chiang Kai-shek, and were doing all they could to resist it, but if the Chinese communists were to press their attacks on the offshore islands, Eisenhower would be faced with 'a very grave decision'.[23] Hood thought that if the Americans got involved in hostilities it might be difficult for them to get support even from friendly countries. Prime Minister Harold Macmillan (who had succeeded Eden as Prime Minister of Great Britain in January 1957) subsequently wrote to Eisenhower, reiterating the British position that had been outlined by Hood.

On 4 September 1958, after several days of sustained bombardment of the offshore islands, the Chinese suddenly and unilaterally declared a 12-nautical-mile limit as their territorial waters. This was apparently decided at a Politburo meeting on the same day following a Chinese assessment that the US response to the bombardment of Quemoy indicated that the Americans were reluctant to go to war with China. According to one Chinese account of this Politburo meeting, Mao declared that an invasion of the offshore islands was not their objective. He said that the offshore islands should be used as a noose to entrap the Americans into committing to defend them, so that 'whenever we wanted to kick them we could do so'.[24] Officially sanctioned Chinese accounts of the strategy that Mao followed will need to be corroborated since such accounts are usually crafted to show Chinese policy in positive light. The show of force that the Americans had built up around the Taiwan Strait and, more generally, in the Western Pacific, would have likely made the Chinese think twice about attempting any landing on the offshore islands. However, the decision to provoke matters by declaring a 12-nautical-mile limit that placed the offshore islands within Chinese territorial waters suggests that the Chinese intended to hold the initiative during the second Taiwan Strait crisis. At the same meeting the Politburo also agreed to a proposal by Zhou Enlai to resume the Warsaw talks, but withheld the announcement in order to study American reactions to their decision regarding the 12-nautical-mile limit of territorial waters.

The Chinese decision precipitated the situation in Washington. In his meeting with the President at Newport, Rhode Island, on 4 September, Dulles recommended that these territorial limits set by China must not be accepted. Dulles thought that the Chinese were preparing to seize the offshore islands and, in his memorandum to the President, Dulles opined that if this were to happen without American intervention it would not only seriously impact the pro-

US regime on Taiwan, but jeopardize the entire anti-communist barrier in the western Pacific. 'The consequences in the Far East would be even more far-reaching and catastrophic than those which followed when the US allowed the Chinese mainland to be taken over by the Chinese communists, aided and abetted by the Soviet Union,' wrote Dulles.[25] Dulles and Eisenhower agreed that the gravity of situation warranted a White House statement. The President asked Dulles to deliver it. The statement said that America was treaty-bound to help Taiwan defend not just the main islands of Taiwan and Penghu, but also to employ forces for securing and protecting 'related positions' such as the offshore islands. But it carefully left the door ajar by adding that it was not yet certain whether the purpose of the Chinese communists was in fact to make an all-out effort to conquer them. Hence, Dulles said, the President had not yet made any finding under the Formosa Resolution of January 1955 that US military forces were required to be employed for the defence of the offshore islands. Nonetheless, the bottom line was made clear not only to China, but for the benefit of the international community, that in the event that naked force was used by China, it would pose a threat that transcended the Taiwan Strait, and that acquiescence therein would, therefore, threaten peace everywhere.[26] The US was prepared to go to war. Tensions ran very high in the first week of September 1958. Orders were passed by the US Joint Chiefs of Staff to the Pacific Command to prepare for the use of atomic weapons.[27]

A reference by the American delegation at a NATO meeting on 2 September about stopping Chinese communism everywhere alarmed the British government. It was anxious over the possibility that the Americans were prepared to go to war and, at the same time, concerned that the widening gap in Anglo-American positions was making it untenable for Britain to publicly stand with America. Macmillan later wrote about the dilemma that confronted Britain. 'If we abandon the Americans—morally I mean, they need no active support, it will be a great blow to the friendship and alliance I have done so much to rebuild and strengthen. If we support them, the repercussions in the Far East, India and through the Afro-Asian group in the Middle East may be very dangerous. At home, parliament and public will be very critical of any change from our public position three years ago. So there we are!'[28] Macmillan's letter of 3 September to Eisenhower was intended to flag the growing breach. But when Dulles, on Eisenhower's orders, replied to the letter, he made it clear that the US had come to the conclusion that the ability to keep Taiwan in friendly hands was not separable from Chiang Kai-shek holding on to the offshore islands, and that if the offshore islands were to fall, it would jeopardize the entire anti-communist barrier. Japan and Southeast Asia would fall into the Sino-Soviet orbit, and New Zealand and Australia, members of the British Commonwealth, would be strategically isolated. Dulles concluded by saying that 'the President and I hope very much that you will, as you suggest, be able to steer your public opinion so that if the worst should happen we could be together. Anything different would be a great catastrophe for both of us.'[29] The American message was that if Britain failed to stand with the US, it also risked losing further influence and allies.

This prompted a further letter from Macmillan, this time directly to Dulles, reiterating concerns 'that we may be on the edge of operations which could be the prelude to a third world war'. He insisted that Formosa (Taiwan) and the offshore islands were in different juridical categories so far as Britain was concerned. He also told Dulles that steering or managing British public opinion was easier said than done in such circumstances. In a replay of the 1955 situation, Britain cloaked itself in the mantle of the Commonwealth, telling Dulles that the Old Commonwealth (Australia, New Zealand, Canada and South Africa) would be 'cautious at best' about supporting the US in a military conflict with China. 'The new Commonwealth countries— India, Malaya, Celyon, Ghana etc.—will of course be against any action.' Macmillan added that he didn't think that this neutralism of the newly independent Commonwealth countries was unexpected, but did add that 'they have a considerable influence in Asiatic opinion'.[30]

It was in this situation of the provocation and counter-provocation by China and the US, and tension between the principal Western allies that, on 6 September, Premier Zhou Enlai released a statement, based on the decision already taken by the Politburo, to offer to resume the ambassadorial talks in Warsaw.[31] The Americans responded positively on the same day. Eisenhower wrote to tell MacMillan, 'I hope this means that the immediate crisis will become less acute, at least temporarily.'[32] But almost immediately, a major escalation seemed to happen with the Soviets jumping into the fray with a long and rambling letter from General Secretary Nikita Khrushchev to Eisenhower on 7 September in which the entire responsibility for the crisis was laid at the feet of the Americans. The warning at the end of the letter that an attack on China would constitute an attack on the Soviet Union sounded ominously like a threat of nuclear war.* The escalating rhetoric from both parties caught the attention

---

* Chinese sources claim that Khrushchev's letter was prompted after Soviet Foreign Minister Andrei Gromyko's air-dash to Beijing where he told Chinese leaders that war with the US was not desirable, and they in turn told him that if it happened China would not involve the Soviets in the war. The Soviets might have concluded, like the British, that a major conflict was imminent (Memoir of Wu Lengxi, 'Inside Story of the Decision Making during the Shelling of Jinmen', 23 August 1958, Wilson Center Digital Archive, Zhuanji Wenxue [Beijing, Biographical Literature], No. 1, 1994, 5–11, https://digitalarchives;wilsoncenter.org/document/117009).

of others. Khrushchev's letter seemed to confirm London's fears of escalation.

One of the suggestions that Macmillan gave in his second letter to the Americans was to seek some means of a solution to the crisis through the demilitarization of the offshore islands* via the UN or some 'friendly but uncommitted government'. In other words, the US might consider some form of mediation to resolve a dangerous crisis. The British had considered the possibility that India might use its good offices and ruled it out. 'As regards the Indians,' stated a telegram from the Commonwealth Relations Office in London to British High Commissioners abroad, 'we have concluded that: (a) in the present state of Sino-Indian relations this would be unlikely to lead to effective action; (b) it might elicit a request from the Indians to seek from the Americans assurances of non-intervention which we know they would be reluctant to give; and (c) by suggesting to the Chinese a divergence of view between western allies might have the opposite effect of that intended.'[33] But while they ruled out using India as an intermediary, the British Foreign Office concluded that India's position on this crisis was broadly consistent with their own.

India was following the developing situation closely and with interest almost from the time the crisis broke out. A telegram from the Indian embassy in Washington reported that the Chinese threat to the offshore islands was causing great alarm in the Eisenhower administration. Rumours were also rife in Washington about possible Indian mediation.[34] Follow-up messages from the Indian embassy in Washington reported that US preparations were underway for military intervention in

---

* Macmillan claimed that the idea had come from Dulles in a conversation with Lord Hood, the British Minister in Washington (Harold Macmillan, 'Chinese Puzzle', Chapter 17, *Riding the Storm, 1956–1959* [Harper and Row], p. 548).

case China invaded the offshore islands.[35] On the other hand, G. Parthasarathi, the Indian Ambassador in Beijing, offered a more sober assessment to New Delhi following his meeting with Vice Foreign Minister Zhang Hanfu on 30 August. Zhang told Parthasarathi that the Chinese bombardment of Quemoy was a retaliatory response to bombardment by the Taiwanese side (which was not true) and blamed the Americans for building up tension in the Taiwan Strait by moving warships from the Mediterranean Sea into the Taiwan Strait. The Chinese wanted India's help to mobilize Afro-Asian support for China in this international crisis. Parthasarathi's assessment was that despite the heightened rhetoric, a major conflict was unlikely. Among reasons that he adduced for this line of thought was that it would be harmful to China to engage in a major military clash, and that the cost of liberating Quemoy would not justify any military action that they might have to undertake.[36] He reiterated this assessment in a second telegram to Foreign Secretary Subimal Dutt on 7 September after the Permanent Representative of Indonesia to the UN, Ali Sastramidjojo, had told the Indian Mission in New York that the Chinese had shared their plans with Indonesia to capture Quemoy and Matsu. Parthasarathi doubted that the Chinese would have given any such indication to the Indonesians. He felt that if China had intended to seize the offshore islands, it would not have waited until Chiang Kai-shek and the Americans had reinforced the islands. 'There are indications,' he told Dutt, 'that Chinese policy in the present crisis has propagandist and diplomatic objectives in mind.'[37]

From the perspective of preserving peace and security in the region, the escalating crisis was Nehru's concern. However, he was in a quandary as to what could be done, noting in one telegram about the crisis: 'I am reluctant to jump in whenever two nations are quarrelling.'[38] Nehru's dilemma was genuine. India was no longer positioned equidistantly between the opposing parties and, hence, in a position to mediate. A series of events had begun to cast long shadows over the India–China friendship. In early July, Chinese troops had crossed over into Indian territory up to Khurnak Fort in Ladakh despite strong Indian objections.[39] Weeks later, the Chinese alleged that India was abetting in the subversive and disruptive activities being carried out by the US and Chiang Kai-shek against China's Tibet region using Kalimpong (in the Indian state of West Bengal) as a base, to 'attain the traitorous aim of separating the Tibet region from the PRC'.[40] Nehru's proposed trip to Tibet at the invitation of the Fourteenth Dalai Lama, which he was greatly looking forward to, seemed to meet with obstacles from China, and had to be eventually postponed because the Chinese claimed that (unidentified) forces were intending bodily harm to Nehru. Nehru wistfully admitted to Apa Pant, India's representative in Sikkim, that 'our relations with China are not as good as they have been in the past, chiefly, because they think that we are conniving at the activities of Tibetan emigres in Darjeeling, Kalimpong etc'.[41] In August, on the eve of the Taiwan Strait crisis, India also objected to inaccurate maps that were published in the prominent Chinese journal *China Pictorial*, showing vast swathes of Indian territory in the northwest and the northeast as part of China.[42]

Nehru was briefed on all these developments by the Ministry of External Affairs. In mid-September, he was leaving for a long visit to Bhutan (since he was unable to visit Tibet, as originally planned). Prior to leaving, he took two actions. First, he endorsed China's claim to the offshore islands as legitimate at his press conference on 7 September. 'That has been our attitude not today,' said Nehru, 'but right from the beginning, for the last eight or nine years.' He said that it must be an 'impossible situation' for China to countenance that islands just off the coast were being used to launch attacks on the mainland, but at the same time he also underscored that this question should be decided peacefully.

Nehru was of the view that intervention was not possible because 'rather rigid attitudes have been taken up on every side'.[43] Zhou thanked the Indian Ambassador in China for Nehru's public support, conveniently choosing to ignore Nehru's pointed comment about the need to settle the question peacefully.[44] Second, he wrote to British Prime Minister Macmillan on 7 September (in reply to a brief message from Macmillan) describing the situation as a 'grave risk' as a result of threats and counter-threats that the two parties were throwing out, and added that 'whatever the merits of the problem may be, I am convinced that no good comes from this type of approach'. He strongly felt that 'all of us should exercise such influence as we have to prevent this catastrophe from happening'.[45] Macmillan was happy to see that Nehru shared his view although, according to him, Nehru's letter did not 'add very much to the solution of my difficulties'.[46]

Zhou's offer to resume the ambassadorial talks in Warsaw provided a window of opportunity for all sides to climb down from escalation, and to weigh their options. The Americans wondered who should make the first move. Dulles felt that if the Americans were to do so, the Chinese might conclude 'we were panting for resumption' and harden their attitude. So, it was finally decided that the new US Ambassador in Warsaw, Jacob D. Beam, would send a copy of Dulles's statement welcoming the Chinese proposal to resume the Warsaw talks to his Chinese counterpart, Wang Bingnan, and leave the initiative to the Chinese side. In the meantime, Dulles internally initiated an important conversation in the State Department on Macmillan's proposal for some kind of demilitarization in the offshore islands. State Department officials rejected the idea, saying that if Chiang's forces withdrew, the PRC could capture these islands later at a time of their choosing. But Dulles had a different reason for pursuing this idea. He told his officials that pursuing Macmillan's idea 'would make the British support of the United States easier'.[47] By then the Americans were beginning to realize how isolated they were in terms of international support in this crisis. They also discussed possible exit options. Defense Secretary Neil McElroy told Eisenhower that the US Joint Chiefs of Staff were of the clear opinion that the offshore islands had no strategic value. The President agreed that it was a 'military debit' to hold them.[48] He in turn told Dulles that America was 'over committed to backing Chiang Kai-shek in a policy of defending Quemoy and Matsu', and that he was quite prepared to abandon them but could not say so publicly during a crisis. Dulles and Eisenhower also mused over the failure of many US allies to stand with them publicly. Dulles told the President that 'we should be thinking of steps to encourage a greater sense of solidarity with our allies lest the several systems of which we are a member begin to fall apart'.[49]

The Chinese leadership was also engaged in similar introspection. It was evident that a military assault on the offshore islands, if that had been their original goal, would meet with very stiff resistance. Mao was not intending to initiate a large-scale conflict with the Americans. He wrote to North Vietnam President Ho Chi Minh on 10 September telling him that 'it is highly unlikely that big war will break out'.[50] With both sides willing to resume talks in Warsaw, the Chinese also understood that the struggle would now shift from the battlefield to the negotiating table. Like Eisenhower, Mao too began to adjust his expectations over the offshore islands. He declared that the next course of action was not to try and seize the offshore islands but to pull the noose tighter around the American neck through diplomatic means.[51] Clear instructions were given by Mao on how these negotiations in Warsaw should be conducted. He wrote to Zhou to make sure that Wang Bingnan and Ye Fei (the Chinese negotiators) understood the 'new policy and new tactics of holding the initiative, keeping the offensive and remaining reasonable. We must conduct our diplomatic struggle from a far-sighted perspective'.[52]

The British Joint Chiefs of Staff had made their own assessment about the situation from the military perspective. They concluded that the offshore islands were of no military value and that their loss (or, for that matter, even the loss of Formosa itself) would not reduce the effectiveness of the island chain from the military perspective. However, they agreed (with the American assessment) that the loss of Taiwan would have serious political implications throughout Southeast Asia which would also affect the British military position,[53] and, therefore, the importance of standing with the US during this crucial turning point in the crisis, although their respective positions on the legal status of the offshore islands were at odds. By 1958, the British had become more dependent on the Americans to protect their Far Eastern interests than was the case a decade earlier. But the British also continued to believe that unless the Americans abandoned the idea of helping Chiang Kai-shek defend the offshore islands, a modus vivendi with China would elude the West. They, therefore, persisted in working privately on the Americans to get them to change their position on the offshore islands, although they were careful to align their public posture with that of the United States. British Foreign Secretary Selwyn Lloyd began his letter to Dulles with the reassurance that 'your troubles are our troubles. In these days this is a matter of hard fact, not just sentiment. Therefore, I want so far as is possible . . . to prevent any open difference of opinion . . . and try to work toward a common position.'

Lloyd conveyed that Britain supported the US effort of building a 'containing line' against communism in the Far East, but suggested that Chiang Kai-shek's insistence on holding on to the offshore islands was weakening, not strengthening, that island chain. Withdrawal from the offshore islands would secure support for the US position among both Asian allies and uncommitted countries and thus strengthen the containment efforts being pursued by the West.* Dulles was still not prepared to concede on this point. He told Sir Harold Caccia, the British Ambassador in Washington, that 'the free world defence line in the Far East was an extremely thin and brittle one . . . In the face of massive communist expansionist pressures it was a hard and delicate task to keep the defence line firm.' But, for the first time in the crisis, Dulles also spoke of extricating the US from the offshore islands' situation but 'without pulling the whole house down'. He told Lloyd that if a formula could be worked out that would provide a reasonable quid pro quo, the Americans might be able to accept it. Third-party intervention was not, however, specifically discussed.[54]

During the week after the Chinese agreed to resume the talks in Warsaw, so far as India was concerned, Nehru had left for Bhutan, and Parthasarathi continued sending sober assessments from Beijing to Foreign Secretary Dutt, telling him that the Chinese are 'realists and will not take risks for which returns would not be commensurate'. In his view they were unlikely to risk major conflict simply to occupy coastal islands. He stuck to his initial view that 'they will continue to keep up tension to gain political and diplomatic ends but will not embark on war unless developments force their hand'.[55] In response to his telegrams, Dutt in turn told Parthasarathi that 'on the whole we agree with your assessment of the situation'.[56] With Nehru away from Delhi, it appeared that India would sit this crisis out. It was at

---

* Lloyd would certainly have had India in mind because it shared Britain's position on the status of the offshore islands. Nehru's position was important to the British effort to bring pressure on the Americans to avoid a war. (Doc. 80, 'Message from Foreign Secretary Lloyd to Secretary of State Dulles', undated, *FRUS, 1958–1960, China, Vol. XIX*).

this point that Krishna Menon, now India's Defence Minister (and also Chief Delegate to the UN), made his entry. He was in London en route to New York for the session of the United Nations General Assembly when he met Lloyd and discussed the Taiwan Strait crisis. He telegraphed Nehru after reaching New York to tell him that Lloyd had expressed grave concern to him over the situation in the Taiwan Strait and 'appeared anxious to convey that we [India] had brought about improvements in 1955 which he said the United States now recognizes in terms "the years were not well used".'* In contrast to the sober assessments being sent by Parthasarathi from Beijing, Menon claimed the British believed that the situation was drifting into a 'shooting war'. Menon also added that 'Selwyn [Lloyd] appeared either on his own or under instructions to want to make us feel that both in regard to Commonwealth relations and Disarmament and China they hoped for and looked to us to help turn the tide and perhaps play decisive role. He was embarrassingly personal about all this.'[57] Menon was hinting that the British were specifically referring to his efforts in 1955. It was evident that Menon was seeking a role for India, and himself, although he couched it in terms of a British request. This happened even as Dutt was informing Parthasarathi on the same day that 'we [Ministry of External Affairs] have no knowledge of any diplomatic move to settle the dispute between US and China over offshore islands'.[58] It looked like India was acting in two unrelated ways.

---

* Dulles had met the Finance Minister of India in Washington on 8 September, and they had discussed the situation in the Taiwan Strait, but made no mention either of India's efforts in 1955 or of seeking India's help in 1958. ('Telegram, Secretary General of MEA from Dayal [Washington]', 9 September 1958, File 649, Part II, Nehru Papers [Miscellaneous Correspondence, 1958 Crisis], Nehru Memorial Museum and Library, New Delhi).

The Sino–US talks that resumed in Warsaw on 14 September offered grounds for hope that the second Taiwan Strait crisis might be resolved through negotiation. Dulles told Beam, the chief American negotiator, that these talks were of great importance and the basic objective should be to rapidly bring about a cessation of hostilities since 'time is running against us'.[59] The Chinese believed, however, that this proposal was intended to draw a permanent ceasefire line between China's mainland on the one hand, and the Quemoy and Matsu islands on the other, in order to realize its scheme of dividing Chinese territory and creating 'two Chinas'. The Chinese totally and categorically rejected this idea.[60] After the initial rounds of discussion Beam reported that there was not the 'slightest change' in the basic Chinese position and that Wang (Bingnan), the Chinese negotiator, 'did not in fact appear to be working under any sense of urgency'.[61] In Warsaw, the Chinese were working to Mao's instructions; namely, they would not discuss the status of the offshore islands but only the withdrawal of US forces from Taiwan. Wang kept insisting that the only point for negotiation between China and the US was the withdrawal of American forces from the Taiwan area, whereas the Americans refused to accept the Chinese position that the status of Taiwan and the offshore islands were an internal matter to be decided by the Chinese on both sides of the Taiwan Strait without US involvement. The Americans, with each passing day, grew more concerned about Chiang's ability to resupply his military forces on Quemoy, and the resentment against America that was building in international opinion. Eisenhower was apprised that the reports from Ambassador Beam did not encourage hopes of a positive outcome.[62] The Indian embassy succinctly captured America's dilemma in its telegram to the Ministry of External Affairs. 'The reduction of the offshore islands by blockade would be as bad as their conquest [by China] by direct assault. Failure of the Americans to resecure would be disastrous to their position in east Asia and the SEATO countries.'[63]

The British sensed the growing frustration and isolation of the Americans and quietly urged them yet again to compromise over the offshore islands. In public, however, the British did not contradict American statements. Lloyd wrote to Macmillan telling him he was 'certain that our handling of the Americans so far has been right. If we had tried to lecture them about the rights and wrongs of their policy past and present, the effect would have been to make them extremely resentful and less liable to take our advice.'[64] Macmillan assured Lloyd that 'the more isolated they feel the more important our friendship will be to them now and in the future'.[65] There is no question that by this time the British were very concerned about Quemoy becoming a casus belli as a result of the lack of progress in the Warsaw talks and in light of the American insistence on protecting the offshore islands. Macmillan told Australian Prime Minister Robert Menzies this was all because the Americans had not profitably used the breathing space they had got in 1955 to make Chiang realize how indefensible Quemoy was.[66]

It was in this state of mind that the British Foreign Secretary, Selwyn Lloyd, met with Eisenhower (and Dulles) at Newport on 21 September (Lloyd was visiting the US for the annual UN General Assembly session). He told Macmillan after his talks that Eisenhower had privately conveyed his firm opposition to the use of even tactical nuclear weapons, which relieved Macmillan of his concern that the Americans would escalate,[67] but there was still the worry that the Chinese (and Soviets) might do that. Lloyd suggested that if the Warsaw talks broke down, it might be a good idea to suggest some other means of negotiations and thought that Nehru might be of assistance.[68] The idea that India (Nehru) should somehow play a role would almost certainly have been the result of the Lloyd–Menon discussion in London since Nehru had not given any indication prior to his departure for Bhutan that India might actively play any role in this crisis. Krishna Menon could have offered such a possibility and Lloyd may have jumped at the idea, in order to calm down a dangerous situation without Britain directly playing a role for fear that it would make its differences with the Americans public. A letter from F. Hoyar Millar, the Permanent Under Secretary of State at the British Foreign Office to Sir Gladwyn Jebb, the British Ambassador in Paris, spelled out that concern. 'Ministers,' he said, 'are anxious that nothing should come out in public that would suggest any split between the Americans and ourselves on this issue.'[69] With Menon in the lead, the British could gently steer the Americans towards a more flexible position on the offshore islands.

In the third week of September, Menon got encouragement from an unexpected quarter—China. Parthasarathi received a summons from Zhou Enlai on the evening of 21 September. Their talk would stretch on to two hours. By the end of it, Zhou would have played two cards that, he hoped, would draw India directly into the Taiwan Strait crisis, from which it had so far stayed way. The first card that Zhou played was to hand over to Parthasarathi a letter from him directly addressed to Krishna Menon, wherein he gave a very detailed exposition of the current state-of-play, including the reasons for the crisis. In his letter to Menon, Zhou outlined the many belligerent actions that the Americans had taken in the Taiwan Strait, and said they were 'playing with fire at the brink of war'. He was especially critical that they had the 'audacity to raise the question of the so-called cease fire in the Taiwan Strait area'.[70] He labelled this as a political plot to confuse the issue. The real issue, said Zhou to Menon, was the massive American military presence in the Taiwan Strait. Once it was withdrawn, China would peacefully liberate Taiwan through negotiation.

Zhou claimed that he was directly addressing his letter to Menon because Nehru was travelling in Bhutan. This was highly irregular. The proper protocol for Zhou would have been to address the letter to his counterpart, Nehru, or to the Minister in Charge of Foreign Affairs since the matter concerned foreign relations, also Nehru. In case Nehru was unreachable, the alternative protocol would have been to address the letter to the interim head of government. Menon was neither interim head of government, nor was he in India. He was India's defence minister. He too was travelling. This was a deliberate breach of protocol by the protocol-conscious Chinese. One could only conclude that they chose to do so because they realized that Krishna Menon was the easiest way to get India embroiled in the crisis. Zhou had an excellent measure of the man with whom he had spent at least twenty hours in one-on-one conversations during the first Taiwan Strait crisis, and he would also have been aware of Menon's frustration and unhappiness at others not acknowledging his diplomatic efforts in 1955. Zhou must have assumed that Krishna Menon, who was in New York where he was also steering the debate on China's admission to the UN, would jump at the opportunity to 'mediate' again, and was the right man in the right place to help China to build international pressure on the US to withdraw from the Taiwan Strait. Zhou's long letter to Menon placed the entire responsibility for the crisis on the US, saying that 'the crucial question in eliminating this crisis is by no means a cease-fire but that the US must cease at once its armed provocations against the PRC, withdrawing all its armed forces from Taiwan, the Penghu islands and the Taiwan Strait and stop interfering in China's internal affairs'.[71] Zhou was hoping this would induce Krishna Menon to build support for China at the UN as a way of putting international pressure on the Americans in order to make them back down.

Just in case this did not work, Zhou had a second arrow to shoot, this one at the Indian Ambassador himself. In his long conversation with Parthasarathi, Zhou spent considerable time setting the stage, speaking about all that the Americans had done to cause the trouble and tension, and all the sincere efforts that China was making to avoid a general war, before he came to the crux of the matter. Zhou told Parthasarathi that if the US attacked the Chinese mainland, there would be a general war. Parthasarathi reported to Dutt: 'Premier [Zhou Enlai] recalled advance intimation he had given during Korean crisis to Panikkar of Chinese intentions and of the action our Prime Minister took.* He said that this was [the] second occasion [after the Korean crisis when the] situation was so grave that he felt our government must be informed. Eisenhower and Dulles seem to think that if they stood firm and ready for military action there would be no war. But they were mistaken if they thought [the] Chinese would be frightened by threats. He quoted [a] Chinese proverb which says "[the] arrow is in the bow" and said that unless [the] Americans change their policy anything might happen.'[72] Zhou's clear intention here was to get a neutral third country—India—to scare the Americans into believing that the Chinese were preparing for war, in order to get them to soften their position regarding the offshore islands. Both of Zhou's actions on 21 September—the letter directly addressed to Krishna Menon and the message to India's Ambassador about the serious danger of war—were nothing more than using India yet again to do China's unpleasant work. Parthasarathi duly reported Zhou's 'grave warning' to New Delhi, saying 'there is no doubt he [Zhou Enlai] expected our government to act as we did in [the] Korean crisis'.† On the same day, to drive home this point Foreign Minister Chen Yi also

---

* On 2 October 1950, Zhou had summoned Indian Ambassador K.M. Panikkar at midnight to tell him that if the American forces crossed the 38th Parallel on the Korean peninsula, the Chinese PLA would attack them and war would ensue. Zhou had wanted India to deliver this message to the Americans.

† It is not clear whether or not this warning was passed on by the Government of India to the Americans.

told a press conference that China would recover the offshore islands, and could not be stopped. Chen declared that only 'such aggression maniacs as Dulles refuse to agree that Quemoy, Matsu and other coastal islands have always belonged to China'. The British representative in Beijing reported to London that so far as the offshore islands were concerned, Chen Yi's statement was uncompromising.[73]

The arrow that Zhou Enlai had fired at Menon hit the intended target. From New York, Menon telegraphed Secretary General Pillai on 26 September to say that there was ominous news from the Far East—despite public opposition to the war, Dulles's statements had reached a stage when the extension of the Formosa resolution to the offshore islands looked 'ominously' possible. 'This,' Menon averred in the telegram to Delhi, 'would bring [a] clash between USA and China dangerously near.'[74] He was, by now, itching with barely concealed desire to enter the diplomatic fray, telling Pillai 'there is widespread if not overwhelming expectation that India should exercise initiative in the present crisis to find a way out which would save face for the USA and be acceptable to the Chinese'. Menon had spread the news in New York about Zhou having written to seek his help. 'It is being sedulously circulated here that Zhou Enlai has sent lots of telegrams to "many" people. This,' Menon said, 'is a kind of counter-blast to the general public demand both in this country (USA) and the UN that the good offices of India should be sought or obtained and also to circulate the view that China is bluffing.'[75] He was suspicious that the British might be in touch with the Chinese and making separate efforts to broker the peace as they had done in 1955. He pressed upon Parthasarathi to find out 'whether they [Chinese] are looking to the British to find a compromise'. It seems he could not bear to compete with others in playing the role of intermediary. He dismissed British efforts as 'playing small politics'.

With barely concealed impatience, Menon told Pillai at the Ministry of External Affairs that 'there is much criticism of us from friendly quarters about our lack of initiative and as some say sitting back contrary to our policies and our previous record'. Claiming that he had 'stayed' his hand for various reasons, including to wait and see whether the US made some move at the official level towards India, he ended his message by saying that in his personal view, 'our lack of initiative involves grave risks in regard to war and would lead to further distortion of Chinese positions. We would also lay ourselves open to severe criticism and much damage to our reputation and our future capacity for working for peace'.[76] Since Nehru was absent from New Delhi and difficult to reach in Bhutan, it is possible that he was, in fact, staking India's claim to mediate in the crisis without Nehru's approval.

By now, officialdom in Delhi was aware of Krishna Menon's penchant to play the diva and, in a tongue-in-cheek response to one of Menon's telegrams bemoaning the American policy, Pillai remarked, 'I am sorry to see that your impression is that American official policy is getting tougher each day. Newspaper reports had encouraged us to hope that you had already succeeded in making a sizable dent in American policy.'[77] Pillai's telegram to Menon was marked to only one other recipient—Nehru. Even given the mutual dislike between Menon and Pillai to which Menon's biographer, Jairam Ramesh, refers in his biography, *A Chequered Brilliance: The Many Lives of V.K. Krishna Menon*, it is rather unlikely that such a verbal rapier thrust could have been made by Pillai if Menon's initiative had Nehru's endorsement. Another indication that Krishna Menon was striking out against the collective advice of the Ministry of External Affairs was an exchange between the British High Commissioner to India, Sir Malcolm MacDonald, and Pillai in early October. Details about Zhou's meeting with the Indian Ambassador on 21 September had been shared with them. London asked MacDonald to inform the Government of India that the reports had been passed on to Washington, but that Britain was not contemplating any formal or public initiative to resolve the matter, since 'there may be a better chance of progress if the two sides can maintain contact under cover of the Warsaw talks'.[78] Pillai was in agreement with this approach. MacDonald telegraphed London to report that 'they [Indians] think the best thing is to leave the Americans and Chinese talking in Warsaw; and they therefore contemplate no initiative themselves at any rate for the present'.[79] According to MacDonald, Pillai had also said 'this is also Krishna Menon's view'. In reality, Krishna Menon was acting the opposite in New York.

The British government could see no clear path out of the impasse in the Taiwan Strait crisis. It was worried that an isolated America might be dragged into the conflict with China. Talks had begun in Warsaw, but after three rounds, neither side showed signs of working towards a compromise. When Lloyd met Dulles in New York on 26 September they discussed whether Nehru would be suitable to undertake the task of helping narrow the differences between the two principal parties in case the Warsaw channel did not produce a satisfactory result. Both agreed that Menon should not be brought into the act.[80] Dulles reluctantly went along with the British proposal to sound out Nehru, perhaps out of a sense of solidarity with his principal ally. However, in Dulles's subsequent meetings in New York—with UN Secretary General Dag Hammarskjöld and Norwegian Foreign Minister Halvard Lange—Dulles was explicit that India was not acceptable as mediator.[81] Menon was hoping that the Americans might make some move at the official level to seek India's assistance after receiving news that Zhou Enlai had written to him. He still refused to acknowledge that the Americans did not want any truck with Menon. He continued to think that he had agency in Washington.

While waiting for the Americans to seek his help, Menon seemed to have concluded that Zhou's letter was adequate to actively mediate the crisis. He thought he saw his opening when Dulles, at a press conference on 29 September, characterized Chiang Kai-shek's decision to put so many troops on the offshore islands as 'rather foolish', and indicated that were there to be a dependable ceasefire in the area, it would not be prudent to keep them there. Menon telegraphed Nehru to say that India's (he meant his own) efforts had made 'an appreciable and fruitful impact' on Dulles, and thought that a similar effort was required with the Chinese.[82] He proposed that Ambassador Parthasarathi should ask Zhou Enlai to publicly state that they were prepared to stop bombarding the offshore islands while Chiang's troops were evacuating them. His idea was that the whole matter would be put to rest if only the Taiwanese could honourably withdraw from the offshore islands, and their subsequent status could be left temporarily undetermined for resolution through subsequent talks. He began to mobilize international support for this idea.

This was not, however, what Zhou intended to happen when he sought to involve Menon by writing the letter. Zhou had wanted to utilize Menon only to secure the support of the international community for China by telling them how reasonable the Chinese were and how unreasonably the Americans were acting in this crisis. Instead, Menon harped on the very idea that alarmed China the most, namely a ceasefire of any kind (even the kind that Menon was proposing). In Beijing's opinion, this would create, de facto, the existence of two Chinas and prevent China from ever using force in the future, which is precisely what China did not want under any circumstance. It was, in one sense, an own goal by Zhou. He had to move swiftly to repair the damage that Menon was causing at the UN in New York. Zhou frantically summoned the Indian Ambassador for a second urgent meeting at 10.30 p.m. on 30 September at the Beijing Hotel. Foreign Minister Chen Yi was in attendance. When Parthasarathi, at Menon's urging, explored the idea of a temporary cessation of hostilities as a first step that would allow Chiang to withdraw his forces from the offshore islands, Zhou emphatically rejected it. 'This is a British idea,' he said, 'and completely impossible to accept.' He described Selwyn Lloyd's activities in New York as 'ill intentioned'. Britain, Zhou said, knew all along that China would never accept this idea, but was 'peddling it to others' (meaning Menon). Zhou reiterated that the issue was not one of ceasing fire since there was no war between China and the US in the first place, but one of unilateral withdrawal by the US of its military forces from Taiwan, so that the whole question of Taiwan might be resolved internally thereafter between the Chinese people on both sides of the Taiwan Strait.[83] The Chinese now wanted Menon off the case. Parthasarathi, therefore, reported to Delhi, and to Menon in New York, that there was no basic change in the Chinese demand that their sovereignty over Taiwan, Penghu and the offshore islands should be conceded (to China) and that the Americans should withdraw their military forces. He said that Zhou had been categorical that Menon's idea of a ceasefire to allow Chiang to withdraw from the offshore islands but without determining their eventual ownership was unacceptable. Directly quoting Zhou, Parthasarathi wrote: 'We can wait. Please ask Mr Menon not to be in a hurry.' Parthasarathi summed up his talk with Zhou, drawing three specific points for Delhi's, and Menon's, attention. First, that China's long-term strategy was one of attrition in the Taiwan Strait, and that it would not risk major war unless its hand was forced; second, China would not be content with piece-meal concessions regarding the offshore islands if it meant permanently freezing the Taiwan issue; and third, that there was no scope for compromise.[84] Parthasarathi, whose analysis of Chinese motivation in the crisis had been consistent, was directly challenging Menon's view that war was imminent unless India did something about it.

The US and China both raced to stop Menon from his misplaced attempt at mediation. On 1 October, the Indian representative to the UN, Arthur Lall (who was close to Menon), approached the US delegation and said that India desired to be helpful by providing informal interpretations for each side of the other's positions, and that Menon or Nehru would be glad to carry a message from them to Zhou. Menon also pushed the idea of temporary cessation of hostilities with the Americans by saying that if Chiang was willing to evacuate the offshore islands, the Chinese might agree to renounce the use of force.[85] Since the Americans already had the read-out of the Parthasarathi–Zhou talks from the British, they knew that this was not an accurate portrayal of the Chinese position. They were already annoyed at Menon for canvassing for votes among the international delegates to support the PRC's admission to the United Nations. They were determined to shut down any Indian efforts at mediation. Dulles issued a direct message to Henry Cabot Lodge, the US Chief Delegate to the UN in New York: 'Department [of State] deeply disturbed over latest activities of Menon and Lall during course of General Assembly consideration [of] Chinese representation issue . . . we are not at all sure as to how aware Nehru is of extent of activity of Menon and Lall in this regard.' (Nehru was to return to Delhi only on 2 October.) Dulles conveyed that the activities of Menon were contributing to an overall deterioration of US–India relations.[86] On 2 October 1958, at a meeting of the National Security Council, Dulles described the conversation between Zhou Enlai and an unnamed individual (presumed to be Indian Ambassador Parthasarathi) as 'planted'.[*] The CIA Director, Allen Dulles, was also convinced that the Chinese were using India for propaganda purposes to embarrass the Americans.[87] Following this meeting, a further message issued from Deputy Secretary of State

---

[*] Part of this record is redacted and hence it is surmised that the 'individual' that was being referred to in the meeting with Zhou was Parthasarathi. The other details in this document clearly suggest this conclusion.

Christian A. Herter for Lodge conveying that 'the department [of state] believes Menon should not be encouraged re any possible role for him or India as mediator in present Taiwan strait crisis'. It added that 'Menon's views not likely to be helpful to us. We believe you should avoid getting into substance [of] Taiwan strait question to degree possible with Menon since he is apt to use what you have to say as means [to] inject himself as third party'.[88] Herter also told Lodge that the American government intended to directly approach Nehru to set the record straight about the Chinese position (which they felt was different from what Menon was conveying from New York). On 13 October, Ellsworth Bunker, the American Ambassador in Delhi, was specifically directed to convey to the Indian government that it did not desire any kind of mediation in the crisis.[89] The British Ambassador in Washington, Sir Harold Caccia, interceded with Dulles, saying that the Indian channel might still be useful to ensure that the Chinese correctly understood the American position, but Dulles said that he thought the Chinese knew the US position pretty well already.[90]

Ironically, the Chinese felt that Krishna Menon was pushing the Western case in the matter of the Taiwan Strait. They felt India was behind an effort by some Afro–Asian delegations in the United Nations, known informally as the Bandung Eight, to introduce a draft ceasefire resolution in the UN General Assembly. Zhou told S.F. Antonov, the Soviet Ambassador in Beijing, about his conversation with Parthasarathi on 30 September. 'Last night the Indian Ambassador informed me of V.K. Krishna Menon's plan [at the UN] . . . He is planning to make a general speech at the UN meeting, including a suggestion that Jiang's [Chiang Kai-shek] troops withdraw from the offshore islands and a request to us to stop fighting with Jiang.' Zhou said that Krishna Menon's plan was actually an American one, and that Menon was helping them to deliver this proposition so as to allow the Americans to better manoeuvre in the crisis in order to make a bargain that benefitted them. Zhou said that he had told Parthasarathi in no uncertain terms that 'we did not want Menon to deliver his proposition'.[91] Chinese anxieties about Menon reached a fever pitch when Parthasarathi, despite two direct conversations with Zhou on 21 and 30 September, was still asked to sound Zhou out on Krishna Menon's intention to speak at the General Debate in the UN General Assembly on 6 October about the idea of a temporary cessation of hostilities to allow Chiang's army to leave the offshore islands. This time Zhou met Parthasarathi at midnight between 4–5 October. He informed New Delhi that 'the Premier was most unhappy [at the idea that Krishna Menon would speak in the General Debate] . . . He went to the extent of saying that if we made such a statement his government would have to counter it, which would not only lead to unpleasantness with a very friendly country but our differences would be exploited by others.'[92] Parthasarathi's closing advice was that if Menon spoke at all, he should not go beyond expressing general support for the Chinese position because any statement or move that advocated a compromise solution would be 'seriously misunderstood' in Beijing.

Oblivious of the anxieties he was causing in both Beijing and Washington, Menon was audacious, or perhaps delusional enough, to propose to Nehru that he might even be permitted to travel to Warsaw 'at some appropriate moment as I did in regard to Geneva, without any claim or pose of mediation'.[93] He had possibly convinced himself that he would repeat his performance in Geneva in 1954 of standing on the doorstep of the ongoing US–China ambassadorial talks and trying to be helpful. It was fortunate that Nehru returned to Delhi, from Bhutan, on 2 October and read the slew of telegrams from Beijing that suggested Menon had upset all sides. He sent an immediate telegram to Menon on 3 October, drawing the latter's attention to the messages from the Indian embassy in China about Zhou being in no hurry for India to take any steps. Nehru, therefore, advised Menon to 'move a little warily'. More importantly, he explicitly conveyed that the 'suggestion that you [Menon] might go to Warsaw does not appeal to me at present'.[94]

Meanwhile, the Chinese side were not sure in what way Menon's efforts were harming their case, and felt they needed to take urgent steps to stop any possibility of a resolution being moved by well-intentioned Afro-Asian delegations on a possible ceasefire. Zhou told the Soviet Ambassador '. . . our assumption is as follows: after Menon makes his proposition, it will be accepted by UN members, and then by most countries in the world'.[95] On the eve of the debate in the UN General Assembly, Chinese Foreign Minister Chen Yi summoned all African–Asian ambassadors in China and reiterated everything that Zhou had conveyed to Parthasarathi. China, he said, would not accept any resolution that did not fully embody the basic principles that Taiwan was an inseparable part of China, and that the US must withdraw all its forces immediately. Chen Yi also categorically informed them that China was neither in any hurry, nor interested in mediation.[96] The Chinese were so concerned by this time about Krishna Menon's efforts in the UN to adopt steps that would permanently freeze the status quo in the Taiwan Strait that they suddenly and unilaterally declared a temporary ceasefire in the Taiwan Strait on the very day that the debate in the UN General Assembly was scheduled. The fact that they shared the announcement in advance with the Indian embassy in Beijing, with the explicit request that it be sent to Krishna Menon,[97] suggests that it was Krishna Menon's activism that may have compelled them to take this step. Menon had succeeded in alienating the main parties even as he was busy claiming that his efforts had 'to a certain extent regained for us [India] the prestige and usefulness to peace, which was really at a low ebb when the [General] Assembly began'.[98]

Menon made a final effort to persuade Nehru to change his mind when, on 13 October, he wrote a personal (top secret) letter

to say that India was losing international prestige because the
pressures exerted by others were deterring India from fulfilling
its responsibilities.[99] But, by this time, Nehru had become more
aware of the Chinese attitude and behaviour towards India and
was losing sympathy for the Chinese. He wrote back to Menon
describing the general Chinese attitude to India 'in many small
matters has not been at all friendly or even sometimes courteous'.[100]
Menon's effort to seek a role in the Taiwan Strait crisis, aside
from adding to India's distrust in Washington and Beijing, had
also distracted India's attention away from a developing bilateral
problem with China. By late October, details emerged in public
about the construction of a motor road by China across eastern
Ladakh (Aksai Chin). An even more concerning matter was the
disclosure, in early November, that two Indian patrol parties of
armed personnel, fifteen in number, who had been missing for five
weeks while on forward patrol in the Ladakh region of India, had
in fact been in Chinese custody since mid-September for 'unlawful
intrusions' into so-called Chinese territory.* The Chinese were
in all likelihood deliberately holding them as a possible pressure
point if India should do anything that harmed Chinese interests
in this crisis. Through the entire Taiwan Strait crisis, even as Zhou
was seeking India's assistance and Nehru was voicing support for
China's case, no information about the missing Indians was shared
by the Chinese government with the Government of India.†

By the third week of October, the Taiwan Strait crisis was
winding down. Dulles visited Taipei. He told Chiang that the

---

* They were deported through the Karakoram Pass on 22 October.

† Evidently, neither Premier Zhou Enlai nor Foreign Minister Chen
Yi had anything to say about this matter even when they dined with
the Indian Ambassador at the embassy residence on 23 October. ('Dutt
from Parthasarathi, Telegram', 24 October 1958, File 657, Part II, JN
Papers [S.G.]).

whole fate of 'Free China' could not be identified with holding 'a few square miles of real estate [he meant the offshore islands] in a highly vulnerable position'.[101] Chiang and he came up with a joint communiqué on 23 October in which the Americans extracted from Chiang the assurance, in writing, that he would abandon the idea of using military force to achieve his mission of liberating China from the communists. Dulles triumphantly informed Eisenhower that 'the Chinese nationalists declared their dependence upon political ideals rather than upon force to liberate the peoples of the China mainland',[102] and that American commitment in future would be limited to the defence of Taiwan.

The Chinese also made a political move—they announced that they would fire artillery at the offshore islands only on odd-numbered days. Mao said this was a 'political battle' to entrap the Americans. 'This time we have caught the wolf [US] in Taiwan and powerfully.'[103] The possibility of a Sino-US war receded by the end of October. Both parties settled down for a prolonged, low-level war of nerves between China and the US. They continued to talk through the Warsaw channel, but no substantive progress was made on finding a sustainable solution. Neither the Chinese nor the Americans sought advice or assistance from India.

From the British perspective, however, the danger of war had merely receded and could reappear at any time because the problem of the offshore islands had still not been satisfactorily addressed. Prior to Dulles's visit to Taipei, the British had even pressed Lord Louis Mountbatten (who, as the Supreme Allied Commander in the Far East, had had dealings with Chiang Kai-shek during the Second World War) into action, to tutor Eisenhower and Dulles on ways of persuading Chiang Kai-shek to give up the offshore islands, but the Americans refused to be drawn into that discussion.[104] The British government was concerned about the constant threat that Sino–US tension still posed to its interests and colonies throughout the Far East. At this point

Dulles informed Lloyd that the US desired to find some way to 'tranquiliz[e] the situation in the Taiwan area' through substantial reduction of forces on the offshore islands,[105] but that there was no question of withdrawing US forces from the Taiwan region as a whole. Lloyd seized upon the idea. His plan was to use the American idea of tranquilizing the Taiwan issue through a tapered reduction of Chiang's forces on the offshore islands, to convince the Commonwealth, and especially India, that China too should be persuaded to provide corresponding assurances in order to lower tensions without taking advantage of the situation. At the same time, Lloyd wanted India to believe that it benefitted from the American military presence, and therefore, simply supporting the Chinese demands for the withdrawal of all US forces was not in India's own security interests. In other words, Lloyd hoped to turn India against the Chinese.

Lloyd told Canadian Prime Minister John Diefenbaker in early November that Asian influence might be used to pressure China by acquainting them with how much the Western security presence in the region benefitted them. 'I said to Mr Diefenbaker that I thought the Asian countries such as India, Burma and Celyon should be brought to realize what was at stake for them. At present they sheltered under the protection of western defensive alliances, whilst not contributing anything to them. They were having it both ways. If those alliances did not exist their position would be much weakened . . . If the Chinese communists felt that Asian public opinion was against them, they might make some reasonable arrangement about the islands but in all events not make an issue of them to promote trouble.'[106]

Lloyd asked British High Commissioner MacDonald to seek a personal interview with Nehru to obtain his reactions. This was to be a 'purely personal sounding operation with no suggestion that we [British] were in any way acting for the Americans or wanted to suggest that the Indians should do anything', since 'Mr Dulles in particular has not shown any great enthusiasm for bringing in the Indians at earlier stages of this affair'.[107] Dulles was consulted in advance. In Lloyd's letter to Dulles on 7 November 1958, he wrote 'some indirect pressure on Peking might be applied if we could mobilize public opinion generally and particularly in Asia in ways more favourable to Nationalists on this issue and less favourable to communists. If the Indians could be brought more to this way of thinking this might have an effect and I have been wondering whether it would not now be a good idea for Malcolm MacDonald to have a personal talk with Nehru not with the object of getting him to intervene with the Chinese (which would not be likely to be very fruitful) but to find out how he is now thinking and to try and influence him in the way suggested.'[108] Dulles agreed to Lloyd's suggestion because his Ambassador in New Delhi had informed him that Nehru was no longer uncritical of Chinese actions in view of the tensions in the bilateral relationship.*[109]

The British did not, eventually, proceed further with the idea of contacting Nehru because they learnt that Bunker as well as the Canadian Prime Minister had already spoken to him on similar lines, and the British Foreign Office thought that another effort might make it look like a deliberate 'ganging-up' by the West on Nehru to get him to do something with the Chinese.[110]

The Chinese eventually got wind of the British attempts to garner Commonwealth support. They understood that the British were playing a duplicitous game using the Commonwealth to

---

* Ambassador Bunker met Nehru on 31 October to brief him on the US stance on the Taiwan Strait situation. Nehru's cryptic note after the meeting with Bunker to Secretary General Pillai and Foreign Secretary Subimal Dutt stated that according to the Americans, the Chinese were giving a distorted version of the talks in Warsaw to the Indian side. Nehru's note suggested that he was not inclined to defend China's position in any way to the Americans ('Talks with the US Ambassador', 31 October 1958, SWJN, Series II, Vol. XLIV, September–October 1958).

disguise their actions. The *People's Daily* editorial pithily described it as a way to 'favour the preservation of Britain's colonial interests and save the foundering wreck of the British Empire'.[111] By that time Ambassador Parthasarathi had admitted to the British representative in Beijing that he was unable to get any Chinese official to talk about the Taiwan Strait crisis after October.[112] By early 1959, with the situation inside Tibet and on the Indo-Tibetan border both flaring up, Britain abandoned all efforts to utilize India. A senior British diplomat rhetorically posed the question as to whether 'in view of recent developments in Tibet and while Mr Nehru was thinking out the question of his relations with China and the problem of the Dalai Lama, did this seem to be a very appropriate moment for pressing him on other aspects of Chinese behaviour?'[113] Britain, which had roped in India as an important instrument of its China policy since early 1949, had finally concluded that it no longer had any uses for India in its own dealings with China.

Epilogue

Aftermath and Why History Is Important

The India–China relationship faced twin crises in 1959 due to the flight of the Dalai Lama to India and the growing friction between the border-guarding forces of India and China in the Himalayan heights. In December 1958, Nehru initiated correspondence with Zhou Enlai on their respective perceptions of the alignment of the India–China boundary. The letters they exchanged revealed the full extent of their disagreement. Nehru claimed Zhou had told him that China would accept the McMahon line as the boundary with India, as it had done with Burma (Myanmar). Zhou flatly rejected Nehru's claim. He also denied China was building a road on Indian territory in the Aksai Chin region of Ladakh, and claimed this road was in Chinese territory.[1] The Dalai Lama's departure from Tibet in March 1959 deepened mistrust because, despite Indian denials, the Chinese believed India was complicit in the troubles in Tibet. During a Politburo meeting on 19 March 1959, Zhou and Deng Xiaoping alleged that India was providing behind-the-scenes support to the West in fomenting trouble. Deng apparently said that 'when the time comes, we will certainly settle accounts with them [India]'.[2] Two incidents between the border-guarding forces, at Longju (Arunachal Pradesh) in August 1959, and a more deadly one at the Kongka Pass (Ladakh) in October 1959, destroyed what remaining trust existed between the two, once friendly, neighbours.

Although the second Taiwan Strait crisis had tapered down, the Chinese leadership was still deeply worried about the threat posed to their eastern flank by the US-backed Chiang Kai-shek regime. A conflict on two fronts would greatly complicate China's strategic problems. In May 1959, at Mao Zedong's specific instance, Pan Zili, the Chinese Ambassador in New Delhi, attempted to mitigate this possibility. He told Foreign Secretary Subimal Dutt that 'the enemy of the Chinese people lies in the east—the US imperialists have many military bases in Taiwan, in south Korea, Japan and in the Philippines which are directed against China. China's main attention and policy of struggle are directed to the east, to the west Pacific region . . . and not to India or any other country in south east Asia or south Asia . . . China [we] will not be so foolish as to antagonize the US in the east and again to antagonize India in the west.' He indicated to Dutt that it suited neither side to open two fronts (the Sino-Pakistan front so far as India was concerned).[3] Dutt thought the Chinese Ambassador was 'highly excited' and that his message was 'extremely irritating'. With Nehru's approval, the Chinese were told their message was discourteous and unbecoming, as if addressed to a hostile country, and that India would not discard or vary any of its policies under external pressure. A deep sense of hurt and betrayal had set in by that time. In 1949, Nehru had optimistically declared that China and India would be co-partners in a resurgent Asia. By October 1959, he was telling his chief ministers that 'it is a fact that our attempts at friendship with the Chinese government have failed and there is unfortunately some actual and a great deal of potential conflict in the air'.[4] The relationship had come full circle in ten years. A similar despondency appeared to overwhelm him insofar as India's role in other international affairs was concerned. In a letter to Krishna

Menon, Nehru said, 'I do not think we can play any decisive role
in it [Cold War] and the tremendous forces that are at play will
continue to go their own way . . . If the cold war leads to an atomic
or other war, there is no help for it.'[5] When Eisenhower wrote
to Nehru in November 1958 urging him to use his influence as
'a world leader for peace in your individual capacity as well as a
representative of the largest of the neutral nations', in preventing
the collapse of nuclear disarmament negotiations in Geneva,[6]
Nehru's response was that 'we naturally hesitate to intervene in
any matter unless we are convinced that such action on our part
will be helpful'.[7] The appetite for 'intervention' diminished with
the realization that China was not a friend, not even a partner,
in the way that India had envisaged in 1949. However, India's
view of the US also changed because of the unfriendly Chinese
attitude to India. India became more willing to look at closer ties,
including military ties, with the US. With Eisenhower's visit to
India in December 1959, it looked as if a new era was dawning in
Indo-US relations in preparation for Kennedy, who saw India as a
counterbalance and contrast to China.[8]

This history of the first ten years of India's interactions with
the United States, Britain and China in the Far East is important
for two reasons. It is a useful repository of knowledge for the
Indian state, and also because hindsight can, sometimes, be useful
for current policy framers.

What can be gleaned from the way the Indian state handled
Far Eastern affairs in the 1950s? It is undeniable that India's
leadership displayed strategic clarity. It recognized that the balance
of power had shifted from the British empire to the Americans.
It saw the new balance of forces taking place within Asia, as free
and independent states replaced colonies. It was rightly concerned
that Cold War politics in Asia would complicate matters. India's
understanding of the situation in China in 1949 was also on the
mark. Nehru accurately assessed that American efforts to stall

the Chinese revolution were unlikely to succeed. The decision to recognize the new regime seemed to fit in well with Nehru's view that 'the emergence of new China is the most important fact in Asia and in the world today'.[9]

But this strategic vision, with regard to the Far East generally and specifically with regard to China, was not accompanied by actionable policy that had well-defined goals and objectives as well as pre-identified resources and capacities to reach them. India's approach to the Chinese question, and more generally to the Far East, was rooted in a vague framework of international relations. This framework was defined by two lines of thinking, namely, that nationalism, or the desire of Asian peoples to be free from colonial rule, not communism, was the most powerful political force in post-World War Asia, and that it was necessary for Asians to determine their own future free from external (Western) interference. Within this general framework, India naturally saw the PRC as, primarily, an Asian partner rather than as a competitor. The US was also seen through the same prism, but not as a fellow democracy as much as an external hegemon. As a result, even sensible advice from Washington, such as the recommendations contained in the American aide-mémoire of 10 October 1949, and reiterated by Truman and Dean Acheson when Nehru visited Washington, that India verify the newly established communist regime's intentions before giving it the legitimacy that it desired, was rejected. Had India heeded American advice, it might have confirmed the existence of a potential boundary problem a decade earlier, and helped craft an appropriate foreign and security policy in the Far East. At the very least, India might not have laboured under the delusion that the communist regime was only interested in abrogating treaties signed between Chiang Kai-shek and the American government and that, by inference, India would face no problem with respect to the Shimla Agreement of 1914 and the McMahon Line. It was, in a classic sense, a case of the ostrich burying its head in the sand.

By the mid-1950s, India had had time to build out a system of foreign policymaking. Yet, diplomacy was driven less by systemic consultation than by individual preference. India was negotiating a key document with China on Tibet in 1953–54. India was also diplomatically engaged on the Korean crisis. Yet, until June 1954, there was practically no direct political contact between the Indian and Chinese leaderships.* Indian policy was not, therefore, built on direct understandings but instead on untested assumptions. In the case of the US and Britain as well, personal preferences played a significant role in making policy. Nehru was not moved by Acheson and disliked Dulles. Thus, the Indian view of US policy in the Far East was shaped not simply from the Cold War perspective but by the view of leading policymakers, about the personalities they were dealing with in Washington. As for Britain, its influence was strongly entrenched even a decade after Independence, and used by it to mould the thinking of the Government of India.

The systemic problem with regard to foreign policymaking in the Government of India was seen during the Indochina crisis, and further mutated during the two Taiwan Strait crises. The principal players—the US, the UK and the PRC—had come to Geneva after full preparation and policy deliberation within their governmental systems. President Eisenhower chaired several meetings of the National Security Council to discuss American policy threadbare. He also consulted senior members of the US Congress and had several rounds of discussion with allied nations prior to defining the American objectives and the ways and means to achieve them. In the case of Britain as well, Eden and Churchill took a policy note to Cabinet for approval on the eve of the conference. China, too, despite Krishna Menon's claim that Zhou did not look like he was acting on instructions from Beijing,[10]

---

* Vijayalakshmi Pandit, Nehru's sister, was the only political figure to meet the Chinese leadership, in Beijing in April 1952. No Chinese political leader visited India until Zhou Enlai in June 1954.

acted on a carefully prepared policy personally drafted by Zhou
Enlai and approved by Mao and other leaders.[11] In fact, Zhou
was in almost daily telegraphic contact with Mao and the party's
central committee during the Geneva Conference.

The Indian approach at the Geneva Conference was ad
hoc and personal. Krishna Menon's participation was not in
any official capacity, but 'informal'.[12] No institutional exercise
was undertaken to determine the policy behind India's informal
involvement. There was no system-wide consultation nor the
preparation of documents outlining objectives. According to
Subimal Dutt, Nehru's Foreign Secretary, Menon carried no
brief with him (at least none that was known by the Ministry
of External Affairs). 'Menon acted mostly on his own and kept
Nehru informed only of the brief outlines of his discussions
with different leaders,' wrote Dutt in his memoirs. 'The Indian
Foreign Office hardly came into the picture.'[13] Krishna Menon,
reportedly, kept no records of his conversations in Geneva.[14]
It appears unlikely that the cabinet was consulted. The prime
minister did speak of it in Parliament and wrote of it in his
letters to the chief ministers, but these did not elaborate upon
the policy behind Krishna Menon's intermediatory role in
Geneva. All information in this regard was confidential and
tightly restricted, indeed so tightly that Nehru personally asked
the British to maintain secrecy on the briefing he gave them
after Zhou Enlai's visit to India. 'Prime Minister [Nehru] this
morning gave me [Acting High Commissioner Middleton] [a]
personal message for Eden . . . In doing so he emphasized that
only he himself, Pillai and the stenographer were aware that this
message had been sent and he was particularly anxious that no
inkling of its existence should leak to the press.'[15] Thus, critical
information required for foreign policymaking was unavailable
to the government as a whole. This was to subsequently become

a pattern. Krishna Menon told Michael Brecher during the Bandung Conference in April 1955 that 'very few people knew what was happening inside the conference; even the Prime Minister [Nehru] knew very little because Mr [Subimal] Dutt was nowhere near these things . . . I told him what was happening and he wrote down what I told him.'[16] Given that Dutt was the incumbent Foreign Secretary, the handing out of selective information to the ministry most concerned with foreign policy pointed to a disturbing absence of process in the crafting of Indian foreign policy.

Krishna Menon had some success in Geneva in 1954, but that was partly because the Americans had effectively withdrawn and the British were steering the conference. Nehru and Menon, however, thought that the successful outcome on Indochina in the Geneva Conference was largely due to their efforts. This encouraged their belief in the idea and value of personalized diplomacy. In the first Taiwan Strait crisis, Krishna Menon formally inserted himself as 'mediator'. Although Nehru felt that India's neutral status (non-alignment) accorded 'a person [Menon] who represents a neutral country a certain advantage in informal discussion',[17] his efforts failed because the US saw India as neither neutral nor unbiased. The idea of neutrality implies a certain benign attitude on the part of the mediator towards all parties. During the 1954–55 Taiwan Strait crisis, India was publicly partial to one side (China) and critical of the other (US). The personality of the 'mediator', V.K. Krishna Menon, compounded the problem. He patronized the Americans, telling Eisenhower and Dulles, repeatedly, that he was acting only out of a desire to extricate America from the crisis in order to save them embarrassment. No less a person that G.L. Mehta, India's Ambassador to the United States, wrote to Nehru in July 1955 that Menon 'is undoubtedly temperamental and sometimes

rather difficult to get on with . . . [and] has been in the past
unnecessarily caustic and harsh about the United States'.[18]

This preference for personal diplomacy over process-driven
foreign policy reached a dangerous level during the second
Taiwan Strait crisis. In late September and early October 1958,
Krishna Menon, assuming he had Nehru's backing, intervened
in the crisis all on his own. During this period, India appeared
to be conducting two, totally unrelated, foreign policies. The
government, represented by the Ministry of External Affairs,
pursued a non-interventionist approach based on the overall
conclusion that while the situation in the Taiwan Strait was
grave, it was not likely to lead to large-scale war. Krishna Menon,
meanwhile, pursued an interventionist approach, claiming the
world was on the verge of major conflict and India was uniquely
placed to act in preventing it. It ended up damaging India's
credibility with everybody. Yet, this dysfunctionality was not
an isolated or individual case, but a manifestation of systemic
disintegration that had begun many years earlier as a result of
the government's failure to develop mechanisms for consultation
within the government (at cabinet or sub-cabinet levels) and with
external stakeholders such as Parliament and strategic experts.

China and Britain took advantage of this to serve their
purposes. Zhou's breach of protocol in directly approaching
Defence Minister Krishna Menon in September 1958 was one
such instance. The decision to bring Ralph Stevenson to India
before a crucial decision on recognizing the new regime in China
in 1949, and Eden's confidential efforts to pressure Nehru for
support in Indochina and the first Taiwan Strait crisis, were other
instances. The proximity to British leaders was understandable
because of India's colonial past, but the over-reliance on their
judgement led to unquestioning acceptance without weighing up
whether these were relevant to or aligned with India's national
interests. By the mid-1950s, the personal dislike that had sprung

up between Dulles and Nehru also gave Britain the opportunity to manipulate Indian thinking. India was always encouraged to look at American policy through a British prism. It practised deception in virtually all the crises, misrepresenting the Indian position to the Americans, withholding crucial information from India or only partially presenting the facts. In a similar manner, India assumed that Chinese interests were aligned to India's simply because both were great Asian states that had suffered from similar colonial experiences. India became the self-appointed spokesperson for the Chinese, defending them in public as well as in private conversations with the American leaders. India's sympathy and public support added credibility to the communist regime. India was over-mindful of Chinese sensitivities, such as when it denied routine overflights for US air force transport planes during the Indochina crisis without actually being asked to do that by China. The government's policy of self-censorship and support to China did not lead to reciprocal Chinese efforts to advance India's interests or be sensitive to Indian concerns. The Chinese leadership always considered India as part of the Western camp. It saw India as a useful diplomatic tool to pass on messages to the West and to build global support for the newly founded People's Republic of China.

The Far East of the 2020s is a very different place. The US is no longer overwhelmingly dominant in the western Pacific. China has developed adequate maritime capacities to challenge American hegemony. Both are invested in each other's economies and China has narrowed the economic gap to a considerable degree. America's diplomatic influence is no longer what it used to be at the end of the twentieth century, and China's is much greater than it was in the 1950s. Britain is reduced to a marginal player with limited economic and diplomatic influence. India is becoming an important player, albeit with limited hard-power capabilities, but with significant economic and diplomatic interests east of the

Malacca Strait. India is no longer under the illusion that China desires friendship with India on the basis of equality and mutual respect. Nor does it see the US as an external hegemon.

The Taiwan Strait, however, is still, possibly, the most dangerous potential flashpoint in the world. China and the US are, again as in the 1950s, in confrontation mode. China thinks that the US is determined to destroy the communist party and weaken China. The US believes that communist China intends to harm American interests in the western Pacific and expel it from this region. Relations between them have, arguably, never been at such a low ebb since the 1950s. In Nehru's words, 'Formosa [Taiwan] stands out as the danger point.'[19] The PRC's goal is to reunify Taiwan with the mainland to symbolically end its humiliation by foreign powers and to mark the true beginning of the Chinese century. The US sees Taiwan as a beacon of democratic resilience against communist authoritarianism, and vital to its security interests as an integral part of the island chain that it built in the 1950s to contain China. For both, then, the 'loss' of Taiwan is an existential problem. Neither side can be certain of decisive victory, but neither has ruled out the use of military force. That makes the situation more fraught with danger.

India has vital stakes in the peace and security of the Taiwan Strait and, more generally, in the western Pacific Ocean. A crisis in the general area of the Taiwan Strait or for that matter in the Far East as a whole could have potentially devastating consequences on India's geopolitical and economic security. Shipping (trade), supply chains (manufacturing), semi-conductors (digital economy) and submarine cables (information technology-enabled services), on which the Indian economy is dependent, may all be crippled in a crisis.[20] Aside from the domestic socio-economic repercussions, the ramifications of a crisis in the western Pacific will also be detrimental to India's geostrategic interests. For India, staying out of this region or, ostrich-like, burying its head in the sand is not an option. In May 1950, Nehru had said that 'all of us who live in this part of the world [Asia] have a great responsibility in shaping and determining it to the extent we can . . . as an independent nation of great potential power we cannot disclaim the responsibilities that come with independence'.[21] This proposition is still valid.

China has made its intentions clear. It is in the midst of a military modernization that will bring the People's Liberation Army (Navy) in strength into the Indian Ocean by the end of this decade, posing a set of challenges to Indian maritime and continental security that it has not confronted after 1947. The intentions of the US are also transparent. Unable to dominate the geopolitical space by itself due to the changes in the relative balance of power, it is seeking to retain its pre-eminence by strengthening alliances and building new partnerships and plurilateral platforms. From India's perspective, this has enhanced its strategic space, allowing it to pursue complex national interests without acting in ways that others might consider destabilizing to peace and security. As a 'swing' state in the Indo-Pacific, India has to craft a foreign policy that balances against China and maintains strategic independence from the US.

One recent development potentially complicates India's geostrategic interests. In this context, the past becomes relevant to the future. In September 2021, the President of the United States and the Prime Ministers of the United Kingdom and Australia announced the creation of AUKUS to 'deepen diplomatic, security and defence cooperation in the Indo-Pacific region'.[22] AUKUS is not simply a plurilateral platform in the Indo-Pacific. It is potentially a new collective defence and security arrangement. Its scope likely covers the full security spectrum from intelligence-gathering to war-fighting. It is directed against China. Concerns in the region that AUKUS might undermine the strategic order in Asia are facile. China's enhanced military capacities, as well as its behaviour and activities in the region, have already undermined the regional strategic balance. AUKUS is intended to preserve Western interests in the Indo-Pacific in the context of an ascendant China. India's concern should focus around what Britain's role will be in this new defence and security arrangement. Britain has not lost its maritime or imperial outlook despite its marginal role in the region after its withdrawal from Hong Kong in 1997. Having exited the European Union, Britain is possibly looking at AUKUS as its path to restore 'Global Britain'. Given the fact that the Indo-Pacific accounts to close to half the world's output, contains half the world's population and will house four of the world's five largest economies by 2030, British interest in this region is natural. But India's historical experience, and the recent British behaviour over the Chagos islands (so-called British Indian Ocean territories), as well as its naval presence in the Indian Ocean region should ring alarm bells in South Block.

Even after Britain formally abandoned its military presence 'east of Suez' in the early 1970s, it retained diplomatic leverages, including through royal connections and the Commonwealth. It remained the principal Western purveyors of Asian diplomacy, the go-to player for advice that the Americans, even the Europeans, needed on Asian geopolitics, aside from China, because it had the experience and knowledge as a result of the colonial past. In pursuit of leverage in the Indian Ocean, it nurtured relationships with the Gulf monarchies, supported Pakistan against India and Singapore against Malaysia, leased its colonial possession in the Chagos Islands to the US for military purposes and joined the American war efforts in Iraq and Afghanistan. Since the beginning of this century, it has reinitiated the process of a strategic shift back to the Indian Ocean. It now has a military presence in Qatar (No. 83 EAG at Al-Udeid airbase), the United Arab Emirates (Al-Minhad airbase), Bahrain (HMS *Jufair*) and Oman (Al-Mussanah airbase and the new Joint Logistics Support Base at Duqm) besides the joint Anglo-American base on Diego Garcia in the

Chagos archipelago. The Duqm facility will be able to support Elizabeth-class aircraft carriers. Britain also has a naval logistics base at Sembawang wharf in Singapore and a garrison in Brunei. Djibouti, where several countries including China and the US have 'facilities', also has a British military presence. In short, despite its claim that the new 'Global Britain' has no military element, it has the military capacity to back its geopolitical role in the Indian Ocean.

In an era of mounting Sino-American competition and declining American capacities, the possibility that Washington might outsource the management of the Indian Ocean to the British can no longer be discounted. Britain requires a geopolitical justification for its enhanced presence in the Indo-Pacific. AUKUS provides that justification. It is an anglosphere in which Britain can anchor its presence in the Indian Ocean with two resident powers with whom the British share an absolute identity of interests. This time, however, we should not permit the British to insert themselves into the Indo-American discourse on the Indo-Pacific. Despite some differences between the two, both in terms of values and interests, a broad-based and intensive dialogue between Washington and New Delhi must become a cornerstone of Indian foreign policy. With China, a more realistic view of its intentions and capabilities is already shaping a pragmatic policy. Dialogue and deterrence should be the twin pillars for the crafting of a new relationship after China's behaviour in the decade of the 2010s systematically ended the modus vivendi that both had built after 1988. This time, when the British come courting India, because we are a principal littoral state in the Indian Ocean, it would be wise to bear Virgil's words: '*Timeo danaos et dona ferentes*' (Beware of Greeks bearing gifts).

Acknowledgements

This book was born out of my curiosity to understand the reasons behind India's decision to recognize the People's Republic of China in December 1949 without any identifiable quid pro quo. Three intrepid young scholars—Tisyaketu Sarkar, Saheb Singh Chadha and Shibani Mehta—helped me to identify and unearth documents from the archives. I owe them a debt of gratitude. Without their efforts it would have been impossible for me to write this book.

I am also indebted to two of India's senior-most diplomats, Maharaj Kumar Rasgotra and Eric Gonsalves, who were witnesses to the making of India's foreign policy during the 1950s. They gave me substantial chunks of their time to help me understand the ethos and circumstances of that period, including the relationships between some of the principal players. These conversations helped me greatly in writing this book.

The Mercator Institute for Chinese Studies in Berlin provided me with the opportunity to do a substantial portion of my writing in their lovely offices in Berlin in March 2023. Carnegie India gave me access to research materials and allowed me to seek the help of their researchers in tracking and obtaining documents relevant to the book.

I thank Ashley Tellis and Rudro Chaudhury for their advice and suggestions when I was writing the book. I am singularly fortunate to know them both and to benefit from their guidance.

My editor, Elizabeth Kuruvilla, encouraged me to write this book after I sent a sketchy synopsis. This is my second book of which she is the editor, and I am grateful to her for all her work in this regard.

My spouse, Vandana, by now is used to my expecting her to manage the home while I write. I am always grateful and feel lucky to be with her.

I dedicate this book to Sahaj who is the best grandson in the whole world.

Notes

Chapter 1: Setting the Stage in the Pacific Theatre

1 'Mr Mao Tse-Tung to the American Ambassador in China (Hurley)', 11 January 1945, *Foreign Relations of the US (FRUS): Diplomatic Papers, 1945, China, Vol. VII.*

2 'Memorandum by Secretary of State to President, "Communist–KMT Relations"', 4 January 1945, *FRUS: Diplomatic Papers, 1945, China, Vol. VII.*

3 'Ambassador in China (Hurley) to President', 14 January 1945, *FRUS: Diplomatic Papers, 1945, China, Vol. VII,.*

4 'Ambassador in China (Hurley) to Secretary of State', 7 February 1945, *FRUS: Diplomatic Papers, 1945, China, Vol. VII.*

5 'Memorandum by Director of Office of Far Eastern Affairs (Ballantine)', 7 March 1945, *FRUS: Diplomatic Papers, 1945, China, Vol. VII.*

6 'Report by Second Secretary of Embassy in China (Service), Subject: View of Mao Tse-tung: America & China', 13 March 1945, *FRUS: Diplomatic Papers, 1945, China, Vol. VII.*

7 'President Roosevelt to Mr Mao Tse-tung', 10 March 1945, *FRUS: Diplomatic Papers, 1945, China, Vol. VII.*

8 'Directive of the CCP Central Committee on Pacific Anti-Japanese Front, 9 December 1941' *Collected Works of Mao Zedong, Vol. VIII* (US Government Joint Publications Research Service [USG JPRS], November 1978), pp. 94–95.

9   'Speech at Cadres Soiree in Yenan in Celebration of October
     Revolution Anniversary, 6 November 1943', *Collected Works of Mao
     Zedong, Vol. IX, Part I* (USG JPRS, November 1978), pp. 151–53.

10   'The China White Paper, August 1949', originally issued as 'US
     Relations with China with Special Reference to Period 1944–1949',
     Department of State Publication 3573, Far Eastern Series 30.

11   'Note of General Marshall's First Conference with Mr Chou
     En-lai', 23 December 1945, *FRUS: Diplomatic Papers 1945, The
     Far East, China, Vol. VII.*

12   'Minutes of Meeting between General Marshall and Chairman
     Mao Tse-tung at Yenan', 4 March 1946, *FRUS: The Far East,
     China, Vol. IX.*

13   'General Marshall to President Truman', 6 May 1946, *FRUS: The
     Far East, China, Vol. IX.*

14   'Statement on US China Aid Bill, 22 June 1946', *Collected Works of
     Mao Zedong, Vol. IX, Part II* (USG JPRS, 1978), pp. 250–51.

15   'The Truth about US Mediation and Future of Civil War in
     China', Talk with US correspondent A.T. Steele, 29 September
     1946, *Selected Works of Mao Zedong, Vol. III* (Beijing: Foreign
     Languages Press).

16   'The China White Paper, August 1949', originally issued as 'US
     Relations with China with Special Reference to Period 1944–1949',
     Department of State Publication 3573, Far Eastern Series 30.

17   'The Ambassador in China (Stuart) to Secretary of State', 1 January
     1947, *FRUS: 1947, The Far East, China, Vol. VII.*

18   'Secretary of State to Ambassador in China (Stuart)', 12 August
     1948, *FRUS: 1948, The Far East: China, Vol. VIII.*

19   'Acting Secretary of State to Ambassador in China (Stuart)',
     20 October 1948, *FRUS: 1948, The Far East: China, Vol. VIII.*

20   'Acting Secretary of State to Ambassador in China (Stuart)',
     20 October 1948, *FRUS: 1948, The Far East: China, Vol. VIII.*

21   'The Ambassador in UK (Winant) to Secretary of State', 19 April
     1945, *FRUS: Diplomatic Papers, 1945, The Far East, China, Vol. VII.*

22   'The Ambassador in China (Hurley), Temporarily in Iran, to
     Secretary of State, Tehran', 14 April 1945, *FRUS: Diplomatic
     Papers, 1945, The Far East: China, Vol. VII.*

23 Robert E. Watson, 'The Foreign Office and Policy Making in China, 1945–1950, Anglo American Relations and Recognition of Communist China', University of Leeds, Institute for International Relations, May 1996, https://etheses.whiterose.ac.uk/1645/1/uk_bl_ethos_269202.pdf accessed 2 May 2023.

24 'No. 1, Memorandum on Present China Situation and on British and American Policies on China, July 7, 1945', *Documents on British Policy Overseas, Series I, Vol. VIII, Britain and China, 1945–1950* (Routledge, 2013).

25 H. Trevelyan, Note titled 'Recent Developments in Relations of the United States of America with China', 23 May 1945, Sino-American Relations, FO 371/46170 (1945).

26 'No. 1, Memorandum on Present China Situation and on British and American Policies on China, July 7, 1945', Chapter 1, *Documents on British Overseas Policy, Series I, Vol. VIII, Britain and China, 1945–1950* (Routledge, 2013), p. 3.

27 'No. 2, Letter to Mr Kitson on Negotiation of New Consular and Commercial Treaties with China, August 30, 1945', Chapter 1, *Documents on British Overseas Policy, Series I, Vol. VIII, Britain and China, 1945–1950* (Routledge, 2013), p. 24.

28 Note by G.V. Kitson, Head, China Department, Foreign Office, 15 January 1946, US Policy in China, FO 371/53678 (1946).

29 Lord Inverchapel, British Ambassador in Washington, to Foreign Office, 8 August 1946, US Policy in China, FO 371/53678 (1946).

30 Note by A.L. Scott, 18 February 1947, FO 371/63318.

31 Telegram from Foreign Office to British Embassy, Washington, 7 February 1947, General Marshall Visit, FO 371/63318 (1947).

32 Telegram from Lord Inverchapel to British Foreign Office, 15 February 1947, General Marshall Visit, FO 371/63318 (1947).

33 'General Marshall to President Truman', 21 November 1946, *FRUS: 1946, The Far East, China, Vol. IX*.

34 'Col. Marshall S. Carter to General Marshall', 21 November 1946, *FRUS: 1946, The Far East, China, Vol. IX*.

35 'No. 28, Sir John Balfour to Mr Bevin, July 16, 1947', Chapter 3, *Documents on British Overseas Policy, Series I, Vol. VIII, Britain and China, 1945–1950* (Routledge, 2013), p. 101.

36 Telegram, 'Political Situation in China', Lord Inverchapel to Foreign Office, 1 February 1948, US Aid to China (1) FO 371/69584 (1948).

37 'No. 45, Letter for Sir Ralph Stevenson to Mr M.E. Dening, May 25, 1948', Chapter 4, *Documents on British Overseas Policy, Series I, Vol. VIII, Britain and China, 1945–1950* (Routledge, 2013), p. 149.

38 Memorandum addressed to Mr M.E. Dening, 1 March 1948, US Aid to China (1) FO 371/69584 (1948).

39 'No. 51, Memorandum by Mr Bevin on Recent Developments in the Civil War in China, December 9, 1948', Chapter 4, *Documents on British Overseas Policy, Series I, Vol. VIII, Britain and China, 1945–1950* (Routledge, 2013), p. 170.

40 'No. 52, Letter from M.E. Dening to H.A. Graves, Counsellor, UK Embassy in the US, December 30, 1948', Chapter 4, *Documents on British Overseas Policy, Series I, Vol. VIII, Britain and China, 1945–1950* (Routledge, 2013), p. 187 in footnotes.

41 'I Go to China', 19 August 1939, *Selected Works of Jawaharlal Nehru (SWJN), Series I, Vol X, July 1939–March 1940.*

42 'Letter to Mao Tse-tung', 11 July 1939, *SWJN, Series I, Vol. X, July 1939–March 1940.*

43 J. Nehru, Interview to *The Hindu*, 24 September 1939, *SWJN, Series I, Vol. X*, July 1939–March 1940.

44 'Speech at Shraddhanand Park', Calcutta, 20 February 1942, *SWJN, Series I, Vol. XII, December 1941–August 1942.*

45 Statement to the *New Chronicle* (London), Allahabad, 28 February 1942.

46 'India's Peaceful Foreign Policy', *New Republic* (New York), 10 February 1947, *SWJN, Series I, Vol. XV, September 1946–January 1947.*

47 'Foreign Policy for India, Reply to Debate on Foreign Policy in Constituent Assembly', 4 December 1947, *SWJN, Series II, Vol. XIV, August–December 1947.*

48 'Message to China, Interview Given to Central News Agency of China', 27 June 1945, *SWJN, Series I, Vol. XIV, June 1945–February 1946.*

49 M.K. Rasgotra, 'Washington DC: Early Warnings of an Indo-US Rift', Chapter 6, *A Life in Diplomacy* (New Delhi: Penguin, 2013).

50 Tanvi Madan, *Fateful Triangle: How China Shaped US–India Relations During the Cold War* (Gurugram: Penguin Random House India, 2020), pp. 16–17.

51 Jawaharlal Nehru, Address at the Sino-Indian Cultural Society, General Body Meeting at Santiniketan, 23 December 1945; Tan Chung, ed., *In the Footsteps of Xuan Zang: Tan Yunshan and India* (www.ignca.gov.in, 1999).

52 Tansen Sen, *Relations between the Republic of China and India, 1937–1949, Routledge Handbook of China-India Relations* (Routledge, 10 March 2020), https://www.routledgehandbooks.com/doi/10.4324/9781351001564-5, accessed on 28 December 2022.

53 K.M. Panikkar, *In Two Chinas: Memoirs of a Diplomat* (London: George Allen & Unwin, 1955), https://archive.org.

54 'The Situation in China', Note to Foreign Secretary, 5 December 1948, *SWJN, Series II, Vol. VIII, October–December 1948.*

55 'Note to Foreign Secretary', 14 December 1948, *SWJN, Series II, Vol. VIII, October–December 1948.*

56 'No. 50, UK Delegation to UN General Assembly (Paris) to Mr Bevin', 20 November 1948, Chapter 3, *Documents on British Overseas Policy, Series I, Vol. VIII, Britain and China 1945–1950* (Routledge), pp. 168–69.

57 'Memorandum by Mr Bevin on Recent Developments in China', 9 December 1948, Chapter 3, *Documents on British Overseas Policy, Series I, Vol. VIII, Britain and China, 1945–1950,* (Routledge, 2013), pp. 170–86.

58 'No. 56, Sir A. Nye (New Delhi) to Sir P. Noel Baker', 15 January 1949, Chapter 3, *Documents on British Overseas Policy, Series I, Vol. VIII, Britain and China 1945–1950,* (Routledge, 2013), pp. 200–02.

Chapter 2: Recognizing the Chinese Communists

1 Subimal Dutt, 'India–Tibet–China', Chapter 7, *With Nehru in the Foreign Office* (Calcutta: Minerva, 1977), pp. 72.

2 Tansen Sen, *Relations between the Republic of China and India, 1937–1949, Routledge Handbook of China-India Relations* (Routledge, 10 March 2020), https://www.routledgehandbooks.com/doi/10.4324/9781351001564-5, accessed on 28 December 2022.

3 Doc. 0027, 16 October 1947, *India–China Relations, 1947–2000, A Documentary Study, Vol. II,* introduced and edited by A.S. Bhasin (New Delhi: Geetika Publishers), pp. 47.

4 Doc. 0029, 21 October 1947, *India–China Relations, 1947–2000, A Documentary Study, Vol. II,* introduced and edited by A.S. Bhasin (New Delhi: Geetika Publishers), pp. 49–51.

5 Doc. 0043, 9 February 1948, *India–China Relations, 1947–2000, A Documentary Study, Vol. II,* introduced and edited by A.S. Bhasin (New Delhi: Geetika Publishers), pp. 71.

6 K.M. Panikkar, *In Two Chinas: Memoirs of a Diplomat* (London: George Allen & Unwin, 1955), https://archive.org.

7 Note of a conversation with His Excellency Dr Wong Wen-Hao and Dr Hu Shih on the situation in China, File No. 703(2)-CJK/49, China, Japa and Korea, Ministry of External Affairs, Public Records, National Archives of India, New Delhi.

8 Doc. 0053, 2 December 1948, *India–China Relations, 1947–2000, A Documentary Study, Vol. II,* introduced and edited by A.S. Bhasin (New Delhi: Geetika Publishers), pp. 85–86.

9 J. Nehru, *Letters to Chief Ministers, Vol. 1, 1947–1949,* edited by G. Parthasarathi (New Delhi: Jawaharlal Nehru Memorial Fund, 1985), hereafter referred to as J. Nehru, *Letters to Chief Ministers, Vol. 1;* letter dated 6 December 1948, pp. 231–32.

10 Doc. 0055, 'Prime Minister's Note to Foreign Secretary on Situation in China', 5 December 1948, *India–China Relations, 1947–2000, A Documentary Study, Vol. II,* introduced and edited by A.S. Bhasin (New Delhi: Geetika Publishers), p. 87.

11 Doc. 0060, Prime Minister's Secretariat, 30 December 1948, *India–China Relations, 1947–2000, A Documentary Study, Vol. II,* introduced and edited by A.S. Bhasin (New Delhi: Geetika Publishers), p. 93.

12 'India, rather suddenly and inevitably becomes the most important country in Asia': J. Nehru, *Letters to Chief Ministers, Vol. 1, 1947–1949*, letter dated 17 January 1949, p. 262.

13 *FRUS, 1949, The Far East: China, Vol. IX,* edited by Francis C. Prescott, Herbert A. Fine and Velma Hastings Cassidy (Washington: USG Printing Office, 1974), hereafter cited as *FRUS, 1949, Vol. IX)*, conversation between British Ambassador (Franks) and Acting Secretary of State (Lovett), 5 January 1949.

14 'No. 58, Minute by Mr Scarlett on the Recognition Question', 17 February 1949, Chapter 5, *Documents on British Policy Overseas, Series I, Vol. VIII, Britain and China, 1945–1950* (Routledge, 2013), p. 204.

15 'No. 59, Memorandum by Mr Bevin on the Situation in China', 9 March 1949, Chapter 5, *Documents on British Policy Overseas, Series I, Vol. VIII, Britain and China, 1945–1950,* (Routledge, 2013), p. 208.

16 'No. 62, Sir O. Franks (Washington) to Mr Bevin', 18 March 1949, Chapter 5, *Documents on British Policy Overseas, Series I, Vol. VIII, Britain and China, 1945–1950* (Routledge, 2013), pp. 229–33.

17 'No. 70, Extract from Conclusions of the Meeting of the Cabinet', 9 May 1949, Chapter 5, *Documents on British Policy Overseas, Series I, Vol. VIII, Britain and China, 1945–1950* (Routledge, 2013), p. 261.

18 Ibid.

19 'No. 72, Memorandum by Mr P.J. Noel Baker on Hongkong', 18 May 1949, Chapter 5, *Documents on British Policy Overseas, Series I, Vol. VIII, Britain and China, 1945–1950,* (Routledge, 2013), p. 268.

20 'No. 82, Memorandum by Mr Noel Baker on Hongkong: Attitude of Other Commonwealth Countries', 17 June 1949, Chapter 5, *Documents on British Policy Overseas, Series I, Vol. VIII, Britain and China, 1945–1950* (Routledge, 2013).

21 *FRUS, 1949, Vol. IX,* 'Note from British Embassy to the Department of State', 19 March 1949.

22 *FRUS, 1949, Vol. IX*, 'Telegram for US Ambassador (Stuart) to Secretary of State', 3 May 1949.

23 *FRUS, 1949, Vol. IX*, 'Circular Telegram from the Secretary of State', 6 May 1949.

24 *FRUS, 1949, Vol. IX*, 'Telegram from Secretary of State to US Ambassador (Stuart)', 13 May 1949.

25 FO 371/75813 (1949), Recognition of Communist Government of (China), July–September 1949 (Folder 4) (Government Papers, National Archives, Kew, 1949), accessed on 11 March 2023, http://www.archivedirect.amdigital.co.uk.proxy.library.georgetown.edu/Documents/Details/FO 371-75813 1949, pp. 6–7, hereafter referred to as FO 371/75813 (1949), Recognition of Communist Government of (China), July–September 1949 (Folder 4) (Government Papers, National Archives, Kew, 1949).

26 'No. 72, Memorandum by Mr P.J. Noel Baker on Hongkong', 18 May 1949, Chapter 5, *Documents on British Policy Overseas, Series I, Vol. VIII, Britain and China, 1945–1950*, (Routledge, 2013), p. 268.

27 *FRUS, 1949, Vol. IX*, 'Telegram from US Ambassador (Stuart) to Secretary of State', 17 May 1949.

28 Tanvi Madan, 'With an Eye to the East: The China Factor and the US–India Partnership, 1949–1979', Dissertation, University of Texas, Austin, May 2012, p. 30.

29 *FRUS, 1949, Vol. IX*, 'Telegram from US Ambassador (Henderson) to Secretary of State', 26 May 1949.

30 Doc. 0078, 'Telegram from Panikkar to K.P.S. Menon, Foreign Secretary', 10 June 1949, *India–China Relations, 1947–2000, A Documentary Study, Vol. II*, introduced and edited by A.S. Bhasin (New Delhi: Geetika Publishers), pp. 114–16.

31 *FRUS, 1949, Vol. IX*, 'Telegram from US Ambassador (Henderson) to Secretary of State', 17 June 1949.

32 Ibid., 21 June 1949.

33 'Transfer of Chinese Capital from Nanking to Canton, Chungking Etc. Appointment of Indian Representative There. Question of Closing Indian Embassy Office at Hong Kong', File No. 711-

CJK/49, China, Japan and Korea, Ministry of External Affairs, Public Records, National Archives of India, New Delhi.

34 J. Nehru, *Letters to Chief Ministers, Vol. 1, 1947–1949,* letter dated 14 May 1949, pp. 343–44.

35 Ibid., letter dated 1 April 1949, p. 307.

36 Ibid., letter dated 14 May 1949, pp. 343–44.

37 Doc. 0080, letter from Prime Minister to Ambassador in the United States Vijayalakshmi Pandit, New Delhi, 1 July 1949, *India–China Relations, 1947–2000, A Documentary Study, Vol. II,* introduced and edited by A.S. Bhasin (New Delhi, Geetika Publishers), p. 117.

38 J. Nehru, *Letters to Chief Ministers, Vol. 1, 1947–1949,* letter dated 13 June 1949, pp. 375–76.

39 Tanvi Madan, 'With an Eye to the East: The China Factor and the US–India Partnership, 1949–1979', Dissertation, University of Texas, Austin, May 2012, p. 28.

40 *FRUS, 1949, Vol. IX,* 'Telegram from Secretary of State to US Ambassador in UK (Douglas)', 20 July 1949.

41 'No. 88, Mr Bevin to Sir Frank Hoyer-Millar (Washington)', 21 July 1949, Chapter 5, *Documents on British Policy Overseas, Series I, Vol. VIII, Britain and China, 1945–1950,* (Routledge, 2013).

42 FO 371/75813 (1949), Recognition of Communist Government of (China), July–September 1949 (Folder 4) (Government Papers, National Archives, Kew, 1949), noting on file dated 27 July 1949, p. 46.

43 *FRUS, 1949, Vol. IX,* 'Telegram from US Ambassador (Douglas) to Secretary of State', 27 July, 1949.

44 FO 371/75813 (1949), Recognition of Communist Government of (China), July–September 1949 (Folder 4) (Government Papers, National Archives, Kew, 1949), note recorded by P.D. Coates, 13 August 1949, p. 100.

45 Ibid., note recorded by Dening, 5 July 1949, p. 9.

46 FO 371/75814 (1949), Recognition of Communist Government of (China), July–September 1949 (Folder 5) (Government

Papers, National Archives, Kew, 1949), Telegram from Stevenson to Dening, 1 September 1949, p. 24.

47   FO 371/75813 (1949), Recognition of Communist Government of (China), July–September 1949 (Folder 4) (Government Papers, National Archives, Kew 1949), Telegram from the Far Eastern Department to the Acting UK High Commissioner to New Zealand, 15 July 1949, pp. 35–36.

48   'No. 94, Memorandum by Mr Bevin on China', 23 August 1949, Chapter 5, *Documents on British Policy Overseas, Series I, Vol. VIII, Britain and China, 1945–1950* (Routledge, 2013), p. 340.

49   *FRUS, 1949, Vol. IX,* telegram from American Charge in London (Holmes) to the Secretary of State, 1 September 1949. Sir William Strang, Permanent Under Secretary of State for Foreign Affairs informed the US charge d'affaires that the memorandum shared with the Americans had been approved by the cabinet and was official British policy.

50   File 710 (2)—CJK—49, hereafter cited as File 710(2)-CJK-49. (1) Note containing HMG's Latest Views on the Situation in China; (2) Exchange of Views between UK and USA (Foreign Secretary Mr Bevin and Mr Acheson) regarding future relations with China; (3) Question of Recognition of the Communist Government in China, National Archives of India, New Delhi.

51   Doc. 0088, 'Telegram from Panikkar to Nehru', 10 August 1949, *India–China Relations, 1947–2000, A Documentary Study, Vol. II,* introduced and edited by A.S. Bhasin (New Delhi: Geetika Publishers, pp. 127–28). Panikkar's advice aligned with Nehru's thinking. Doc. 0090, 'Telegram from New Delhi for Panikkar', *India–China Relations, 1947–2000, A Documentary Study, Vol. II,* introduced and edited by A.S. Bhasin (New Delhi: Geetika Publishers), p. 130.

52   Doc. 0089, 'Telegram from Prime Minister to Vijayalakshmi Pandit', 12 August 1949, *India–China Relations, 1947–2000, A Documentary Study, Vol. II,* introduced and edited by A.S. Bhasin (New Delhi: Geetika Publishers), pp. 129–30.

53   *FRUS, 1949, Vol. IX,* 'Circular Telegram from Secretary of State to Certain Diplomatic and Consular Officers', 19 August 1949.

54   File 710 (2)—CJK—49, Noting by K.P.S. Menon.

55   Ibid., Noting by Girija Shankar Bajpai.

56   Mao Tse Tung, 'On the People's Democratic Dictatorship: In Commemoration of the 28th Anniversary of the Communist Party of China', www.marxists.org.

57   Doc. 0078, 'Telegram from Panikkar to K.P.S. Menon', 10 June 1949, *India–China Relations, 1947–2000, A Documentary Study, Vol. II*, introduced and edited by A.S. Bhasin (New Delhi: Geetika Publishers), pp. 114–16.

58   J. Nehru, *Letters to Chief Ministers, Vol. 1, 1947–1949*, letter dated 14 May 1949, pp. 343–44.

59   Doc. 0084, 'Telegram from Panikkar to Menon', 17 July 1949, *India–China Relations, 1947–2000, A Documentary Study, Vol. II*, introduced and edited by A.S. Bhasin (New Delhi: Geetika Publishers), pp. 122–23.

60   Doc. 0088, 'Telegram from Panikkar to Nehru', 10 August 1949, *India–China Relations, 1947–2000, A Documentary Study, Vol. II*, introduced and edited by A.S. Bhasin (New Delhi: Geetika Publishers), pp. 127–28.

61   Doc. 0094, Panikkar's note to K.P.S. Menon, 7 September 1949, *India–China Relations, 1947–2000, A Documentary Study, Vol. II*, introduced and edited by A.S. Bhasin (New Delhi: Geetika Publishers), pp. 129–30.

62   *FRUS, 1949, Vol. IX*, 'Memorandum of Conversation by Director of Office for Far Eastern Affairs (Butterworth) with Dening, Assistant Under Secretary for Foreign Affairs in Charge of Far Eastern Matters', British Foreign Office, 9 September 1949.

63   Note recorded by Peter Scarlett, dated 31 August 1949: 'Secretary of State wishes to canvass the support of our friends in the commonwealth countries before he sees Mr Acheson.' FO 371/75813 (1949), Recognition of Communist Government of (China), July–September 1949 (Folder 4) (Government Papers, National Archives, Kew, 1949), p. 125.

64   File 710 (2)—CJK—49, Letter from Frank Roberts to Foreign Secretary K.P.S. Menon, 2 September 1949.

65   Ibid., Note Handed to Ministry of External Affairs by
      British Deputy High Commissioner Frank Roberts, 25
      August 1949.

66   *FRUS, 1949, Vol. IX*, 'Memorandum of Conversation by
      Director of Office for Far Eastern Affairs (Butterworth) with
      Dening, Assistant Under Secretary for Foreign Affairs in Charge
      of Far Eastern Matters', United Kingdom Foreign Office,
      9 September 1949.

67   FO 371/75815 (1949), Recognition of Communist Government
      of (China), July–September 1949 (Folder 6) (Government
      Papers, National Archives, Kew, 1949), 'Conversation between
      Mr Dening and Mr Butterworth at the State Department on the
      Afternoon of 9 September 1949', p. 47.

68   *FRUS, 1949, Vol. IX,* 'Memorandum of Conversation by Secretary
      of State with UK Foreign Secretary (Bevin)', 13 September 1949.

69   FO 371/75815 (1949), Recognition of Communist Government
      of (China), July–September 1949 (Folder 6) (Government
      Papers, National Archives, Kew, 1949), 'Record of Meeting Held
      at the State Department', Washington, 13 September 1949,
      'China', pp. 38–39.

70   Ibid.

71   *FRUS, 1949, Vol IX*, 'Memorandum of Conversation by
      Secretary of State with UK Foreign Secretary (Bevin)',
      17 September 1949.

72   FO 371/75815 (1949), Recognition of Communist Government
      of (China), July–September 1949 (Folder 6) (Government
      Papers, National Archives, Kew, 1949), 'Record of Meeting Held
      at the State Department', Washington, 17 September 1949,
      pp. 89–90.

73   FO 371/75816 (1949), Recognition of Communist Government
      of (China), July–September 1949 (Folder 7) (Government
      Papers, National Archives, Kew, 1949), Telegram from British
      Foreign Office to Nanking, 1 October 1949, pp. 31–32.

74   FO 371/75815 (1949), Recognition of Communist Government
      of (China), July–September 1949 (Folder 6) (Government

Papers, National Archives, Kew, 1949), telegram from Stevenson in Nanking to the British Foreign Office, 20 September 1949, pp. 54–55.

75   FO 371/75816 (1949), Recognition of Communist Government of (China), July–September 1949 (Folder 7) (Government Papers, National Archives, Kew, 1949), telegram from Stevenson in Nanking to the British Foreign Office, 1 October 1949, pp. 40–42.

76   Ibid.

77   Ibid., p. 63.

78   FO 371/75816 (1949), Recognition of Communist Government of (China), July–September 1949 (Folder 7) (Government Papers, National Archives, Kew, 1949), telegram from British Foreign Office to British Embassy in Washington, 4 October 1949, p. 44.

79   *FRUS, 1949, Vol. IX,* telegram from US charge in London (Douglas) to Secretary of State, 10 October 1949.

80   Ibid.

81   *FRUS, 1949, Vol. IX,* 'Memorandum by Secretary of State of Conversation with President Truman', 17 October 1949.

82   FO 371/75816 (1949), Recognition of Communist Government of (China), July–September 1949 (Folder 7) (Government Papers, National Archives, Kew, 1949), notes by P.D. Coates and Vallat, p. 126.

83   Ibid.

84   *FRUS, 1949, Vol. IX,* 'Telegram from the Acting Secretary of State to the Charge d'Affaires in India', 7 October 1949.

85   *FRUS, 1949, Vol. IX,* 'Telegram from US Charge Donovan to Secretary of State', 10 October 1949.

86   J. Nehru, *Letters to Chief Ministers, 1947–1964, Vol. 1, 1947–1949,* letter dated 6 December 1948, pp. 231–32.

87   J. Nehru, *Letters to Chief Ministers, 1947–1964, Vol. 1, 1947–1949,* letter dated 1 April 1949, pp. 231–32.

88   Doc. 0095, *India–China Relations, 1947–2000, A Documentary Study, Vol. II,* introduced and edited by A.S. Bhasin (New Delhi:

Geetika Publishers), letter from Prime Minister to Finance Minister John Mathai, 10 September 1949, p. 144.

89 Doc. 0096, Telegram from Indian Embassy in Nanking to K.P.S. Menon', 12 September 1949, *India–China Relations, 1947–2000, A Documentary Study, Vol. II,* introduced and edited by A.S. Bhasin (New Delhi: Geetika Publishers), p. 145.

90 Doc. 0104, Telegram from Prime Minister to Ambassador K.M. Panikkar, New Delhi', 2 October 1949, *India–China Relations, 1947–2000, A Documentary Study, Vol. II,* introduced and edited by A.S. Bhasin (New Delhi: Geetika Publishers), pp. 153–54.

91 *FRUS, 1949, Vol. IX,* 'Memorandum of Conversation by Secretary of State (with Nehru)', Washington, 12 October 1949.

92 *FRUS, 1949, Vol. IX,* 'Memorandum of Conversation between President Truman, Secretary of State Acheson, Jawaharlal Nehru and G.S. Bajpai', 13 October 1949.

93 M.K. Rasgotra, 'Washington DC: Early Warnings of an Indo-US Rift' Chapter 6, *A Life in Diplomacy* (New Delhi: Penguin, 2013).

94 *FRUS, 1949, Vol. IX,* 'Telegram from US Charge (Donovan) to Secretary of State', 18 October 1949.

95 File 710 (2)—CJK—49, letter from the High Commissioner of the United Kingdom to the Foreign Secretary, 13 October 1949.

96 File 710 (2)—CJK—49, note by C.S. Jha, in notes portion of file.

97 File 710 (2)—CJK—49, note recorded by Foreign Secretary K.P.S. Menon on a noting by Joint Secretary (N) C.S. Jha, 17 October 1949.

98 File 710 (2)—CJK—49, note by C.S. Jha, Joint Secretary (N), 10 November 1949.

99 File 710 (2)—CJK—49, note by K.M. Panikkar, 11 November 1949.

100 *FRUS, 1949, Vol. IX,* 'Telegram from US Charge (Donovan) to Secretary of State', 7 November 1949.

101 'No. 110, Memorandum by Mr Bevin on Recognition of the Chinese Communist Government, 24 October 1949, Chapter 5, *Documents on British Policy Overseas, Series I, Vol. VIII, Britain and China, 1945–1950* (Routledge, 2013), p. 397.

102 File 710 (2)—CJK—49, note given by Deputy High Commissioner Roberts to Foreign Secretary K.P.S. Menon, 4 November 1949.

103 File 710 (2)—CJK—49, letter from K.P.S. Menon to Sir Archibald Nye, 4 November 1949.

104 File 710 (2)—CJK—49, note given by Deputy High Commissioner Roberts on Outcome of Bukit Serene Conference in Singapore.

105 File 710 (2)—CJK—49, telegram from High Commission of India, London, 15 November 1949.

106 *FRUS, 1949, Vol. IX,* 'Memorandum of Conversation by Deputy Assistant Secretary of State for Far Eastern Affairs (Merchant) with British Political Counsellor (Graves)', 23 November 1949.

107 File 710 (2)—CJK—49.

108 Doc. 0129, 'Telegram from Nehru to Attlee', December 1949, *India–China Relations, 1947–2000, A Documentary Study, Vol. II,* introduced and edited by A.S. Bhasin (New Delhi: Geetika Publishers), p. 203.

109 *FRUS, 1949, Vol. IX,* 'Telegram, US Charge (Donovan) to Secretary of State', 4 November 1949

110 *FRUS, 1950, Vol. VI, East Asia and the Pacific,* 'Telegram from the Ambassador in India (Henderson) to the Office-in-Charge of India–Nepal Affairs (Weil)', 30 December 1950.

111 Doc. 0115, 'Note by Prime Minister Dated 17 November 1949', *India–China Relations, 1947–2000, A Documentary Study, Vol. II,* introduced and edited by A.S. Bhasin (New Delhi: Geetika Publishers), pp. 182–83.

112 Doc. 0115, 'Note by Prime Minister Dated 17 November 1949', *India–China Relations, 1947–2000, A Documentary Study, Vol.*

II, introduced and edited by A.S. Bhasin (New Delhi: Geetika Publishers), pp. 182–83.

113   File 710 (2)—CJK—49, note by Girija Shankar Bajpai, 19 November 1949.

114   Doc. 0124, 'Letter from Prime Minister Jawaharlal Nehru to Deputy Prime Minister Vallabhbhai Patel', 6 December 1949, *India–China Relations, 1947–2000, A Documentary Study, Vol. II*, introduced and edited by A.S. Bhasin (New Delhi: Geetika Publishers), p. 196.

115   File 710 (2)—CJK—49.

116   File 710 (2)—CJK—49, telegram from Ministry of External Affairs to certain missions, 20 November 1949.

117   J. Nehru, *Letters to Chief Ministers, 1947–1964, Vol. 1, 1947–1949*, letter dated 1 December 1949, pp. 480–81.

118   Doc. 0140, 'Note on the Meeting Held by the Prime Minister with Foreign Secretary (K.P.S. Menon), K.M. Panikkar and Political Officer (H. Dayal) on 30 December 1949 to Discuss "Policy on Tibet"', *India–China Relations, 1947–2000, A Documentary Study, Vol. II*, introduced and edited by A.S. Bhasin (New Delhi: Geetika Publishers), pp. 217–18.

119   *FRUS, Vol. IX, 1949*, 'Memorandum from Assistant Secretary of State for Far Eastern Affairs (Butterworth) to Secretary of State', December 5, 1949, 'Subject: Reply to Note for Indian Embassy on Question of Recognition of Chinese Communist Regime'.

120   File 710 (2)—CJK—49, top secret telegram from Indian embassy in Washington to New Delhi, 1 December 1949.

121   Doc. 0128, 'Message from the British Prime Minister to the Prime Minister', 18 December 1949, *India–China Relations, 1947–2000, A Documentary Study, Vol. II*, introduced and edited by A.S. Bhasin (New Delhi: Geetika Publishers), pp. 201–02.

122   Doc. 0129, 'Telegram from Nehru to Krishna Menon Containing Message to Mr Attlee, (undated)', *India–China Relations, 1947–2000, A Documentary Study, Vol. II*, introduced and edited by A.S. Bhasin (New Delhi, Geetika Publishers), p. 203.

123   Doc. 0138, 'Telegram from Nehru to Zhou Enlai through the Indian Representative in Nanking', 29 December 1949, *India–China Relations, 1947–2000, A Documentary Study,*

Vol. II, introduced and edited by A.S. Bhasin (New Delhi, Geetika Publishers), p. 214.

124 'No. 114, Mr Bevin to Sir O. Franks (Washington), 16 December 1949, Chapter 5, *Documents on British Policy Overseas, Series I, Vol. VIII, Britain and China, 1945–1950* (Routledge, 2013), p. 432.

Chapter 3: Geneva and Indochina

1   Kevin Ruane, Antony Eden, 'British Diplomacy and the Origins of the Geneva Conference of 1954', *The Historical Journal, March 1994, Vol. 37, No. 1, Cambridge University Press*, pp. 153–72.

2   Doc. 0133, 'Letter, Nehru to Soekarno', 22 December 1949, *India–China Relations, 1947–2000, A Documentary Study, Vol. II*, introduced and edited by A.S. Bhasin (New Delhi: Geetika Publishers), pp. 206–07.

3   *SWJN, Series II, Vol. XIV, Part II, April–July 1950*, 'Cable to Mr Bevin', New Delhi, 24 May 1950, pp. 371–72.

4   *SWJN, Series II, Vol. XIV, Part I, November 1949–April 1950*, 'Note by A.V. Pai, Principal Private Secretary, of Nehru's Remarks to Ambassador Loy Henderson', 8 February 1950, *SWJN, Series II, Vol. XIV, Part II*, April–July 1950.

5   C. Mary Turnbull, *Britain and Vietnam, 1948–1955, War and Society*, 6:2, 104–124, DOI: 10.1179/106980488790304904.

6   No. 1, 'Indo-China: Annual Review for 1954, Sir Hubert Graves to Mr Eden', 5 January 1954, *British Documents on Foreign Affairs (BDFA), Part V (1951–1956, Series E, Asia 1954, Vol. VII)*, LexisNexis, 2008.

7   No. 2, 'Comments on Possible Chinese Aggression and Future French Policy in Indo-China', 12 January 1954, Sir Oliver Harvey to Mr Allen, *BDFA, Part V (1951–1956, Series E, Asia 1954, Vol. VII)*, LexisNexis, 2008.

8   Doc. 499, 'Memorandum of Discussion at 179th Meeting of the NSC', 8 January 1954, *FRUS, 1952–1954, Indochina, Vol. XIII, Part I*.

9   *Doc. 512*, 'Memorandum by C.D. Jackson, Special Assistant to the President', 18 January 1954, *FRUS, 1952–1954, Indochina, Vol. XIII, Part I*.

10   No. 3, 'American Intentions in Indo-China, Sir Roger Makings to Mr Eden', 8 February 1954, *BDFA, Part V (1951–1956, Series E, Asia 1954, Vol. VII)*, LexisNexis, 2008.

11   Doc. 585, 'Memorandum of Discussion at 186th Meeting of the NSC', 26 February 1954, *FRUS, 1952–1954, Indochina, Vol. XIII, Part I*.

12   'Appeal for Ceasefire, Reply to Debate on President's Address in Lok Sabha', 22 February 1954, *SWJN, Series II, Vol. XXV, February 1954–May 1954*.

13   'Cable to Raghavan', 25 February 1954, *SWJN, Series II, Vol. XXV, February 1954–May 1954*.

14   No. 4, 'Nehru's Proposals for a Ceasefire, Sir Hubert Graves to Mr Eden', 27 February 1954, *BDFA, Part V (1951–1956, Series E, Asia 1954, Vol. VII)*, LexisNexis, 2008.

15   No. 7, 'Conversation between the Secretary of State and the Indian High Commissioner', 10 March 1954, 'Telegram from Eden to Sir Hubert Graves', Saigon, *BDFA, Part V (1951–1956, Series E, Asia 1954, Vol. VII)*, LexisNexis, 2008.

16   Anthony Eden, Book 1, Chapter 5, 'War in Indo-China', *Full Circle: The Memoirs of Anthony Eden* (Boston: Houghton Mifflin Co., 1960), pp. 86–120.

17   No. 7, 'Conversation between the Secretary of State and the Indian High Commissioner', 10 March 1954, 'Telegram from Mr Eden to Sir H. Graves', Saigon, *BDFA, Part V (1951–1954, Series E, Asia 1954, Vol. VII)*, LexisNexis 2008.

18   'Principles of Foreign Policy, Intervention in the Lok Sabha', 24–25 March 1954, *SWJN, Series II, Vol. XXV, February–May 1954*.

19   Doc. 649, 'Hagerty Diary', 26 March 1954, *FRUS, 1952–1954, Indochina, Vol. XIII, Part I*.

20   G.L. Mehta, 'Foreign Policy of Dulles', *India Quarterly*, Vol. XIX, No. I (January–March 1963), pp. 3–20, https://www.jstor.org/stable/45068256.

21   Minutes, 'Chairman Mao Zedong's Second Meeting with Nehru', 23 October 1954, Chinese Foreign Ministry Archive 204—00007—15(1), Doc. 0751, *India–China Relations, 1947–2000, A Documentary Study, Vol. II*, introduced and edited by A.S Bhasin (New Delhi: Geetika Publishers), p. 1295.

22   Thomas K. Robb and David J. Gill, 'Divided Action', Chapter 6, *Divided Allies* (Cornell University Press).

23   Anthony Eden, 'War in Indo-China', Book 1, Chapter 5, *Full Circle: The Memoirs of Anthony Eden* (Boston: Houghton Mifflin Co., 1960), pp. 86–120.

24   No. 14 (1) and (2), 'US Views on South-east Asia, Sir Roger Makins to Mr Eden', 3 April 1954, *BDFA, Part V (1951–1956, Series E, Asia 1954, Vol. VII)*, LexisNexis, 2008.

25   Doc. 663, 'The Ambassador in India (Allen) to Department of State', 31 March 1954, *FRUS, 1952–1954, Indochina, Vol. XIII, Part I.*

26   No. 20, 'Indian Views of US Policy, UK High Commissioner in India to CRO', 9 April 1954, *BDFA, Part V (1951–1956, Series E, Asia 1954, Vol. VII)*, LexisNexis, 2008.

27   Doc. 680, 'The Secretary of State to the Embassy in India', 2 April 1954, *FRUS, 1952–1954, Indochina, Vol. XIII, Part I.*

28   'Statement by Dulles, Meeting of the Congress Parliamentary Party', 9 April 1954, *SWJN, Series II, Vol. XXV, February–May 1954.*

29   No. 20, 'UK Views of the Political and Military Situation', CRO to UK High Commissioner in India, 10 April 1954, *BDFA, Part V, 1951–1956, Series E, Asia 1954, Vol. VII)*, LexisNexis 2008.

30   Doc. 686, 'Memorandum for File of Secretary of State', 5 April 1954, *FRUS, 1952–1954, Indochina, Vol. XIII, Part I.*

31   Doc. 692, Secretary of State to the Embassy in the UK, April 4, 1954.

32   Doc. 705, 'Memorandum of Discussion at 192nd Meeting of the NSC', 6 April 1954, *FRUS, 1952–1954, Indochina, Vol. XIII, Part I.*

33   From Richard Nixon's memoirs, as mentioned in footnote to Doc. 705, 'Memorandum of Discussion at 192nd Meeting of the NSC, 6 April 1954, *FRUS, 1952–1954, Indochina, Vol. XIII, Part I.*

34   Doc. 704, 'The Ambassador in the UK (Aldrich) to Department of State', 6 April 1954, *FRUS, 1952–1954, Indochina, Vol. XIII, Part I.*

35   'Indo-China, Memorandum for Cabinet by Secretary of State for Foreign Affairs, Top Secret, C. (54) 134', 7 April 1954, Cabinet

Memoranda, CAB 129/67, Original Reference C 101 (54)—150 (54), 15 March–14 April 1954, National Archives, Kew, United Kingdom. The Cabinet Papers, CAB 129 post-war memoranda (nationalarchives.gov.uk).

36   Doc. 741, 'The Secretary of State to the Department of State', 13 April 1954, *FRUS, 1952–1954, Indochina, Vol. XIII, Part I.*

37   Doc. No. 15, 'Communiqué Issued by Mr Dulles and Mr Eden, London, 13 April 1954, Documents relating to British Involvement in the Indo-China Conflict, 1945–1965, Misc. No. 25 (1965), Presented to Parliament by the Secretary of State for Foreign Affairs, December 1965, London, pp 66–67.

38   Doc. 690, 'Editorial Note', *FRUS, 1952–1954, Indochina, Vol. XIII, Part I.*

39   Cabinet Note by Secretary of State for Foreign Affairs, 'South East Asia', Secret, C. (54) 196, June 14, 1954, Cabinet Memoranda, CAB 129/68, Original Reference C 151 (54)—200 (54), 21 April–15 June 1954, National Archives, Kew, United Kingdom. The Cabinet Papers, CAB 129 post-war memoranda (nationalarchives.gov.uk).

40   Anthony Eden, 'War in Indo-China', Book 1, Chapter 5, *Full Circle: The Memoirs of Anthony Eden* (Boston: Houghton Mifflin Co., 1960), pp. 86–120.

41   Doc. 758, 'Memorandum of Conversation, by Assistant Secretary of State for European Affairs (Merchant)', 18 April 1954, *FRUS 1952–1954, Indochina, Vol. XIII, Part I.*

42   Doc. 770, 'The Secretary of State to the Department of State', 22 April 1954, *FRUS, 1952–1954, Indochina, Vol. XIII, Part I.*

43   Anthony Eden, 'War in Indo-China', Book 1, Chapter 5, *Full Circle: The Memoirs of Anthony Eden* (Boston: Houghton Mifflin Co., 1960), pp. 86–120.

44   Doc. 6 (3), 'South East Asia Defence, Mr Eden to Mr Gore Booth', 21 April 1954, *BDFA, Part V (1951–1956, Series E, Asia, 1954, Vol. VII),* 'Further Correspondence Respecting South East Asia and the Far East (General)', Part VIII, January–December 1954, LexisNexis 2008.

45   No. 16, Indo-China: Attitude of HMG—Paper Prepared by the Foreign Secretary, April 1954, 'Documents relating to British Involvement in the Indo-China Conflict, 1945–1965', Misc. No. 25 (1965), Presented to Parliament by the Secretary of State for Foreign Affairs, December 1965, London, pp. 67–68.

46   Indo-China, Note by the Secretary of the Cabinet, Top Secret, C (54) 155, 27 April 1954, Cabinet Memoranda, CAB 129/68, Original Reference C 151 (54)—200 (54), 21 April–15 June 1954, National Archives, Kew, United Kingdom. The Cabinet Papers, CAB 129 post-war memoranda (nationalarchives.gov.uk).

47   Cabinet Note by Secretary of State for Foreign Affairs, 'South East Asia', Secret, C. (54) 196, 14 June 1954, Cabinet Memoranda, CAB 129/68, Original Reference C 151 (54)—200 (54), 21 April–15 June 1954, National Archives, Kew, United Kingdom. The Cabinet Papers, CAB 129 post-war memoranda (nationalarchives.gov.uk).

48   Anthony Eden, 'Geneva Conference', Book 1, Chapter 6, *Full Circle: The Memoirs of Anthony Eden* (Boston: Houghton Mifflin Co., 1960), pp. 120–64.

49   Doc. 833, 'Record of Secretary of State Briefing for Members of Congress', 5 May 1954, *FRUS, 1952–1954, Indochina, Vol. XIII, Part I.*

50   Doc. 838, 'Memorandum of Discussion at the 195th Meeting of the NSC', 6 May 1954, *FRUS, 1952–1954, Indochina, Vol. XIII, Part I.*

51   M. Brecher, 'Geneva Conference on Indochina', Chapter 4, *India and World Politics: Krishna Menon's View of the World* (London: Oxford University Press, 1968), pp. 44–51.

52   Doc. 0657, 'Telegram, Raghavan from Prime Minister', 16 April 1954, *India–China Relations, 1947–2000, A Documentary History, Vol. II,* edited by A.S. Bhasin (New Delhi: Geetika Publishers, 2018).

53   'Proposals on Indochina, Statement in Parliament', 24 April 1954, *SWJN, Series II, Vol. XXV,* February–May 1954.

54   Doc. 0710, 'Fifth Round of Talks between Prime Minister and
      Chinese Premier Chou Enlai', New Delhi, 27 June 1954, *India–
      China Relations, 1947–2000, A Documentary History, Vol. II,*
      edited by A.S. Bhasin (New Delhi: Geetika Publishers, 2018),
      pp. 1197–1198.

55   'Personal Message for Mr Nehru from Mr Eden', dated
      16 May 1954, Krishna Menon Papers, File No. 920 Part I, Nehru
      Memorial Museum and Library (NMML), New Delhi.

56   Anthony Eden, 'Geneva Conference', Book 1, Chapter 6, *Full
      Circle: The Memoirs of Anthony Eden* (Boston: Houghton Mifflin
      Co., 1960), p. 120.

57   Subimal Dutt, 'Indo-China', Chapter 6, *With Nehru in the
      Foreign Office* (Calcutta: Minerva, 1997), pp. 60–71.

58   M. Brecher, 'Geneva Conference on Indochina', Chapter 4, *India
      and World Politics: Krishna Menon's View of the World* (London:
      Oxford University Press, 1968), pp. 44–51.

59   Subimal Dutt, 'Indo-China', Chapter 6, *With Nehru in the
      Foreign Office* (Calcutta: Minerva, 1997), pp. 60–71.

60   K.S. Shelvankar, 'Armistice in Indochina, Negotiations at
      Geneva', *The Hindu,* 18 May 1954.

61   K.S. Shelvankar, 'Settlement in Indochina, Menon's Mission',
      The Hindu, 25 May 1954.

62   *Indian Views of Sino-Indian Relations*, No. 1, February 1956,
      Indian Press Digests, Monograph Series, Institute of International
      Studies, University of California, Berkeley, accessed at the Hoover
      Institution, Stanford University, 12 October 2023.

63   K.S. Shelvankar, 'Private Talks in Geneva, India's Initiative
      Welcomed by Delegates', *The Hindu*, 27 May 1954.

64   K.S. Shelvankar, 'Eden-Molotov Accord, An Encouraging
      Feature', *The Hindu*, 30 May 1954.

65   Doc. 596, Smith–Menon Meeting, Geneva, US Delegation to
      Department of State, 25 May 1954, *FRUS, 1952–1954, Geneva
      Conference, Vol. XVI.*

66   Doc. 607, Smith–Eden–Chauvel Meeting, Geneva, US
      Delegation to the Department of State, 26 May 1954, *FRUS,
      1952–1954, Geneva Conference, Vol. XVI.*

67 *The Hindu,* 'Settlement in Indochina, Vital Role of India', 21 July 1954.

68 Doc. 866, 'Memorandum of Conversation by Secretary of State', 11 May 1954, *FRUS, 1952–1954, Indochina, Vol. XIII, Part I.*

69 M. Brecher, 'Geneva Conference on Indochina', Chapter 4, *India and World Politics: Krishna Menon's View of the World* (London: Oxford University Press, 1968), pp. 44–51.

70 Doc. 6 (10), 'Mr Eden to Foreign Office (Message Meant for Mr Casey)', 22 May 1954, *BDFA (Part V, 1951–1956, Series E, Asia, 1954, Vol. VII),* 'Further Correspondence Respecting South East Asia and the Far East (General)', Part VIII, January–December 1954, LexisNexis 2008.

71 Cabinet Memorandum by Secretary of State for Foreign Affairs, 'The Geneva Conference', Secret, C. (54) 177, 24 May 1954.

72 Anthony Eden, 'Geneva Conference', Book 1, Chapter 6, *Full Circle: The Memoirs of Anthony Eden* (Boston: Houghton Mifflin Co., 1960), p. 120–64.

73 Cable from Zhou Enlai, 'Regarding High Level Meeting with Foreign Secretary Eden', 1 May 1954, Wilson Center Digital Archive, PRC FMA 206-Y049, translated by Gao Bei, https://digitalarchive.wilsoncenter.org/document/110604.

74 'Notes on Conversation between Mr Krishna Menon and Mr Chou Enlai, 14 July 1954 (2–3.20 p.m.)', Krishna Menon Papers, File No. 916, NMML, Delhi.

75 'Notes on Conversation between Mr Krishna Menon and Mr Chou Enlai, 15 July 1954 (11.30 a.m. to 1.10 p.m.)', Krishna Menon Papers, File No. 916, NMML, Delhi.

76 Cable from Zhou Enlai, 'Regarding Situation of the First Plenary Situation, 9 May 1954, Wilson Center Digital Archive, PRC FMA 206-Y0049, translated by Chen Zhihong, https://digitalarchive.wilsoncenter.org/document/110607

77 'Cable from Zhou Enlai, Premier's Intentions and Plans to Visit India', 22 June 1954, Wilson Center Digital Archive, PRC FMA 203-00005-01, translated by Jeffrey Wang, https://digitalarchive.wilsoncenter.org/document/112347.

78   M. Brecher, 'Geneva Conference on Indochina', Chapter 4, *India and World Politics: Krishna Menon's View of the World* (London: Oxford University Press, 1968), pp. 44–51.

79   Footnote to cable to V.K. Krishna Menon, 21 June 1954, *SWJN, Series II, Vol. XXVI, June–September 1954.*

80   To C. Rajagopalachari, 29 July 1954, *SWJN, Series II, Vol XXVI, June–September 1954.*

81   *Indian Views of Sino-Indian Relations*, No. 1, February 1956, Indian Press Digests, Monograph Series, Institute of International Studies, University of California at Berkeley, accessed at the Hoover Institution, Stanford University, 12 October 2023.

82   To G.L. Mehta, June 29, 1954, *SWJN, Series XII, Vol. XXVI, June–September 1954*, pp. 355–56.

83   G.L. Mehta papers, NMML, Delhi.

84   Cable to V.K. Krishna Menon, 20 July 1954, p. 358.

85   G.L. Mehta papers, NMML, Delhi.

86   'Notes on Conversation between Mr Nehru and Mr Chou Enlai, 16 July 1954 (10 p.m.)', Krishna Menon Papers, File No. 916, NMML, Delhi.

Chapter 4: The First Taiwan Strait Crisis

1   *Foreign Relations of the United States, 1952–1954, China and Japan, Vol, XIV Part I*, edited by David W. Mahon and Harriet Schwar (Washington: USG Printing Office, 1985), hereafter cited as *FRUS, 1952–1954, Vol. XIV, Part I.*

2   'Statement by the President, Truman on Korea', 27 June 1950, Wilson Center Digital Archive, Public Papers of the Presidents, Harry S. Truman, 1945–1953, https://digitalarchive.wilsoncenter.org/document/116192.

3   Doc. 68, 'Memorandum of Conversation by Assistant Secretary of State for Far Eastern Affairs (Allison)', 28 January 1953, *FRUS, 1952–1954, Vol. XIV, Part I.*

4   'Annual Message to the Congress of the State of the Union', 2 February 1953, https://eisenhowerlibrary.gov.

5   Doc. 73, 'Memorandum by Assistant Secretary of State for Far Eastern Affairs (Allison) to President', 2 February 1953, *FRUS, 1952–1954, Vol. XIV, Part I.*

6   Doc. 130, 'The Secretary of State to Certain Diplomatic and Consular Officers', 29 July 1953, *FRUS, 1952–1954, Vol. XIV, Part I.*

7   Doc. 149, 'Statement of Policy by NSC—US Policy Towards Communist China', 6 November 1953, *FRUS, 1952–1954, Vol. XIV, Part I.*

8   Doc. 150, 'Statement of Policy by National Security Council: US Objectives and Courses of Action with Reference to Formosa', 6 November 1953, *FRUS, 1952–1954, Vol. XIV, Part I.*

9   Doc. 173, Memorandum by Assistant Secretary for Far Eastern Affairs (Robertson) to Secretary of State, 'Bilateral Pact with China', 25 February 1954, *FRUS, 1952–1954, Vol. XIV, Part I.*

10   Doc. 182, 'Memorandum by Assistant Secretary for Far Eastern Affairs (Robertson) to Secretary of State: Bilateral Pact with China', 31 March 1954, *FRUS, 1952–1954, Vol. XIV, Part I.*

11   Letter, Trevelyan to Eden, Peking, 31 August 1954, FO 371/110216, 'Foreign Policy of the Chinese People's Government', 1954 (National Archives, Kew), pp. 66–67, accessed on April 2023.

12   Doc. 196, 'Memorandum of Conversation by Special Assistant to the President for National Security Affairs (Cutler)', 22 May 1954, *FRUS, 1952–1954, Vol. XIV, Part I.*

13   'Telegram, CCP Central Committee to Zhou Enlai, Concerning Policies and Measures in the Struggle against the United States and Chiang Kai-shek after the Geneva Conference', 27 July 1954, Wilson Center Digital Archive, PRC FMA, translated by Chen Zhihong, https://digitalarchive.wilsoncengter.org/document/111050.

14   'Memorandum of Conversation, between Soviet Premier Georgy Malenkov and Zhou Enlai', 29 July 1954, Wilson Center Digital Archive, AVPRF f. 06, o. 13a, d. 25, II. 8, obtained by Paul Wingrove and translated by Gary Goldberg, https://digitalarchive.wilsoncenter.org/document/111272.

15 'Telephone Conversation between Dulles and British Ambassador Shri Roger Makins', 26 July 1954, *FRUS, 1952–1954, Vol. XIV, Part I.*

16 Doc. 284, 'The President to the Acting Secretary of State', 8 September 1954, *FRUS, 1952–1954, Vol. XIV, Part I.*

17 Doc. 298, 'Memorandum by Assistant Secretary of State for European Affairs (Merchant) to Roderic L O'Connor, Special Assistant to the Secretary of State', 19 September 1954, *FRUS, 1952–1954, Vol. XIV, Part I.*

18 'Memorandum of Discussion, 214th Meeting of the National Security Council', 12 September 1954, *FRUS, 1952–1954, Vol. XIV, Part I.*

19 Docs 305, 307, 'Secretary of State to Department of State', London, 27 September and 29 September 1954.

20 Doc. 261, 'Memorandum by Acting Secretary of State to Assistant Secretary of State for Far Eastern Affairs (Robertson)', 1 September 1954, *FRUS, 1952–1954, Vol. XIV, Part I.*

21 Doc. 345, 'Memorandum by Acting Secretary of State to President', 15 October 1954, *FRUS, 1952–1954, Vol. XIV, Part I.*

22 PRO, CAB 128/27, CM (54) 66, 15 October 1954, in footnote, 'Anglo American Tensions over the Chinese Offshore Islands', Tracie Lee Steele, London School of Economics, September 1991 (ProQuest LLC, 2014), p. 37.

23 'US Policy towards Nationalist China in Formosa (Taiwan): Situation in Quemoy (Kinmen); Resolution before UN Security Council; UK Position, November 1954' (Government Papers, National Archives, Kew, FO 371/110327, Folder 7), p. 5.

24 Ibid., 'Telegram from Eden to the British Ambassador in Washington', 4 November 1954, p. 12.

25 Ibid., 'Telegram from British Foreign Secretary Eden to the British Ambassador in Washington', 4 November 1954, p. 42.

26 Ibid., 'Telegram from the British Ambassador in Washington to Eden', 5 November 1954, pp. 45–46.

27 Doc. 383, 'Memorandum of Conversation by Assistant Secretary of State for European Affairs (merchant), November 5, 1954, *FRUS, 1952–1954, Vol. XIV, Part I.*

28   'US Policy towards Nationalist China in Formosa (Taiwan): Situation in Quemoy (Kinmen); Resolution before UN Security Council; UK Position, November 1954)' (Government Papers, National Archives, Kew, FO 371/110327, Folder 7), 'Telegram from British Ambassador in Washington to the Foreign Office', 6 November 1954, p. 70.

29   'Personal Message from Jawaharlal Nehru to Anthony Eden', 26 June 1954, 'Political Relations between India and the Chinese People's Government' (Government Papers, National Archives, Kew, FO 371/112210), accessed on 16 January 2023.

30   Doc. 0708, 'Third Session of Talks between Prime Minister and Zhou Enlai', Delhi, 26 June 1954, *India–China Relations, 1947–2000, A Documentary Study, Vol. I,* introduced and edited by A.S. Bhasin (New Delhi: Geetika Publishers, 2018), pp. 1199–200.

31   Doc. 0751, 'Chinese Version of the Second Meeting between Nehru and Mao Tse-tung', Peking, 23 October 1954, Chinese Foreign Ministry Archive, PRC FMA 204-0000715 (1), p. 1303.

32   Doc. 1009, 'The US Charge in India (Taylor) to Department of State', 26 May 1952, *FRUS, 1952–1954, Africa and South Asia, Vol. XI, Part II.*

33   Doc. 80, 'The Ambassador in India (Bowles) to Department of State', 10 February 1953, *FRUS, 1952–1954, China and Japan, Vol XI, Part I.*

34   M.K. Rasgotra, 'Washington DC: Early Warnings of an Indo-US Rift', Chapter 6, *A Life in Diplomacy* (New Delhi: Penguin, 2013).

35   Doc. 1044, *FRUS, 1952–1954, Africa and South Asia, Vol. XI, Part II.*

36   *SWJN, Series II, Vol. XXIII,* July–September 1953.

37   Doc. 1059, 'Secretary of State to US Embassy in India', 3 September 1953, *FRUS, 1952–1954, Africa and South Asia, Vol. XI, Part II.*

38   Doc. 404, 'Communist Courses of Action in Asia through 1957', National Intelligence Estimate, 23 November 1954, *FRUS, 1952–1954, China and Japan, Vol. XIV, Part I.*

39   J. Nehru, *Letters to Chief Ministers, Vol II, 1950–1952,* edited by G. Parthasarathi (New Delhi: Jawaharlal Nehru Memorial Fund); letter dated 15 July 1950, pp. 142–44.

40   'Talks between Jawaharlal Nehru and Chou Enlai', Delhi, 27 June 1954, *India–China Relations, 1947–2000, A Documentary Study, Vol. II,* introduced and edited by A.S. Bhasin (New Delhi: Geetika Publishers), p. 1191.

41   Doc. 0751, 'Chinese Version of the Second Meeting between Nehru and Mao Tse-tung', Peking, 23 October 1954, Chinese Foreign Ministry Archive, PRC FMA 204-0000715 (1), pp. 1294–295.

42   J. Nehru, *Letters to Chief Ministers, Vol II, 1950–1952,* edited by G. Parthasarathi (New Delhi: Jawaharlal Nehru Memorial Fund); letter dated 18 August 1950, p. 167.

43   Ibid., letter dated 1 February 1951.

44   Doc. No. 264, 'Memorandum by Assistant Secretary of State for Near East, South Asia and African Affairs (Jernegan) to Assistant Secretary of State for Far Eastern Affairs (Robertson)', 27 August 1954, *FRUS, 1952–1954, China and Japan, Vol XI, Part I.*

45   'Text of Prime Minister's Speech in Lok Sabha on Foreign Affairs Debate', 29 September 1954; 'Statements by Mr Nehru and Others on Indian Foreign Policy; Political Relations between India and China; Attitude towards Foreign Possessions in India', July–December 1954 (Government Papers, National Archives, Kew, FO 371-112197, Folder 2).

46   'Telegram for the UK High Commissioner to the Commonwealth Relations Office', I October 1954, 'Nehru's Statement in the Lok Sabha', 1 October 1954, 'Statements by Mr Nehru and Others on Indian Foreign Policy; Political Relations between India and China; Attitude towards Foreign Possessions in India', July–December 1954 (Government Papers, National Archives, Kew, FO 371-112197, Folder 2).

47   'Text of Prime Minister's Speech in Lok Sabha on Foreign Affairs Debate', 29 September 1954, 'Statements by Mr Nehru and Others on Indian Foreign Policy; Political Relations between India and China; Attitude towards Foreign Possessions in India', July–December 1954 (Government Papers, National Archives, Kew, FO 371-112197, Folder 2).

48   Doc. 0759, 'Note by Prime Minister Jawaharlal Nehru on Implications of His China Visit', Delhi, 14 November 1954, *India–China Relations, 1947–2000, A Documentary Study, Vol. II*, introduced and edited by A.S. Bhasin (New Delhi: Geetika Publishers), pp. 1355–358.

49   'Note by Sir Ian Kilpatrick to Eden', 24 November 1954, FO 371/110216, 'Foreign Policy of the Chinese People's Government' (Government Papers, National Archives, Kew, 1954), accessed on 22 April 2023.

50   'Memo recorded by Mr Desmond Donnelly', 20 November 1954, 'Statements by Mr Nehru and Others on Indian Foreign Policy; Political Relations between India and China; Attitude towards Foreign Possessions in India', July–December 1954 (Government Papers, National Archives, Kew, FO 371-112197, Folder 2).

51   Doc. 393, 'British High Commissioner in India (Clutterbuck) to Commonwealth Relations Office', 10 November 1954, *FRUS, 1952–1954, China and Japan, Vol XI, Part I.*

52   'Interview with Mr Nehru, Taya Zinkin', *Manchester Guardian*, 16 November 1954, 'Statements by Mr Nehru and Others on Indian Foreign Policy; Political Relations between India and China; Attitude towards Foreign Possessions in India', July–December 1954 (Government Papers, National Archives, Kew, FO 371-112197, Folder 2).

53   Doc. 411, 'World Reactions to Certain Possible US Courses of Action against Communist China', National Intelligence Estimate, 28 November 1954, *FRUS, 1952–1954, China and Japan, Vol XI, Part I.*

54   'Telegram from Commonwealth Relations Office to UK High Commissioner in Delhi', 5 November 1954, 'US Policy towards Nationalist China in Formosa (Taiwan), Situation in Quemoy (Kinmen), Resolution before the UN Security Council; UK Position, November 1954' (Government Papers, National Archives, Kew, FO371,10327, Folder 7), p. 116.

55   'Political Relations between India and the United Kingdom',
      Government Papers, National Archives, Kew, accessed on 16
      January 2023, 'Minute by Mr J. Garner on Talk with Sir R.
      Pillai', London, 29 November 1954, File 371/112213.

56   Letter from Mehta to Nehru, 1 December 1954, 'Top Secret,
      No. 149-A/54', G.L. Mehta Papers, File 1, Nehru Memorial
      Museum and Library, New Delhi.

57   'Memorandum by Deputy Secretary of State (Murphy) to
      Assistant Secretary of State for Near East, South Asia and African
      Affairs (Byroade)', 18 November 1954, *FRUS, 1952–1954,
      China and Japan, Vol XI, Part I.*

58   'Zhou Enlai's Speech to the CPPCC', 26 December 1954,
      FO 371/110216, 'Foreign Policy of the Chinese People's
      Government' (National Archives, Kew, 1954).

59   'Telegram from Trevelyan to British Foreign Office',
      7 December 1954, 'US Policy Towards Nationalist China in
      Formosa (Taiwan; Situation I Quemoy (Kinmen)', Resolution
      before the UN Security Council, UK Position, December 1954'
      (Government Papers, National Archives, Kew, 371/110241,
      Folder 11), accessed on 16 January 2023.

60   'Transcript of Conversation between Zhou Enlai and Humphrey
      Trevelyan', 5 January 1955, Wilson Center Digital Archive,
      Zhou Enlai Waijiao Wenxuan (Selected Diplomatic Papers
      of Zhou Enlai), translated by Simon Schuchat (Beijing:
      Zhongyang Wenxuan, 1990), pp. 94–105, https://digitalarchive.
      wilsoncenter.org/document/260506.

61   Doc. 12, 'US Policy towards Formosa and Government
      of Republic of China', National Security Council Report,
      15 January 1955, *FRUS, 1955–1957, China, Vol. II*, edited
      by Harriet Schwar (Washington: USG Printing Office, 1986),
      hereafter referred to as *FRUS, 1955–1957, China, Vol. II*; Doc.
      54, 'Memorandum of Conversation between the Secretary of
      State and the British Ambassador (Makins)', 28 January 1955,
      FRUS, 1955–1957, China, Vol. II.

62   Doc. 25, 'Memorandum of Conversation, Department of State',
      20 January 1955, *FRUS, 1955–1957, China, Vol. II.*

63   Doc. 34, 'Message from President to Congress', 24 January 1955, *FRUS, 1955–1957, China, Vol. II.*

64   Doc. 41, 'Letter from President Eisenhower to British Prime Minister Churchill', 25 January 1955, *FRUS, 1955–1957, China, Vol. II.*

65   Doc. 51, 'Memorandum from the British Embassy in Washington to Department of State', 28 January 1955, *FRUS, 1955–1957, China, Vol. II.*

66   'Telegram from the British Embassy in Peking to the Foreign Office', 25 January 1955, 'US Policy Towards Nationalist China in Formosa (Taiwan); Position of Quemoy (Kinmen) and Matsu Islands; Discussion on the Future with Communist China'; UK and Commonwealth Views on the Future of Formosa, January 1955 (Taiwan, Folder 3) (Government Papers, National Archives, Kew, FO 371/115025), p. 62, accessed on 1 February 2023.

67   Doc. 51, 'Memorandum from the British Embassy in Washington to the Department of State', 28 January 1955, *FRUS, 1955–1957, China, Vol. II.*

68   'Telegram from the British Embassy in Peking to the Foreign Office', 25 January 1955, 'US Policy Towards Nationalist China in Formosa (Taiwan); Position of Quemoy (Kinmen) and Matsu Islands; Discussion on the Future with Communist China'; UK and Commonwealth Views on the Future of Formosa', January 1955 (Taiwan, Folder 3) (Government Papers, National Archives, Kew, FO 371/115025), pp. 82–83), accessed on 1 February 2023.

69   'Telegram from Sir Roger Makins, British Ambassador in Washington to the Foreign Office', 9 February 1955, FO 371-115035, February 1955 (Government Papers, National Archives, Kew, Folder 13), accessed on 1 February 2023.

70   Doc. 54, 'Memorandum of Conversation between the Secretary of State and the British Ambassador (Makins)', 28 January 1955, *FRUS, 1955–1957, China, Vol. II.*

71   Note from A. Rumbold to J.S. Mehta, 25 January 1955, 'US Policy towards Nationalist China in Formosa (Taiwan); Position of Quemoy (Kinmen) and Matsu Islands; Discussion on the Future with Communist China'; UK and Commonwealth Views on the Future of Formosa, January 1955 (Taiwan, Folder 3)

(Government Papers, National Archives, Kew, FO 371/115025),
pp. 97–98, accessed on 1 February 2023.

72   'Message (Personal) from Eden to Nehru', 2 February 1955,
File 371-115033, Taiwan, February 1955 (Government Papers,
National Archives, Kew, Folder 11), pp. 77–78, accessed on
31 January 2023.

73   Doc. 76, 'Telegram from US Ambassador in the UK (Aldrich)
to Department of State', 3 February 1955, *FRUS, 1955–1957,
China, Vol. II.*

74   Doc. 82, 'Telegram from US Ambassador in the UK (Aldrich)
to Department of State', 4 February 1955, *FRUS, 1955–1957,
China, Vol. II.*

75   Doc. 0798, 'Telegram from Prime Minister to Raghavan',
London, 10 February 1955, *India–China Relations, 1947–
2000, A Documentary Study, Vol. II,* introduced and edited by
A.S. Bhasin (New Delhi: Geetika Publishers), pp. 1436–437.

76   Doc. 83, 'Memorandum from Assistant Secretary of State for
European Affairs (Merchant) to Secretary of State', 4 February
1955, *FRUS, 1955–1957, China, Vol. II.*

77   Doc. 84, 'Telegram from Acting Secretary of State to US
Ambassador in the UK (Aldrich)', 4 February 1955, *FRUS,
1955–1957, China, Vol. II.*

78   Doc. 104, 'Letter from President Eisenhower to Prime Minister
Churchill', 10 February 1955, *FRUS, 1955–1957, China, Vol. II.*

79   Trevelyan reported his conversation with the Indian Ambassador
in Beijing in early February to the British Foreign Office, saying
that Zhou Enlai had told the Indians that China was more or less
in agreement with the Soviet idea. 'Telegram from Trevelyan to
the British Foreign Office', 8 February 1955, File 371-115003,
February 1955 (Taiwan) (Government Papers, National
Archives, Kew, Folder 111).

80   'Telegram from US Ambassador to USSR (Bohlen) to Department
of State', 5 February 1955, *FRUS, 1955–1957, China, Vol. II.*

81   'Telegram from British Foreign Office to the UK Delegation
to the United Nations', 11 February 1955, File 371-115035,

Taiwan, 1955 (Government Papers, National Archives, Kew, Folder 13), accessed on 1 February 2023.

82   Doc. 152, 'Memorandum of Conversation, Department of State', 14 March 1955, *FRUS, 1955–1957, China, Vol. II.*

83   Doc. 156, 'Memorandum of Conversation, Department of State', 16 March 1955, *FRUS, 1955–1957, China, Vol. II.*

84   Doc. 0794, 'Extracts from the Minutes of the Commonwealth Prime Ministers Conference', London, 31 January 1955, *India–China Relations, 1947–2000, A Documentary Study, Vol. II,* introduced and edited by A.S. Bhasin (New Delhi: Geetika Publishers), pp. 1427–430.

85   'Note to Indira Gandhi', *SWJN, Series II, Vol. XXVIII*, February–May 1955, pp. 158–59.

86   'Cable to N. Raghavan', 3 February 1955, *SWJN, Series II, Vol. XXVIII*, February–May 1955, pp. 160–61.

87   'Cable to Raghavan', 10 February 1955, *SWJN, Series II, Vol. XXVIII*, February–May 1955, pp. 168–69.

88   'Note by Canadian Foreign Minister Lester Pearson to the Canadian High Commissioner to India', 21 February 1955, 'United States Policy towards Nationalist China in Formosa (Taiwan); Position of Quemoy (Kinmen) and Matsu Islands, Discussion on Future with Communist Chinese; UK and Commonwealth Views on Future of Formosa', February–March 1955 (Taiwan) (Government Papers, National Archives, Kew, 1955, Folder 18), FO 371/115040, Folder 18), pp. 58–60, accessed on 16 January 2023.

89   'Canadian High Commissioner Reports on Meetings with Nehru and Pillai', 26 February 1955, 'United States Policy towards Nationalist China in Formosa (Taiwan); Position of Quemoy (Kinmen) and Matsu Islands; Discussion on Future with Communist Chinese; UK and Commonwealth Views on Future of Formosa', February–March 1955 (Taiwan) (Government Papers, National Archives, Kew, 1955, FO 371/115040, Folder 18), pp 65–67, accessed on 16 January 2023.

90   Doc. 104, 'Letter from Eisenhower to Churchill', 10 February 1955, *FRUS, 1955–1957, China, Vol. II.*

91 'United States Policy towards Nationalist China in Formosa (Taiwan); position of Quemoy (Kinmen) and Matsu Islands; Discussion on Future with Communist Chinese; UK and Commonwealth Views on Future of Formosa', February–March 1955 (Taiwan) (Government Papers, National Archives, Kew, FO 371-115040, Folder 18), accessed on 30 January 2023, hereafter cited as (Government Papers, National Archives, Kew, FO 371-115040, Folder 18), accessed on 30 January 2023.

92 Doc. 119, 'Telegram from Secretary of State to the US Ambassador to the UK', 18 February 1955, *FRUS, 1955–1957, China, Vol. II.*

93 'Telegram from Secretary of State Anthony Eden to Prime Minister Churchill', Bangkok, 25 February 1955 (Government Papers, National Archives, Kew, FO 371-115040, Folder 18), pp. 4–7, accessed on 30 January 2023.

94 'Record of Conversation between Zhou Enlai and Trevelyan', Beijing, 25 February 1955, (Government Papers, National Archives, Kew, FO 371-115040, Folder 18), pp. 38–40, accessed on 30 January 2023.

95 'Record of Interview with Zhou Enlai', 28 February 1955, 'United States Policy towards Nationalist China in Formosa (Taiwan); position of Quemoy (Kinmen) and Matsu Islands; Discussion on Future with Communist Chinese; UK and Commonwealth Views on Formosa', February–March 1955 (Government Papers, National Archives, Kew, 1955, FO 371-115040, Folder 18), pp. 136–38, accessed on 16 January 2023.

96 'Telegram from Commonwealth Relations Office to UK Missions in the Commonwealth', 2 March 1955, 'United States Policy towards Nationalist China in Formosa (Taiwan); Position of Quemoy (Kinmen) and Matsu Islands; Discussion on Future with Communist Chinese; UK and Commonwealth views on Future of Formosa', February–March 1955 (Taiwan) (Government Papers, National Archives, Kew, 1955, FO 371-115040, Folder 18), pp. 162, accessed on 16 January 2023.

97 Doc. 143, 'Letter from British Ambassador (Makins) to Secretary of State', 7 March 1955, *FRUS, 1955–1957, China, Vol. II.*

98   'Telegram from Commonwealth Relations Office to UK High Commissioner in New Delhi', 11 March 1955, 'United States Policy towards Nationalist China in Formosa (Taiwan); Position of Quemoy (Kinmen) and Matsu Islands; Discussion on Future with Communist Chinese; UK and Commonwealth Views on Future of Formosa', February–March 1955 (Taiwan) (Government Papers, National Archives, Kew, 1955, FO 371-115040, Folder 18), pp. 183–84, accessed on 16 January 2023.

99   'Letter from Mehta to Prime Minister Nehru, Top Secret, No. 53-A/55', 17 March 1955, *G.L. Mehta Papers*, File 1 (New Delhi: Nehru Memorial Museum and Library).

100 Doc. 165, 'Memorandum of Conversation, Department of State', 24 March 1955, *FRUS, 1955–1957, China, Vol. II*.

101 Ibid.

102 Doc. 168, 'Message from Foreign Secretary Eden to Secretary of State', 25 March 1955, *FRUS, 1955–1957, China, Vol. II*.

103 Doc. 177, 'Letter from President Eisenhower to Prime Minister Churchill', 29 March 1955, *FRUS, 1955–1957, China, Vol. II*.

104 Doc. 157, 'United Kingdom Appreciation of Far Eastern Situation', Memorandum received from the British Ambassador (Makins), 16 March 1955, *FRUS, 1955–1957, China, Vol. II*.

105 Doc. 158, 'Communist Capabilities and Intentions with Respect to the Offshore Islands and Taiwan through 1955, and Communist and Non-communist Reactions with Respect to the Defence of Taiwan', National Intelligence Estimate, 16 March 1955, *FRUS, 1955–1957, China, Vol. II*.

106 Doc. 189, 'Memorandum from the President to the Secretary of State', 5 April 1955, *FRUS, 1955–1957, China, Vol. II*.

107 Doc. 193, 'Memorandum of Conversation, Department of State', 7 April 1955, *FRUS, 1955–1957, China, Vol. II*.

108 Doc. 216, 'Telegram from Ambassador in Indonesia (Cummings) to Department of State', 23 April 1955, *FRUS, 1955–1957, China, Vol. II*.

109 Chapter 7, *Diplomacy of Contemporary China*, edited by Han Nianlong (Hong Kong: New Horizon Press, 1990), pp. 99–100.

110 Doc. 222, 'Editorial Note', *FRUS, 1955–1957, China, Vol. II.*

111 Doc. 232, 'Telegram from Secretary of State to US Embassy in Pakistan', 30 April 1955, *FRUS, 1955–1957, China, Vol. II.*

112 'Summary of the Views of Afro-Asian Countries on the Taiwan Issue at the Afro-Asian Conference', 27 May 1955, Wilson Center Digital Archive, PRC, FMA 207-00018-01, 1-4, obtained by Amitav Acharya and translated by Yang Shanhou, https://digitalarchive.wilsoncenter.org/document/114694.

113 J. Nehru, *Letters to Chief Ministers, Vol. IV, 1954–56*, edited by G. Parthasarathi (New Delhi: Jawaharlal Nehru Memorial Fund); letter dated 28 April 1955.

114 Ibid., letter dated 20 May 1955.

115 Doc. 234, /Telegram from Ambassador in India (Cooper) to Department of State', 1 May 1955, *FRUS, 1955–1957, China, Vol. II.*

116 Doc. 244, 'Telegram from Acting Secretary of State to US Embassy in India', 7 May 1955, *FRUS, 1955–1957, China, Vol. II.*

117 No. 3, 'Krishna Menon's Interview with Premier Chou En-lai on Wednesday, 18 May 1955', File 347, Part II, Nehru Memorial Museum and Library, New Delhi.

118 No. 1, 'Krishna Menon's Interview with Premier Chou En-lai on Thursday, 12 May 1955', File 347, Part II, Nehru Memorial Museum and Library, New Delhi.

119 Ibid.

120 No. 2, 'Krishna Menon's Interview with Premier Chou En-lai on Sunday, 15 May 1955', File 347, Part II, Nehru Memorial Museum and Library, New Delhi.

121 No. 3, 'Krishna Menon's Interview with Premier Chou En-lai on Wednesday, 18 May 1955', File 347, Part II, Nehru Memorial Museum and Library, New Delhi.

122 No. 4, 'Krishna Menon's Interview with Premier Chou En-lai on Thursday, 19 May 1955', File 347, Part II, Nehru Memorial Museum and Library, New Delhi.

123 'Minutes of Conversation between Premier Zhou Enlai and British Charge d'Affaires Humphrey Trevelyan, 26 May 1955,

Wilson Center Digital Archive, PRC, FMA 207-00010-16, 61-69, translated by Yafeng Xia, https://digitalarchive.wilsoncenter.org/document/110837.

124   Doc. 257, 'Telegram from Secretary of State to Embassy in India', 24 May 1955, *FRUS, 1955–1957, China, Vol. II.*

125   'Letter from Indian Ambassador (Mehta) to President Eisenhower', 27 May 1955, *FRUS, 1955–1957, China, Vol. II.*

126   Chapter 9, *Diplomacy of Contemporary China*, edited by Han Nianlong (Hong Kong: New Horizon Press, 1990), pp. 121–22. This outreach was made known to Washington but was withheld from New Delhi.

127   *The MacMillan Diaries: The Cabinet Years, 1950–1957*, edited by Peter Catterall (MacMillan, 2003), p. 433.

128   Doc. 262, 'Memorandum of Substance of Conversation', Peking, 26 May 1955, *FRUS, 1955–1957, China, Vol. II.*

129   'Top Secret Note No. 119-A/55', 14 June 1955, recorded by G.L. Mehta, Indian Ambassador in Washington, *G.L. Mehta Papers*, File 1, Nehru Memorial Museum and Library, New Delhi.

130   Doc. 269, 'Memorandum of a Conversation with the President', White House, 14 June 1955, *FRUS, 1955–1957, China, Vol. II.*

131   'Top Secret Note No. 119-A/55, 14 June 1955, recorded by G.L. Mehta, Indian Ambassador in Washington, *G.L. Mehta Papers*, File 1, Nehru Memorial Museum and Library, New Delhi.

132   Doc. 269, 'Memorandum of a Conversation with the President', White House, 14 June 1955, *FRUS, 1955–1957, China, Vol. II.*

133   Doc. 270, 'Memorandum of a Conversation, Department of State', 14 June 1955, *FRUS, 1955–1957, China, Vol. II.*

134   *The MacMillan Diaries: The Cabinet Years, 1950–1957*, edited by Peter Catterall, (MacMillan, 2003), p. 439.

135   Doc. 273, 'Memorandum of Conversation between President and Secretary of State', San Francisco, 19 June 1955, *FRUS, 1955–1957, China, Vol. II.*

136   *The MacMillan Diaries: The Cabinet Years, 1950–1957*, edited by Peter Catterall (MacMillan, 2003), pp. 440–41.

137   Doc. 283, 'Memorandum of Conversation, Department of State', 1 July 1955, *FRUS, 1955–1957, China, Vol. II.*

138   Ibid.

139   'Top Secret Note No. 124-A/55', 1 July 1955, Note Recorded by G.L. Mehta, Indian Ambassador in Washington, on Conversation with Secretary of State Dulles on 1 July 1955, *G.L. Mehta Papers*, File 1, Nehru Memorial Museum and Library, New Delhi.

140   Doc. 283, 'Memorandum of Conversation, Department of State', 1 July 1955, *FRUS, 1955–1957, China, Vol. II.*

141   'Top Secret Note No. 124-A/55', 1 July 1955, Note Recorded by G.L. Mehta, Indian Ambassador in Washington, on Conversation with Secretary of State Dulles on 1 July 1955, *G.L. Mehta Papers*, File 1, Nehru Memorial Museum and Library, New Delhi.

142   'Top Secret Telegram from Krishna Menon to Prime Minister Nehru', 2 July 1955, File No. 359, *Krishna Menon Papers*, Nehru Memorial Museum and Library, New Delhi.

143   'Top Secret Note No. 125-A/55, 6 July 1955, Note Regarding Mr Krishna Menon's Conversation with Secretary of State Dulles on 6 July, *G.L. Mehta Papers*, File 1, Nehru Memorial Museum and Library, New Delhi.

144   Doc. 288, 'Memorandum of Conversation, Department of State', 6 July 1955, *FRUS, 1955–1957, China, Vol. II.*

145   Michael Brecher, 'Suez 1956', Chapter 6, *India and World Politics: Krishna Menon's View of the World* (London: Oxford University Press, 1968), pp. 62–77.

146   'Top Secret Note No. 126-A/55, 6 July 1955, Note Regarding Mr Krishna Menon's Conversation with President Eisenhower on 6 July, *G.L. Mehta Papers*, File 1, Nehru Memorial Museum and Library, New Delhi.

147   Eisenhower Library, Ann Whitman Diary Series, Box 6: ACW Diary July 1955(3), DDE/caw, 14 July 1955, quoted in Tracy Lee, *Anglo-American Tension over the Offshore Islands, 1954–1958*, London School of Economics, September 1991, published by ProQuest LLC (2014).

148   File 361, 'Miscellaneous Correspondence, Late 1955 Crisis', *Krishna Menon Papers*, Nehru Memorial Museum and Library, New Delhi.

149 Doc. 289, 'Telegram from the Secretary of State to the Embassy of Italy', 7 July 1955, *FRUS, 1955–1957, China, Vol. II.*

150 Doc. 235, 'Memorandum of Conversation, Department of State', May 3, 1955, *FRUS, 1955–1957, China, Vol. II.*

151 Doc. 274, 'Memorandum of Conversation between Secretary of State and British Foreign Secretary MacMillan', San Francisco, 20 June 1955, *FRUS, 1955–1957, China, Vol. II.*

152 Doc. 291, 'Telegram from Secretary of State to the US Embassy in London', 8 July 1955; Doc. 273, 'Memorandum of Conversation between Secretary of State and British Foreign Secretary MacMillan', San Francisco, 20 June 1955, *FRUS, 1955–1957, China, Vol. II.*

153 'Telegram from Krishna Menon to Prime Minister', 12 July 1955, London, File 361, Miscellaneous Correspondence, Late 1955 Crisis, *Krishna Menon Papers*, Nehru Memorial Museum and Library, New Delhi.

154 'Telegram, Raghavan from Prime Minister, 14 July 1955, Message to Be Conveyed to Zhou Enlai', File 361, Miscellaneous Correspondence, Late 1955 Crisis, *Krishna Menon Papers*, Nehru Memorial Museum and Library, New Delhi.

155 'Cable to Zhou Enlai', *SWJN, Series II, Vol XXIX*, June–August 1955, p. 360.

156 *The MacMillan Diaries: The Cabinet Years, 1950–1957*, edited by Peter Catterall (MacMillan, 2003), p. 448.

157 'Plan for the Sino-US Ambassadorial Talks in Geneva', 18 July 1955, Wilson Center Digital Archive, PRC, FMA 111-00014-01, 2–5, obtained and translated by Yafeng Xia, https://digitalarchive.wilsoncenter.org/document/120388.

158 'Telegram, Krishna Menon from Raghavan', 16 July 1955, File 361, Miscellaneous Correspondence, Late 1955 Crisis, *Krishna Menon Papers*, Nehru Memorial Museum and Library, New Delhi.

159 'Cable from the Chinese Foreign Ministry to Wang Bingnan, "Talking Points for the Fifth Meeting"',10 August 1955, Wilson Center Digital Archive, PRC, FMA 111-00016-06, 21–24, translated by Yafeng Xia, https://digitalarchive.wilsoncenter.org/document/110855.

Chapter 5: The Second Taiwan Strait Crisis

1   Doc. 268, 'Address by the Secretary of State', San Francisco, 28 June 1957, 'Our Policies Toward Communism in China', *Foreign Relations of the United States, 1955–1957, China, Volume III.*

2   Doc. 271, 'Telegram from U. Alexis Johnson to Department of State', Geneva, 11 July 1957, *FRUS, 1955–1957, China, Vol. III.*

3   Doc. 287, 'Memorandum of Discussion at 338th Meeting of the National Security Council', 2 October 1958, *FRUS, 1955–1957, China, Vol. III.*

4   Doc. 299, 'Memorandum from Director of Intelligence & Research (Cumming) to Undersecretary of State (Herter)', 29 November 1957, *FRUS, 1955–1957, China, Vol. III.*

5   FO 371/133523, 'Defence of Formosa (Taiwan) against China', March–August 1958 (Government Papers, National Archives, Kew, 1958, Folder 2), p. 32, accessed on 9 April 2023.

6   Doc. 23, 'Telegram from Department of State to Embassy in ROC', August 2, 1958, *FRUS, 1958–1960, China, Vol. XIX*, edited by Harriet D. Schwar (USG Printing Office, 1996).

7   'Letter, Mao Zedong to Peng Dehuai and Huang Kecheng', 27 July 1958, Wilson Center Digital Archive, *Zhonggong Zhongyang Wenxian Yanjiushi*, ed. Jianguo Yilai Mao Zedong Wengao (Mao Zedong's Manuscripts since the Founding of the PRC), Vol. 7 (Beijing: Zhongyang Wenxian Chubanshe, 1992), pp. 326–27, https://digitalarchive.wilsoncenter.org/document/117011.

8   Doc. 24, 'Telegram from Commander Taiwan Defense Command (Smoot) to C-in-C Pacific (Stump)', 4 August 1958, *FRUS, 1958–1960, China, Vol. XIX.*

9   Doc. 26, 375th Meeting of the National Security Council, 7 August 1958.

10   FO 371/133523, 'Defence of Formosa (Taiwan) against China', March–August 1958, (Government Papers, National Archives, Kew, 1958, Folder 2), p.42, accessed on 9 April 2023.

11   Doc. 27, 'Memorandum from Assistant Secretary of State for Far Eastern Affairs (Robertson) to Secretary of State', August 8, 1958, *FRUS, 1958–1960, China, Vol. XIX.*

12   Doc. 31, 'Memorandum of Conference with President Eisenhower', 12 August 1958, *FRUS, 1958–1960, China, Vol. XIX.*

13   Doc. 36, 'Memorandum for the Record', 14 August 1958, *FRUS, 1958–1960, China, Vol. XIX.*

14   Doc. 38, 'Memorandum from Assistant Secretary of State for Far Eastern Affairs (Robertson) to Secretary of State', 20 August 1958, *FRUS, 1958–1960, China, Vol. XIX.*

15   Doc. 43, 'Memorandum of Meeting', White House, 25 August 1958, 'Summary of Meeting at White House on Taiwan Straits Situation', *FRUS, 1958–1960, China, Vol. XIX.*

16   Doc. 47, 'Possible Developments in the Taiwan Strait Area', Special National Intelligence Estimate, 26 August 1958, *FRUS, 1958–1960, China, Vol. XIX.*

17   'Instructions, Mao Zedong to Peng Dehuai', 18 August 1958, Wilson Center Digital Archive, Jianguo Yilai Mao Zedong Wengao, Vol. VII (Beijing: Zhongyang Wenxian Chubanshe), p. 348, https://digitalarchives.wilsoncenter.org/document/117014.

18   Memoir by Wu Lengxi, 'Inside Story of the Decision Making during the Shelling of Jinmen', 23 August 1958, Wilson Center Digital Archive, Zhuanji Wenxue (Biographical Literature, Beijing), No. 1, 1994, 5–11, https://digitalarchives.wilsoncenter.org/document/117009.

19   Doc. 52, 'Memorandum of Meeting', White House, 29 August 1958, 'Summary of Meeting at White House on Taiwan Straits Situation', *FRUS, 1958–1960, China, Vol. XIX.*

20   FO 371/133523, 'Defence of Taiwan (Formosa) against China', March–August 1958 (Government Papers, National Archives, Kew, Folder 2), p. 74, accessed on 9 April 2023.

21   Doc. 54, 'Memorandum of Conversation', 30 August 1958, *FRUS, 1958–1960, China, Vol. XIX.*

22   FO 371/133524, 'Defence of Formosa (Taiwan) against China, August 1958' (Government Papers, National Archives, Kew, Folder 3), pp. 64–65, accessed on 9 April 2023.

23   Ibid., pp. 58–60.

24   Memoir by Wu Lengxi, 'Inside Story of the Decision Making during the Shelling of Jinmen', 23 August 1958, Wilson Center Digital Archive, Zhuanji Wenxue (Biographical Literature, Beijing), No. 1, 1994, 5–11, https://digitalarchives.wilsoncenter.org/document/117009.

25   Doc. 67, 'Memorandum Prepared by Secretary of State Dulles', Newport, Rhode Island, 4 September 1958, *FRUS, 1958–1960, China, Vol. XIX.*

26   Doc. 68, 'Statement by Secretary of State', White House Press Release, Newport, Rhode Island, 4 September 1958, *FRUS, 1958–1960, China, Vol. XIX.*

27   Doc. 44, 'Orders Given by Joint Chiefs of Staff to Commander-in-Chief Pacific (Felt)', *FRUS, 1958–1960, China, Vol. XIX.*

28   Harold Macmillan, 'Chinese Puzzle', Chapter 17, *Riding the Storm, 1956–1959* (Harper and Row), p. 544.

29   Doc. 69, 'Letter from Dulles to Prime Minister MacMillan', Washington, 4 September 1958 *FRUS, 1958–1960, China, Vol. XIX.*

30   Doc. 70, 'Message from MacMillan to Dulles', London (undated), *FRUS, 1958–1960, China, Vol. XIX.*

31   Text by NCNA in *Documents on International Affairs, 1958* (London: OUP, 1962), pp 179–82.

32   *FRUS, 1958–1960, China, Vol. XIX.*

33   FO 371/133526, 'Defence of Formosa (Taiwan) against China', August–September 1958 (Government Papers, National Archives, Kew, Folder 5), pp. 37–38, accessed on 9 April 2023.

34   'Telegram from Embassy of India, Washington (Dayal), to Foreign Secretary', 28 August 1958, File 646, Part I (Miscellaneous Correspondence, 1958 Crisis), Nehru Memorial Museum and Library, New Delhi.

35   'Telegram from Dayal (Washington) to Foreign Secretary', 4 September 1958, File 648, Part I (Miscellaneous Correspondence, 1958 Crisis), Nehru Memorial Museum and Library, New Delhi.

36   'Telegram from Parthasarthi to Dutt', 31 August 1958, File 646, Part II (Miscellaneous Correspondence, 1958 Crisis), Nehru Memorial Museum and Library, New Delhi.

37   'Telegram from Parthasarathi to Dutt', 7 September 1958, File 649, Part I (Miscellaneous Correspondence, 1958 Crisis), Nehru Memorial Museum and Library, New Delhi.

38   'Noting by Jawaharlal Nehru', 7 September 1958, File 649, Part I (Miscellaneous Correspondence, 1958 Crisis), Nehru Memorial Museum and Library, New Delhi.

39   Doc. 1037, 'Note Verbale Handed by MEA to Chinese Counsellor in India', 2 July 1958, *India–China Relations, 1947–2000, A Documentary Study, Vol. II,* introduced and edited by A.S. Bhasin (New Delhi: Geetika Publishers, 2018), p. 1877.

40   Doc. 1040, 'Note Given by Chinese MFA to the Indian Counsellor in Peking', 10 July 1958, *India–China Relations, 1947–2000, A Documentary Study, Vol. II,* introduced and edited by A.S. Bhasin (New Delhi: Geetika Publishers, 2018), pp. 1880–882.

41   Doc. 1041, 'Letter from Prime Minister to Political Office in Sikkim', 11 July 1958, *India–China Relations, 1947–2000, A Documentary Study, Vol. II,* introduced and edited by A.S. Bhasin (New Delhi: Geetika Publishers, 2018), p. 1883.

42   Doc. 1051, 'Note Given by MEA to Chinese Counsellor in India', 21 August 1958, *India–China Relations, 1947–2000, A Documentary Study, Vol. II,* introduced and edited by A.S. Bhasin (New Delhi: Geetika Publishers, 2018), pp. 1896–897.

43   'Press Conference', 7 September 1959, New Delhi, *SWJN, Series II, Vol. XLIV*, September–October 1958, pp. 97–98.

44   'Telegram from Parthasarathi to Dutt', 9 September 1958 (Miscellaneous Correspondence, 1958 Crisis), Nehru Memorial Museum and Library, New Delhi.

45 FO 371/133531, 'Defence of Formosa (Taiwan) against China', September 1958 (Government Papers, National Archives, Kew, Folder 10), pp. 20–21, accessed on23 January 2023.

46 Harold Macmillan, 'Chinese Puzzle', Chapter 17, *Riding the Storm, 1956–1959* (Harper and Row), p. 550.

47 Doc. 76, 'Memorandum of Conversation, Washington', 8 September 1958, 'Resumption of Ambassadorial Talks with Chinese Communists', *FRUS, 1958–1960, China, Vol. XIX.*

48 Doc. 78, Editorial Note, *FRUS, 1958–1960, China, Vol. XIX.*

49 Doc. 79, 'Memorandum of Conversation between President Eisenhower and Secretary of State Dulles', 11 September 1958, *FRUS, 1958–1960, China, Vol. XIX.*

50 'Telegram, Mao Zedong to Ho Chi Minh', 10 September 1958, *Jianguo Yilai Mao Zedong Wengao* (Mao Zedong's Manuscripts since the Founding of the PRC), Vol. VII, edited by Zhonggong Zhongyang Wenxian Yanjiushi (Beijing: Zhongyang Wenxian Chubanshe, 1992), p. 413, https://digitalarchives.wilsoncenter.org/document/117016.

51 Memoir of Wu Lengxi, 'Inside Story of the Decision Making during the Shelling of Jinmen', 23 August 1958, Wilson Center Digital Archive, Zhuanji Wenxue (Biographical Literature, Beijing), No. 1, 1994, 5–11, https://digitalarchives.wilsoncenter.org/document/117009.

52 'Letter, Mao Zedong to Zhou Enlai', 18 September 1958, Wilson Center Digital Archive, *Mao Zedong Waijiao Wenxuan* (Selected Works of Mao on Diplomacy) (Beijing: Zhongyang Wenxian Chubanshe, 1994), p. 353, https://digitalarchives.wilsoncenter.org/document/117020.

53 FO 371/133531, 'Defence of Formosa (Taiwan) against China', September 1958 (Government Papers, National Archives, Kew, Folder 10), accessed on 23 January 2023.

54 Doc. 82, 'Memorandum of Conversation', 12 September 1958, *FRUS, 1958–1960, China, Vol. XIX.*

55 'Telegram, Parthasarthi to Dutt', 14 September 1958, File 650, Part II (Miscellaneous Correspondence, 1958 Crisis), Nehru Memorial Museum and Library, New Delhi.

56   'Telegram, Parthasarathi from Dutt', 16 September 1958, File 650, Part II (Miscellaneous Correspondence, 1958 Crisis), Nehru Memorial Museum and Library, New Delhi.

57   'Telegram, Prime Minister from Krishna Menon', New York, 15 September 1958, File 651, Part 1, Nehru Papers (Miscellaneous Correspondence, 1958 Crisis), Nehru Memorial Museum and Library, New Delhi.

58   'Telegram, Parthasarathi from Dutt', 16 September 1958, File 651, Part I, Nehru Papers, (Miscellaneous Correspondence, 1958 Crisis), Nehru Memorial Museum and Library, New Delhi.

59   Doc. 89, 'Telegram from Secretary of State Dulles to Embassy in Poland', 14 September 1958 (Personal), *FRUS, 1958–1960, China, Vol. XIX.*

60   Chapter 9, *Diplomacy of Contemporary China*, edited by Han Nianlong (Hong Kong: New Horizon Press, 1990), p. 134.

61   Doc. 104, 'Telegram from Embassy in Poland to Department of State', 18 September 1958, *FRUS, 1958–1960, China, Vol. XIX.*

62   Doc. 122, 'Memorandum of Conversation', 23 September 1958, *FRUS, 1958–1960, China, Vol. XIX.*

63   'Telegram, Dayal to Foreign Secretary', 17 September 1958, Nehru Papers (Miscellaneous Correspondence, 1958 Crisis), File 651, Part I.

64   'Telegram, Selwyn Lloyd, New York, to Foreign Office', London, 19 September 1958, FO 371/133531, 'Defence of Formosa (Taiwan) against China', September 1958 (Government Papers, National Archives, Kew, 1958, Folder 10), pp. 118–20, accessed 23 January 1958.

65   FO 371/133531, 'Defence of Formosa (Taiwan) against China', September 1958 (Government Papers, National Archives, Kew, 1958, Folder 10), p. 123, accessed on 23 January 1958

66   FO 371/133537, 'Defence of Formosa (Taiwan) against China', September–October 1958 (Government Papers, National Archives, Kew, 1958, Folder 16), accessed on 23 January 2023.

67   Harold Macmillan, 'Chinese Puzzle', Chapter 17, *Riding the Storm, 1956–1959* (Harper and Row), p. 555.

68 Doc. 115, 'Memorandum of Conversation', Newport, Rhode Island, 21 September 1958, *FRUS, 1958–1960, China, Vol. XIX.*

69 FO 371/133539, 'Defence of Formosa (Taiwan) against China', September–October 1958 (Government Papers, National Archives, Kew, 1958), accessed on 23 January 2023.

70 'Telegram, Dutt from Parthasarathi', 21 September 1958, File 651, Part II, Nehru Papers, (Miscellaneous Correspondence, 1958 Crisis), Nehru Memorial Museum and Library, New Delhi.

71 Ibid.

72 Ibid.

73 'Telegram from Peking to Foreign Office', 21 September 1958, FO 371/133531, 'Defence of Formosa (Taiwan) against China, September 1958 (Government Papers, National Archives, Kew, 1958, Folder 10), accessed on 23 January 2023.

74 'Telegram, Personal, Secretary General Pillai from Krishna Menon', New York, 26 September 1958, File 651, Part 1, Nehru Papers (Miscellaneous Correspondence, 1958 Crisis), Nehru Memorial Museum and Library, New Delhi.

75 'Telegram, Personal, Pillai from Krishna Menon', 27 September 1958, File 651, Part II, Nehru Papers (Miscellaneous Correspondence, 1958 Crisis), Nehru Memorial Museum and Library, New Delhi.

76 'Telegram, Personal, Pillai from Krishna Menon', 27 September 1958, File 651, Part II, Nehru Papers (Miscellaneous Correspondence, 1958 Crisis), Nehru Memorial Museum and Library, New Delhi.

77 'Telegram, Personal, Krishna Menon from N.R. Pillai', 28 September 1958, File 651, Part II, Nehru Papers (Miscellaneous Correspondence, 1958 Crisis), Nehru Memorial Museum and Library, New Delhi.

78 'Telegram from CRO to High Commission in Delhi', 3 October 1958, FO 371/133537, 'Defence of Formosa (Taiwan) against China', September–October 1958 (Government Papers, National Archives, Kew, 1958, Folder 16), p. 48, accessed on 23 January 2023.

79   'Telegram from MacDonald to CRO', 4 October 1958, 371/133537, 'Defence of Formosa (Taiwan) against China', September–October 1958 (Government Papers, National Archives, Kew, 1958 Folder 16), p. 51, accessed on 23 January 2023.

80   Doc. 130, 'Memorandum of Conversation: Secretary's Trip to New York', 26 September 1958, *FRUS, 1958–1960, China, Vol. XIX.*

81   Doc. 134, 'Memorandum of Conversation: Secretary's Trip to New York', 27 September 1958, *FRUS, 1958–1960, China, Vol. XIX.*

82   'Prime Minister from Krishna Menon', New York, Telegram, 1 October 1958, File 653, Part I, JN Papers (S.G.).

83   'Memorandum of Conversation: Premier Zhou Receives Indian Ambassador to China, Parthasarathi', 30 September 1958, Wilson Center Digital Archive, PRC-FMA 110-00713-02, translated by Anna Beth Keim, https://digitalarchive.wilsoncenter.org/document/116576.

84   'N.R. Pillai from Parthasarathi, Telegram' (also repeated to Menon in New York, 2 October 1958, File 653, Part I, JN Papers (S.G.).

85   Morton H. Halperin, *The 1958 Taiwan Strait Crisis: A Documented History* (Santa Monica, CA: Rand Corporation, 1966), p. 329.

86   Doc. 37, 'Telegram from Department of State to US Mission to UN', 1 October 1958, *FRUS, 1958–1960, UN and General International Matters, Vol. II.*

87   Doc. 148, 'Editorial Note', *FRUS, 1958–1960, China, Vol. XIX*, edited by Harrier Dashiell Schwar and Glenn W. LaFantasie (Government Printing Office, 1996).

88   Doc. 154, 'Department of State to US Delegation to United Nations General Assembly', 3 October 1958, *FRUS, 1958–1960, China, Vol. XIX.*

89   Morton H. Halperin, *The 1958 Taiwan Strait Crisis: A Documented History* (Santa Monica, CA: Rand Corporation, 1966), pp. 515–16.

90   Doc. 171, 'Memorandum of Conversation', 9 October 1958, *FRUS, 1958–1960, China, Vol. XIX.*

91   'Meeting Minutes, Zhou Enlai's conversation with S.F. Antonov, on Taiwan Issue (excerpt)', 5 October 1958, Wilson Center Digital Archive, *Zhou Enlai Waijian Wenxuan* (Selected Works of Zhou Enlai on Diplomacy) (Beijing: Zhongyang Wenxian Chubanshe, 1990), pp. 262–67, https://digitalarchive.wilsoncenter.org/document/117018.

92   'Pillai from Parthasarathi, Telegram', 5 October 1954, File 653, Part II, JN Papers (S.G.).

93   'Prime Minister from Krishna Menon', New York, Telegram, 1 October 1958, File 653, Part I, JN Papers (S.G.).

94   'Krishna Menon from Prime Minister', New Delhi, Telegram, 3 October 1958, File 653, Part I, JN Papers (S.G.).

95   'Meeting Minutes, Zhou Enlai's Conversation with S.F. Antonov, on Taiwan Issue (excerpt)', 5 October 1958, Wilson Center Digital Archive, *Zhou Enlai Waijian Wenxuan* (Selected Works of Zhou Enlai on Diplomacy) (Beijing: Zhongyang Wenxian Chubanshe, 1990), pp. 262–67, https://digitalarchive.wilsoncenter.org/document/117018.

96   'Telegram, Peking to Foreign Office', 7 October 1958, FO 371/133537, 'Defence of Formosa (Taiwan) against China', September–October 1958 (Government Papers, National Archives, Kew, 1958, Folder 16), pp. 104–05, accessed on 23 January 2023.

97   Doc. 215, 'Letter from Dulles to Lloyd', 24 October 1958, *FRUS, 1958–1960, China, Vol. XIX*. File 653, Part II, JN Papers (S.G.).

98   'Prime Minister from Krishna Menon', New York, Telegram, 1 October 1958, File 653, Part I, JN Papers (S.G.).

99   'Panditji from Krishna, Top Secret and Personal', 13 October 1958, File 655, Part II, JN Papers (S.G.).

100   'Letter, Krishna Menon from Prime Minister, Personal and Secret', 14 October 1958, File 655, Part II, JN Papers (S.G.).

101   Doc. 207, 'Memorandum of Conversation', Taipei, 23 October 1958, *FRUS, 1958–1960, China, Vol. XIX*.

102   Doc. 201, 'Telegram from Secretary of State to Department of State (for President)', 23 October 1958, *FRUS, 1958–1960, China, Vol. XIX*.

103 'Memorandum of Conversation of Mao Zedong with Six Delegates of Socialist Countries', China, 2 October 1958, Wilson Center Digital Archive, GARF f.9576, op. 18, 1958, d. 26, 1.312-322, obtained and translated by Austin Jersild, https://digitalarchive.wilsoncenter.org/document/116826.

104 Doc. 192, 'Memorandum of Conversation', 17 October 1958, *FRUS, 1958–1960, China, Vol. XIX.*

105 Doc. 215, 'Letter from Dulles to Lloyd', 24 October 1958, *FRUS, 1958–1960, China, Vol. XIX.*

106 'Record of Conversation between British Foreign Secretary Selwyn Lloyd and Canadian PM Diefenbaker', 4 November 1958, FO 371/133544, 'Defence of Formosa (Taiwan) against China', November 1958 (Government Papers, National Archives, Kew, 1948), pp. 4–7, accessed on 1 April 2023.

107 'Note by P.G.F. Dalton', FO 371/133544, 'Defence of Formosa (Taiwan) against China', November 1958 (Government Papers, National Archives, Kew, 1948), pp. 85–86, accessed on 1 April 2023.

108 'Message from Selwyn Lloyd to Dulles through British Embassy in Washington', 7 November 1958, FO 371/133544, 'Defence of Formosa (Taiwan) against China', November 1958 (Government Papers, National Archives, Kew, 1958, pp. 98–99, accessed on 1 April 2023.

109 'Letter from Dulles to Lloyd', 19 November 1958, FO 371/133546, 'Defence of Formosa (Taiwan) against China' (Government Papers, National Archives, Kew, 1958, Folder 25), p. 24, accessed on 1 April 2023.

110 'Telegram, MacDonald to CRO', 3 December 1958, FO 371/133546, 'Defence of Formosa (Taiwan) against China' (Government Papers, National Archives, Kew, 1958, Folder 25), p. 37, accessed on 1 April 2023.

111 Editorial, *People's Daily*, 12 December 1958, FO 371/133546, 'Defence of Formosa (Taiwan) against China' (Government Papers, National Archives, Kew, 1958, Folder 25), pp. 77–78, accessed on 1 April 2023.

112 'Letter from A.D. Wilson, British Charge d'Affaires in Peking, to P.G.F. 'Dalton, 13 December 1958, FO 371/133546, 'Defence of Formosa (Taiwan) against China' (Government Papers,

National Archives, Kew, 1958, Folder 25), pp. 107–08, accessed on 1 April 2023.

113 'Note by P.G.F. Dalton', 23 April 1959, FO 371/141391, 'Defence of Formosa (Taiwan) against China', January–February 1959 (Government Papers, National Archives, Kew, 1959, Folder 1), pp. 39–40.

Epilogue: Aftermath and Why History Is Important

1 Subimal Dutt, 'India–China Border Dispute', Chapter 9, *With Nehru in the Foreign Office*, pp. 108–38.

2 R.S. Kalha, *India–China Boundary Issues: Quest for Settlement* (New Delhi: ICWA/Pentagon Press, 2014), p. 97.

3 Doc. 1409, 'Statement by Chinese Ambassador to Foreign Secretary', 16 May 1959, *India–China Relations, 1947–2000, A Documentary Study, Vol. II,* introduced and edited by A.S. Bhasin (New Delhi: Geetika Publishers, 2018), pp. 2478–482.

4 Ibid.

5 'Letter from Prime Minister to Krishna Menon, Secret and Personal', 26 November 1958, Nehru Papers, extracts, File 662, Part I, Nehru Memorial Museum and Library, New Delhi.

6 'Letter from Ellsworth Bunker, US Ambassador in India, to Nehru, forwarding message from President Eisenhower', 28 November 1958, Nehru Papers, extracts, File 664, Part 1, Nehru Memorial Museum and Library, New Delhi.

7 'Telegram, Chagla from Pillai, 3 December 1958, transmitting message from Nehru to Eisenhower', 28 November 1958, Nehru Papers, extracts, File 664, Part I, Nehru Memorial Museum and Library, New Delhi.

8 Tanvi Madan, 'With an Eye to the East: The China Factor and the US–India Partnership, 1949–1979', Dissertation, University of Texas, Austin, May 2012, pp. 275–76.

9 J. Nehru, *Letters to Chief Ministers, Vol. II, 1950–1952*, edited by G. Parthasarathi; letter dated 2 February 1950, p. 16.

10 Michael Brecher, 'Geneva Conference on Indochina', Chapter 4, *India and World Politics: Krishna Menon's View of the World* (London: Oxford University Press, 1968), p. 47.

11   'Preliminary Opinions on Assessment and Preparations for the
      Geneva Conference, prepared by the PRC, MFA (drafted by
      Premier and Foreign Minister Zhou Enlai, excerpt)', 2 March
      1954, Wilson Center Digital Archive, PRC FMA 206-Y0054,
      translated by Chen Zhihong, https://digitalarchive.wilsoncenter.
      org/document/111963.

12   J. Nehru, *Letters to Chief Ministers, 1952–1954, Vol. III*; letter
      dated 3 June 1954.

13   Subimal Dutt, 'Indochina', Chapter 6, *With Nehru in the Foreign
      Office* (Calcutta: Minerva), pp. 60–61.

14   Jairam Ramesh, Chapter 13, Part V, *A Chequered Brilliance: The
      Many Lives of V.K. Krishna Menon* (Penguin).

15   'Telegram, UK (Acting) High Commissioner to Secretary of
      State for Foreign Affairs, Top Secret', No. 615, 26 June 1954,
      'Political Relations between India and the Chinese Peoples
      Government' (Government Papers, National Archives, Kew,
      1954), accessed on 16 January 2023.

16   Michael Brecher, 'Bandung 1955', Chapter 5, *India and World
      Politics: Krishna Menon's View of the World* (London: Oxford
      University Press, 1968), p. 54.

17   J. Nehru, *Letters to Chief Ministers, 1952–1954, Vol. III*; letter
      dated 3 June 1954.

18   'Letter to Prime Minister from G.L. Mehta, Secret and Personal',
      7 July 1955, Nehru Papers, extracts, File 360, Part I, Nehru
      Memorial Museum and Library, New Delhi.

19   J. Nehru, *Letters to Chief Ministers, 1950–1952, Vol. II*; letter
      dated 18 August 1950, Nehru Memorial Museum and Library,
      New Delhi, p. 167.

20   Vijay Gokhale, 'What Should India Do before the Next Taiwan
      Strait Crisis?', April 2023, Carnegie India, 2020.

21   J. Nehru, *Letters to Chief Ministers, 1950–1952, Vol. II*; letter
      dated 30 May 1950, Nehru Memorial Museum and Library,
      New Delhi, pp. 109–10.

22   'Joint Leaders Statement on AUKUS', White House, Washington,
      15 September 2021.

Scan QR code to access the
Penguin Random House India website